WA 1093093 0

D0507782

Achieving Quality Improvement

Achieving Quality Improvement

Improvement

A practical guide

Roland Caulcutt

BP Chemicals Lecturer
University of Bradford Management Centre
Bradford
UK

CHAPMAN & HALL

London · Glasgow · Weinheim · New York · Tokyo · Melbourne · Madras

658.562
CAU

Published by Chapman & Hall, 2–6 Boundary Row, London SE1 8HN, UK

Chapman & Hall, 2–6 Boundary Row, London SE1 8HN, UK

Blackie Academic & Professional, Wester Cleddens Road, Bishopbriggs, Glasgow G64 2NZ, UK

Chapman & Hall GmbH, Pappelallee 3, 69469 Weinheim, Germany

Chapman & Hall USA, One Penn Plaza, 41st Floor, New York NY 10119, USA

Chapman & Hall Japan, ITP-Japan, Kyowa Building, 3F, 2-2-1 Hirakawacho, Chiyoda-ku, Tokyo 102, Japan

Chapman & Hall Australia, Thomas Nelson Australia, 102 Dodds Street, South Melbourne, Victoria 3205, Australia

Chapman & Hall India, R. Seshadri, 32 Second Main Road, CIT East, Madras 600 035, India

First edition 1995   1 0 9 3 0 9 3 0

© 1995 Roland Caulcutt

Typeset in 10/12pt Palatino by ROM-Data Corporation Ltd, Falmouth

Printed in Great Britain by Clays Ltd, St Ives plc

ISBN 0 412 55930 7

Apart from any fair dealing for the purposes of research or private study, or criticism or review, as permitted under the UK Copyright Designs and Patents Act, 1988, this publication may not be reproduced, stored, or transmitted, in any form or by any means, without the prior permission in writing of the publishers, or in the case of reprographic reproduction only in accordance with the terms of the licences issued by the Copyright Licensing Agency in the UK, or in accordance with the terms of licences issued by the appropriate Reproduction Rights Organization outside the UK. Enquiries concerning reproduction outside the terms stated here should be sent to the publishers at the London address printed on this page.

The publisher makes no representation, express or implied, with regard to the accuracy of the information contained in this book and cannot accept any legal responsibility or liability for any errors or omissions that may be made.

A catalogue record for this book is available from the British Library

Learning Resources
Centre

∞ Printed on permanent acid-free text paper, manufactured in accordance with ANSI/NISO Z39.48-1992 and ANSI/NISO Z39.48-1984 (Permanence of Paper).

17/5/95

Contents

Contents

Preface

In manufacturing industry it is now accepted that change is the norm. Furthermore, it is widely realized that the momentum of change needed to remain competitive, requires that everyone must be committed to quality improvement. We can carry no passengers. Indeed, those companies that cannot harness the full potential of their human resources, may fall behind in this never-ending race. The devil takes the hindmost.

This book is written for those who need help to achieve quality improvement. It is based on my experience as a quality management consultant with many companies, in many industries. I have chosen to write the book as a series of conversations with hypothetical clients in imaginary companies. So, it is a work of fiction. Nonetheless, it is based on fact, and on real experience with real managers in real companies. I have tried to cover a wide spectrum of problems that are encountered in many companies and I have set these problems in several industries. Obviously, my selection of industries was influenced by my recent experience.

Chapters 2, 3, 6 and 7 are set in an imaginary chemical company. Chapters 4 and 5 deal with quality problems in a company that makes tin cans. In Chapter 8, I visit a water company to advise on sewage treatment and, in Chapter 9, I consult with a manufacturer of vehicle components who is attempting to improve a welding process. Chapter 1 is an introduction which attempts to set quality improvement in the wider context of total quality management (TQM) and Chapter 10 summarizes the more important points made in Chapters 2 to 9.

How can you, a busy reader, gain maximum benefit from this book without reading all ten chapters? Naturally, you will read any chapters which are set in your particular industry. However, if you read only those chapters, you will miss much that could be helpful to you. If you already have some experience in the use of data analysis for process improvement, you could well start at Chapter 10 and allow the back references therein to steer you into earlier chapters. Even a beginner could benefit from starting at Chapter 10. I hope, however, that many readers will start at Chapter 1 and find that the narrative style carries them through to the end.

Many people have helped me in the writing of this book. I received encouragement and support from my colleagues at the European Centre for Total Quality Management, Bradford University and O&F Quality Management Consultants. Constructive comments on certain chapters were made by Howard Coulson of Exxon Chemical, Malcolm Gall of Hydro Polymers and Colin Pitts of BP Chemicals. I tested many of my ideas on process improvement during discussions with Henry Neave and David Kerridge of the British Deming Association. I am very grateful to all these people, but I know that they would not agree with everything I have written.

Mrs Barbara Ward and Mrs Wendy Docherty of Bradford University have produced such excellent typescript from my incoherent scribbles. Neil Chapman of Adept Scientific helped me to produce an enormous number of diagrams in an electronic format acceptable to the publisher. My heartfelt thanks to all three.

Finally I would like to record my gratitude to BP Chemicals for their continued sponsorship of my lectureship at Bradford University, Management Centre. Without this support I would have to do much more consultancy but I would never find time to write about it.

Roland Caulcutt
University of Bradford
Management Centre
Bradford

Chapter 1

People and processes

The consultant is not visiting clients today. He stays at home and thinks about the nature of total quality management (TQM) and the reasons why so many companies are progressing so slowly. He considers the view that many managers do not have the breadth of knowledge and understanding that are required, if we are to obtain a good return on our investment in people and processes.

1.1 INTRODUCTION

There is really no need for me to wake so early. I am not planning to catch an early train. I am not intending to drive through Leeds before the morning rush hour. In fact, I do not anticipate going anywhere today. However, waking early has become a habit. So, by 6:30 I have had a light breakfast and I am sat at my desk.

I expect to be sat at my desk for many hours, reading and writing and thinking. However, experience has taught me that it is difficult to plan these three activities. Correction! It is easy to plan, but sometimes I have great difficulty sticking to a plan that requires me to produce creative ideas. So, I hope to do quite a lot of thinking, but will not be too upset if the thoughts fail to materialize and I find, by the end of the day, that I have spent more time reading and writing.

What will be the focus of my thinking? Well, it is quite some time since I had a day completely free, so I could start by reflecting upon my recent activities. Today is Friday. On Thursday I visited a food manufacturing company to discuss their training requirements. I spent Wednesday at the university, teaching TQM to MBA students and preparing a short course in 'Culture Change for Quality Improvement'. I also made many phone calls and despatched, to a journal editor, a research paper that I hope will now be acceptable for publication. I was at home on Tuesday, correcting and amending the research paper that I posted on Wednesday. Monday was a very interesting day. I attended a meeting in London to discuss the writing of a new training module in team leadership. This will be produced by a Communications Consultancy for BP Chemicals, who sponsor my lectureship at Bradford University.

'Was this a typical week?', you may wonder. Well, I suppose it was typical, in the variety of experience that it offered. Certainly next week will be very different, as I shall be spending three days in The Netherlands, whilst the following week will include four days at the university. If variety is the spice of life, my . . .

I consider that I am very fortunate to be able to pursue such varied and interesting work. I am very grateful to my sponsors and to all the other companies who have employed me in the past. I realize that many of the managers I advise, would dearly love to have as much time as I have to think about the activities in which they are involved. Perhaps they would share my view that the best learning comes, not from experience, but from reflecting on experience. On the other hand, I believe that there are many managers who are entirely happy that their days are filled with activity. Perhaps they can reflect as they act. I cannot. Clearly all managers are different, at least in some respects, just as all workers are different and all companies and all processes are unique in certain ways. If you believe that all people are like you, and if you believe that all processes are identical, you will certainly have difficulty implementing TQM.

1.2 WHAT IS TOTAL QUALITY MANAGEMENT (TQM)?

'There is nothing new in TQM.' This view has been expressed by so many reputable business managers, that it needs to be given serious consideration. However, if we eventually conclude that there is little of real novelty in TQM, then we must also acknowledge that the quality gurus have performed a very valuable service by bringing together the essential elements of TQM and presenting them as a coherent strategy for business improvement.

What are these essential elements? John Oakland, Head of the European Centre for TQM at Bradford University, presents these essential elements in a diagram or model (Fig. 1.1). He suggests that a TQM initiative requires commitment, culture and communication. The commitment to quality, is required of people at all levels, but particularly among senior managers. This commitment is essential if a culture for quality improvement is to be developed around an ethos of open communication. Of course, it may be difficult, if not impossible, to change a culture by direct action. Perhaps improvement is more easily achieved if we focus on the more tangible elements in the model: teamwork, systems and tools or techniques. For example, achieving registration of your company, or unit, or site, to BS 5750 (ISO 9000), together with extensive training of your people in teamwork and the use of quality tools, may well help to create a total quality culture.

At the centre of Oakland's model we find processes, which link together chains of customers and suppliers. The concept of the internal customer is

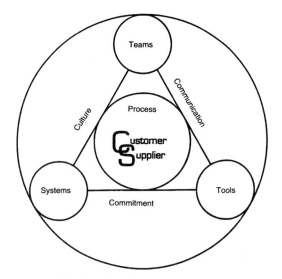

Fig. 1.1 Oakland's model of total quality management.

fundamentally important if these chains and processes are to be meaning-ful. Furthermore, the idea that processes need to be identified, clearly defined and managed, must be a cornerstone of any total quality initiative, be it in manufacturing or services.

So, what would other quality experts think of Oakland's model of TQM? Unfortunately, the eminent quality gurus seem reluctant to speak of each other in public, so we would need to ask the question discreetly, and in private. However, it is hard to imagine any quality consultant suggesting that communication was unimportant, or that teamwork had no part to play, or that management commitment was irrelevant to quality improve-ment. Certainly, different writers in the quality field have given different emphasis to the elements in Oakland's model, but few writers would suggest that any one element could be eliminated.

Having recently read Deming's latest book, *The New Economics* (Deming, 1993), I suspect that this most senior of quality gurus would wish to add a fourth 'C' to communication, commitment and culture. Deming places great emphasis on co-operation. I would have to agree with such an extension of the model. In my experience the health of a company culture can be measured by the extent of the co-operation that exists. Co-operation between departments and co-operation between people at different levels are both indicative of an open culture with true customer focus.

Deming has now set aside his famous 14 points for management, which formed the structure of his earlier book *Out of the Crisis* (Deming, 1986). His latest writing is built upon the four pillars of his 'system of profound knowledge'. There is no conflict between the two texts but, clearly, a list of four essential components is more easily remembered than one of 14. The four pillars of profound knowledge are:

1. Appreciation for a system
2. Knowledge about variation
3. Theory of knowledge
4. Psychology.

The above list is expressed in Dr Deming's own words. If you are not familiar with his earlier writings you might appreciate some explanation of these four essential elements. First, Deming uses the words 'system' and 'process' interchangeably. So both he and Oakland, and many other writers, are suggesting that all managers need to understand processes. Deming defines a system (process) as 'a network of interdependent components that work together to try to accomplish the aim of the system'. In this simple definition, only the word 'interdependent' hints at the complexity of many processes, in which we find feedback loops, time delays and interactions between components. With such complexity, a small change at one location can have unforeseen effects at some other place and at a later time. Small wonder that the 'workers' trapped within such a process are almost powerless to achieve or improve quality without the support of 'management' who are outside the process and can view the bigger picture.

If you have studied systems engineering you may be entirely happy with Deming's suggestion that all managers need 'an appreciation for a system'. For the many managers who have not yet embarked on such studies, Deming offers the consoling thought that 'one need not be eminent in any part of profound knowledge in order to understand it and apply it'.

Second, when Deming says that every manager should have 'knowledge about variation', he is recommending that you should study the techniques for quality improvement. A knowledge of these techniques (which are the focus of this book) can help you to reduce variation in your products and services, to the benefit of your customers. This knowledge will also help you to appreciate what can reasonably be expected from a process, or from people working within the process.

Third, the theory of knowledge is concerned with the way people learn, and the use of scientific method for gaining process understanding. Quality improvement and cost reduction come from process improvement that follows from increased knowledge of process relationships. Thus the TQM culture must be a learning culture.

Fourth, by listing psychology as the final pillar of profound knowledge, Deming is reminding us that every employee can make an important contribution to customer satisfaction and company profitability. Thus a basic understanding of human motivation is essential for any manager. The effect on employee motivation of a manager's unreasonable expectations is good reason for studying psychology and variation together. Further reason for extending this joint study to include processes, is provided by the obvious difficulty of separating the contribution of the individual from that of other elements in the process.

So, TQM is concerned with people, processes and performance. But it also focuses on communication, commitment, co-operation and company culture. Furthermore, it is characterized by leadership, learning and long-term objectives.

Clearly, TQM is not easily defined in one sentence. Nonetheless, all quality consultants sincerely believe that your company can gain enormous benefits from the pursuit of total quality. In the past ten years many companies have followed the advice of quality gurus and consultants. Are they entirely satisfied with the benefits they have gained?

1.3 WHY IS PROGRESS SO DISAPPOINTING?

Speakers at quality conferences claim that a high percentage of TQM initiatives have failed. The quoted percentage varies from speaker to speaker, but it seems to average about 70%. Many of the speakers mention a recent survey that offers support for their assertions of failure. Unfortunately none of the speakers have time to give further details, or to say precisely what they mean by 'failure', but they certainly leave the impression that TQM has no built-in guarantee of success.

My experience offers only partial support for this total quality gloom. The companies I visit as a consultant are all making progress. Of this, I have no doubt. Some of the companies are making, what could reasonably be described as, good progress, or significant progress. They are now better able to compete than they were five years ago. Management style has changed, company culture has changed, and change itself is now accepted as the norm.

However, I must report that, despite this undoubted progress, there is not widespread satisfaction. Within the companies I advise, there is considerable disappointment.

Senior managers are disappointed. They perceive that the benefits resulting from the TQM initiative do not match the expectations that were raised at the outset. Of course, it is difficult to assess the benefits gained, because it is impossible to know just where the company would have been if it had not embarked on the total quality journey.

People on the 'shop floor' are disappointed. It is true that they are now treated with more respect, but this was little consolation to those who were recently made redundant. (Cynics have remarked that restructuring is now executed more quickly and with even greater secrecy, than it would have been before total quality was introduced.) Undoubtedly, a number of managers have changed their attitude towards their staff and the growth of teamwork has led to more openness, but progress is often localized.

Oases of excellence may be surrounded by a desert of indifference, defensiveness or even fear.

I can only speak for the companies with which I have had contact, of course. These are certainly not a representative sample of all British companies. Many of my clients are manufacturing companies and many are large. The two smaller companies I have visited recently are distinctly different, and one can recognize the possibility of their rapid transformation to a total quality culture. However, within the larger companies, there is an inertia that does not inspire such confidence. It has often been suggested that we might have to wait ten or more years for a whole generation of senior managers to retire before we see much progress towards a total quality culture, in larger companies. I wonder if this prediction is propagated by middle managers, who would benefit most from the retirements. Let us hope that there will be no such delay, for I believe that our recent progress needs to be accelerated, not retarded.

Many of my clients operate in truly global markets. To match the performance of their European competitors, may no longer guarantee consistent profitability, or even survival. Competition from the Middle East and the Pacific Rim could well prove to be the major threat in the near future. There can be little doubt that, in some industries at least, oriental competitors are demonstrating quite alarming rates of progress in product development, cost reduction and quality improvement.

If we accept that total quality must be a never-ending journey then the word 'failure' would not seem to be appropriate. How can an initiative be said to have failed if it is not yet completed? Perhaps 'abandonment' is a better word to describe what is reported to have happened in some companies. The absence of any obvious short-term benefits from their total quality initiative may have led to its formal closure or to its death by neglect. Alternatively, the long-term TQM programme may have been postponed until survival had been secured. However, it is hard for me to accept that TQM has been set aside in 80% of the companies that were attracted to the total quality philosophy.

So, I cannot accept that the failure, or abandonment, of TQM is so widespread as many believe it to be. Nonetheless, I am intensely interested in the reasons why the expectations associated with so many TQM initiatives, have not been met. I would like to suggest that lack of understanding by managers, of people and processes, may be a contributory cause.

1.4 UNDERSTANDING PROCESSES

Philip Crosby, the American quality guru, who has influenced many large manufacturing companies in Britain, defines a process as 'simply a series of actions or operations conducted to produce a desired result'. He lists the essential elements of a process as inputs, equipment/facilities, training/

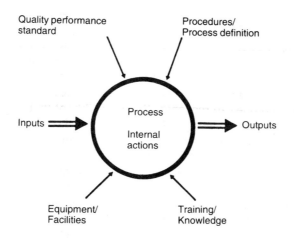

Fig. 1.2 Crosby's process model.

knowledge, procedures/process definition, quality performance standard and outputs. Crosby suggests that the inputs are consumed in the creation of the output, whereas the equipment, training, procedures and standards are more enduring.

While Crosby's process model does not specifically mention people, it clearly implies that they may well be involved in the internal actions. Why else would we need training or written procedures? Oakland, in the second edition of *Total Quality Management*, also gives us a pictorial model that leaves us in no doubt that people have an important part to play. He defines a process as 'a process is the transformation of a set of inputs, which can include actions, methods and operations, into outputs that satisfy customer needs and expectations in the form of products, information, services or – generally – results'.

Thus, it is stressed by Deming, Crosby, Oakland and many other quality professionals that a process must have an output, and an aim or purpose. It is important that the desired output should be clearly defined and the purpose, or aim, be clearly understood by those people within the process. The aim of the process is to produce the defined output. Deming has often said, 'Without an aim there is no process.' We might extend this maxim: 'Without a clearly defined output there can be no agreed aim.'

Having read the comments of Deming, Crosby and Oakland, would you now recognize a process if you saw one? Before you rush to answer 'Yes, of course I would', you should bear in mind that business processes vary enormously in size and complexity. Furthermore, any process can be broken down into sub-processes or, alternatively, can be regarded as being part of a larger process. While many business processes contain all of the elements in Oakland's model (Fig. 1.3), and additional elements such as

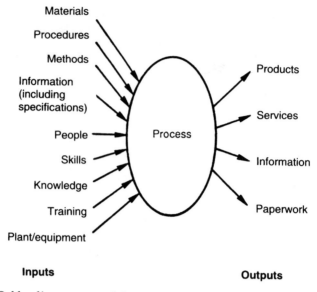

Inputs   Outputs

Fig. 1.3 Oakland's process model.

packaging, delivery and collection, it is always possible to subdivide such a process into much simpler processes. Some of the sub-processes may consist of little more than one person or one machine.

Consider, for example, the service you are given in a shop or department store. You receive goods from a 'serving person' and offer money in payment. Clearly, this exchange of goods and cash takes place within a 'serving process'. We could study this process, we could manage the process, and we could improve the process, using techniques described in subsequent chapters. We could reflect upon the aim, or aims, of the process, which might include the 'delight of customers'. However, no matter how high or low the customer delight, it is clear that this 'serving process' needs to be supported by other processes. These would put goods on the shelves, take cash to the bank, clean the store, train the staff, promote the products, etc. The 'serving person' might also work within one or more of these other processes. Several of these processes could be grouped together and re-garded as a larger process. Taking this to the extreme, we could regard the whole company as one process. Perhaps it would be useful to regard the whole city or the whole country as one process, 'UK Ltd', or 'USA Inc.'. It has been suggested that competing companies within Japan co-operate with each other much more than do competitors within western countries. Thus Japan could be regarded as a much more efficient process than USA or UK.

One fundamental message of TQM is that managers must manage processes. The quality gurus maintain that managers are not managing processes sufficiently well. However, in fairness to the many capable and

Fig. 1.4 A simple process.

conscientious managers that I meet, I would like to suggest that managing processes may be much more difficult than many people imagine. The difficulties arise because of the complexity of the processes. Rarely do I meet a process as simple as that in Fig. 1.4.

The simple process can be broken down into three sub-processes, SP1, SP2 and SP3. Let us say that, in SP1, an employee unpacks large parcels of items received from suppliers. In SP2, a second employee gathers together small groups of items and packs them. In SP3, a third employee despatches the small packages to customers. This is a very simple process and is relatively easy to manage. If, for example, a customer is dissatisfied, it may be reasonable for the manager to try to find out which of the three employees has failed, and take appropriate action. However, in my experience, few processes are so simple and rarely is such management behaviour appropriate.

The more complex process in Fig. 1.5 can be regarded as seven sub-processes that are located in three departments. Though each department has a manager, no one is responsible for managing the whole process. Each manager strives to optimize the performance of his or her department. When a customer dissatisfaction is revealed it may be extremely difficult to discover which employee, if any, has failed. Indeed it may not be appropriate to speak of human failure. The fault may be inherent to the process. The fault may more reasonably be attributed to a non-existent procedure, which was not written, by the non-existent process manager.

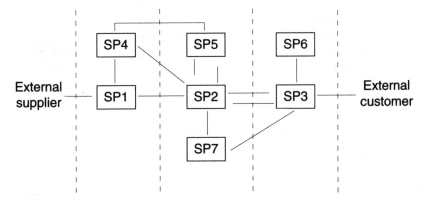

Fig. 1.5 A more complex process.

So, what is needed, in order to improve the performance of the process in Fig. 1.5? The following suggestions are worthy of consideration.

- It is important that one manager should be responsible for the whole process.
- The process manager, assisted by a process improvement team, should study the performance of the whole process and assess the capability of the process to meet customer requirements.
- To control the process, and to improve the process it will be necessary, at times, to focus on one or more sub-processes. Thus the manager must be able to shift his attention from the whole process (the big picture) to individual components (a detailed picture). Whereas, the employees within the process may only see individual trees, the manager must stand back and study the whole forest.
- It is essential for the manager to realize that optimizing each of the sub-processes will not optimize the performance of the whole process. The failure of management to study the whole process will result in sub-optimization with inferior service to the customer.
- For optimum performance of the whole process the departmental managers must be prepared to co-operate with each other, giving the aim of the main process priority over the aim of a sub-process whenever there is conflict.

If you are to manage any process successfully, you need to understand relationships between cause and effect. Practising managers must act upon causes to produce desired effects. The techniques and methods discussed in later chapters of this book will help you to establish the links between the quality of your products/services and the many factors that you can manipulate in order to improve your quality and decrease your costs. These techniques are well proven and their use will be illustrated in many industries. They give you permanent benefits by increasing your knowledge of your process, which enables you to improve the process, which in turn improves the quality of your goods or services. The chain of events is illustrated in Fig. 1.6.

The learning, which is an essential component of Fig. 1.6, can only occur in the minds of employees. Thus employees must be motivated to learn if quality improvement is to occur. Do managers fully understand the factors that motivate human behaviour?

1.5 UNDERSTANDING PEOPLE

How are we to assess the effectiveness of TQM? I believe that TQM will only be judged truly successful if it benefits all stakeholders. TQM will be worth pursuing only if it benefits your customers, suppliers, shareholders, employees and those who share your environment. To disappoint any one

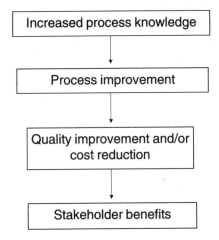

Fig. 1.6 Learning for quality improvement.

group of stakeholders, for any length of time, could undermine the progress of your company. Perhaps your shareholders are the stakeholders most lacking in patience. They are prepared to sell their holding in your company as soon as they are given an unsatisfactory answer to the question, 'What's in it for me?' The larger shareholders may even employ a computer to ask this question, with a disturbing frequency and persistence.

Your customers also ask 'What's in it for me?' whenever they decide whether or not to place an order for your goods or services. They wonder, 'Would we obtain better quality, delivery or price from a competitor?' Your suppliers question whether or not you will be able or willing to pay for the materials you have ordered. People living within the vicinity of your manufacturing sites and storage depots ask what effect your activities are having on the environment and whether or not it would be wise to file a complaint.

With all these stakeholders asking so many questions about your company would you not also expect your employees to be asking 'What's in it for me?' If your employees are not openly asking this question, perhaps you should reflect on the reason for their silence. A company culture that does not encourage openness may suppress creativity, contribution and co-operation.

If you accept my assertion that all of your stakeholders are asking 'What's in it for me?', then you will wish to understand their personal objectives, which they pursue in order to obtain the benefits that they regard as important. This is an age old problem, of course. No doubt you have often asked yourself what other people hope to gain by behaving in the way that they do. If you assume that other people are motivated exactly as you are, then their behaviour will often appear incomprehensible. It is much safer to assume that every person has a unique set of personal objectives and motives, though you will obviously find similar objectives among people from similar backgrounds or cultures.

How could Mr A, a manager, gain a better understanding of the personal objectives of a member of his department, Mr B? Obviously, he could ask. Mr A could ask Mr B direct and simple questions designed to reveal the subordinate's motivation. This is unlikely to be very successful. First, B might not be able to describe the forces that motivate him or the objectives he hopes to achieve. Second, B might not wish to pass to A this information, which would surely increase the power that A could exert on B, for good or bad. Clearly this reluctance would be greater in a culture of fear.

Could the study of psychology help Mr A towards a greater understanding? The answer must be 'Yes', but psychology is a vast discipline with many specialisms. Mr A, a busy manager, will never have the time needed to study many texts on motivation. Of course, he may already have a little knowledge. Perhaps he is aware of the writings of McGregor (1960), Maslow (1970) and Hertzberg (1968), but this is more likely to have been gained from three slides flashed on the screen at a short course or conference, rather than a deep study of their original works.

Douglas McGregor (1960) suggested that a manager's behaviour would be driven by his or her assumptions or theories about human nature. His research led him to believe that almost all managers subscribe to one or other of two basic theories, which he labelled Theory X and Theory Y. Supporters of Theory X maintain that the average employee has an inherent dislike of work and will only make an effort to achieve the company's objectives if threatened, punished or coerced. Thus managers need to exercise constant vigilance and control over a workforce that is motivated only by money and insecurity. Theory Y, on the other hand, suggests that the average employee is not averse to physical work. On the contrary he or she may enjoy a sense of achievement from both physical and mental effort. Furthermore, an employee will exercise self-discipline and responsibility in the pursuit of objectives to which he or she is committed and may well exhibit considerable creativity if allowed to realize a personal potential, which is often greatly undervalued.

McGregor's ideas on Theory X and Theory Y are known by many managers. But McGregor had much more to say about motivation and personal development. Writing about management by objectives as early as 1957, he pointed out the need to align personal and company objectives:

'The effective development of managers does not include coercing them into acceptance of the goals of the enterprise, nor does it mean manipulating their behaviour to suit organizational needs. Rather it calls for creating a relationship within which a man can take responsibility for developing his own potentialities, plan for himself, and benefit from putting his plans into action. By this process he can gain a genuine sense of satisfaction, for he is using his own capabilities to achieve simultaneously both his objectives and those of the organization.'

Thus, McGregor implies that all employees, including managers, will pursue their own personal objectives. This is in accord with my earlier assertion that all human behaviour is motivated by self-interest, as evidenced by the universal questioning of 'What's in it for me?' For maximum utilization of your company's human resources, therefore, you need a culture in which all employees are simultaneously pursuing both their own objectives and the company objectives. Clearly this can only occur if the two sets of objectives are closely aligned. Creating a TQM culture is, I believe, largely a matter of clarifying and aligning objectives.

Abraham Maslow (1970) is also well known to many managers. His hypothesis, that human needs can be usefully classified as a hierarchy, seems to accord with common sense and everyday experience. Maslow suggested five levels of need:

1. Physiological needs – sleep, hunger, thirst, etc.
2. Safety needs – security
3. Social needs – belonging, social interaction, friendship, love, etc.
4. Self-esteem needs – respect, self-respect, recognition, status, etc.
5. Self-actualization needs – growth, development, achievement of potential, etc.

Maslow suggested that we can pay attention to the higher needs, only when the lower needs are satisfied. Thus a person might risk greater danger to obtain food if the hunger need were acute, but he or she would not take such risks on a full stomach. Similarly, an employee who is an effective team member whilst he or she is attempting to satisfy social and self-esteem needs, may become much less effective if the threat of redundancy focuses attention on lower needs. The implications for managers of such hierarchical issues are thoroughly discussed in Maslow's *Motivation and Personality* (1970).

Frederick Hertzberg (1968), the third of our well-known psychologists, carried out extensive research on the attitudes of employees towards their jobs. His findings led him to a clear distinction between the factors that people complain about when they are unhappy at work and the factors that lead to job satisfaction. The former include salary, overtime and working conditions. Hertzberg labelled these 'hygiene' factors. He concluded that improvements in the hygiene factors might help to prevent unhappiness, but they would not motivate employees to work harder or smarter. That would only result from 'motivating' factors, and the two universal motivating factors are achievement and recognition.

Hertzberg asked employees at all levels to describe a bad day at work and a good day at work. He found that deficiencies in hygiene factors often characterized the bad days but, almost without exception, a sense of achievement and/or recognition were associated with the good days. Thus, an employee carrying out an apparently meaningless and unimportant task, will not be motivated to achieve higher standards or strive for process improvement, nor will he or she experience much job satisfaction. On the other hand, an employee who can see how the task relates to the needs of customers and who receives recognition from other team members, will be motivated to strive for greater achievement.

The important writings of McGregor, Maslow and Hertzberg were published long ago. They are well-known among managers and you might argue that they are rather old hat. It is true that many managers are aware of these three psychologists, but it is also true that their advice on motivation has not been acted upon, to any great extent. Within many companies, perhaps your own company, you can still find Theory X managers, if you look below the surface. You will find departments or sections in which higher needs and recognition do not appear too high on the manager's list. I would argue that one hour of reflection on the theory of motivation and his or her experience, could lead any manager to a very long list of objectives that staff are pursuing within the company.

Suppose that your company were introducing TQM and you were asked to explain the benefits that employees would gain. On the assumption that every member of your audience would be wondering 'What's in it for me?', would you not expect that some would wish to know if TQM would give them:

- greater job security,
- a feeling of importance,
- higher salary,
- greater control,
- better working conditions,
- greater understanding of where the company is going,
- clear and agreed objectives,
- greater sense of achievement,
- reduced risk of injury,
- more variety in their work,
- more opportunity for progression,
- greater freedom to schedule their work, and so on.

Is it not possible that everyone in your company is motivated by one or more of the above needs? Clearly the list is incomplete. You might well be able to add needs that I have not included. Perhaps there are employees in your company who are wondering if TQM will result in their being:

- more confident,
- less afraid of not meeting their targets,
- able to question why things are done this way,
- less guilt-ridden when things go wrong,

- able to voice their opinions without fear of retribution,
- treated with more respect,
- able to work with others on job improvement,
- listened to, when they make suggestions,
- given more responsibility,
- given feedback on their performance,
- given due recognition for their contribution,
- free to learn and fully utilize their intellect, and so on.

These needs, which serve as drives or motivators, and determine the personal objectives of your employees, must be given consideration by any manager who wishes to promote quality improvement. Can you reasonably expect open communication if staff do not receive due recognition for their contribution? Are you likely to see external customers treated with respect if those who serve them are not similarly treated by their managers? How are junior employees to attach due importance to their many tasks if they do not have clear objectives based on an understanding of where the company is going?

Obviously my description of human motivation does not do full justice to the true complexity of the forces that drive our behaviour. For example, it is an oversimplification to suggest that only one need is operating at any point in time. It is possible to satisfy several needs simultaneously. Furthermore, it is possible to pursue, at the same time, several objectives that may not be entirely compatible. Clearly, it is not possible to have your cake and eat it. Nor is it possible to have both the halfpenny and the gingerbread. The conflict between competing objectives is often a conflict between short-term and long-term needs. For example, you might wish to spend money on food, drink or entertainment for immediate pleasure and you might also wish to invest money in a pension or a house purchase. Clearly you cannot use the same £1 for both purposes. A person severely addicted to drugs pursues short-term objectives with total disregard to the long-term effects. The very same conflict exists in every business company, of course. Dollars, or pounds, paid out in dividends or salaries cannot also be spent on research and development or plant that would enhance future income.

Clearly, all of the needs I have listed are consistent with the teachings of McGregor, Maslow and Hertzberg. All three would agree, I believe, with my assertion that the frustration of any one of these needs could lead to reduced co-operation, less effective communication and missed opportunities for quality improvement, cost reduction and/or customer service. Can you afford to ignore the personal objectives of your colleagues, your subordinates and the managers to whom you report? Can you deny the need for a culture in which everyone's personal objectives are aligned as closely as possible with the objectives of the company?

We have looked at the work of three psychologists in the field of motivational psychology. Many other branches of psychology offer alternative perspectives on human behaviour and each can shed some light on the culture that is required for quality improvement. It is beyond the scope of this book to discuss all of these specialisms in any depth, but a brief mention of two or three, with indications for further reading would be appropriate.

Theory of personal constructs

For those who need to appreciate the fragility of human communication, some acquaintance with George Kelly's *Theory of Personal Constructs* (1955) is desirable. Perhaps this is most readily available in Bannister and Fransella's popular book *Inquiring Man* (1986). Kelly suggests that each person views the world through his or her own unique system of personal constructs. These constructs help us to predict or anticipate future events. The effectiveness of this prediction will depend upon the nature of a person's constructs and the way they are hierarchically structured. People with similar personal constructs should be able to communicate more easily with each other. A company with a 'common language of quality' will have acquired this through extensive training, which has changed the personal constructs of the employees. Perhaps your own system of personal constructs will change as you read this book. I hope so. If your constructs do not change you will not have been influenced by my writing.

So what exactly is a personal construct? Let us carry out a small experiment that will elicit one of your personal constructs. Write down the names of three people who are important in your life. You may have listed your wife or husband, a parent, a friend, a barman, an accountant, etc. Now ask yourself, 'Which of the three is most different to the other two?' Clearly there are many ways in which you could make this decision. The choice is yours.

Having selected the 'odd' one, you must now decide in what way he or she is different. No doubt there are many ways in which the 'odd' one differs from the other two. Choose only one, then write it down. Then write down how the other two differ from the 'odd' one. You may consider this second factor to be the opposite of the first. Perhaps you have written one of the following:

- happy – unhappy
- smokes – does not smoke
- tall – short
- friendly – aggressive
- dependable – like Richard
- practices TQM – has rejected TQM

Any one of the above could constitute a personal construct for someone. It is likely that you wrote something quite different. However, what you did write down was one of your many personal constructs. By considering other groups of three, you would elicit additional constructs. This could go on forever and your list of constructs would obviously differ from someone else's list. Your set of personal constructs is as unique as your fingerprints, and gives you a unique perspective. Clearly, you cannot see a problem in exactly the same way that someone else perceives it. Are you then to conclude that you are right and everyone else is wrong, or are you driven to show greater respect for the other person's point of view?

Transactional analysis

Transactional analysis (TA) is another branch of psychology that is readily accessible through a popular text. You may have read, or heard of, *I'm OK, You're OK* by Thomas Harris (1973). TA focuses on the basic person-to-person communication, or transaction, in which each party adopts one of three possible 'states' described as 'child', 'parent' or 'adult'. Only in an 'adult'–'adult' transaction are both parties in touch with the reality of the problem or situation under discussion. If either party is in 'parent' or 'child' state then unsatisfied needs from earlier experiences will distract from the sharing of information. For successful problem solving in teams, it is necessary that employees should be able to remain in the 'adult' for extended periods, but this will not be possible if their 'child' and/or 'parent' be triggered by other team members or external circumstances.

With a little practice you can detect changes of state within yourself and others. In a meeting watch out for such 'parent' words as should, ought, always, never, etc. Listen for 'child' phrases such as I wish, I want, I don't care, I guess, and excessive use of superlatives such as biggest, best, etc. Only in the 'adult' state can people handle information at all objectively and whilst doing so will use 'adult' words such as where, when, what, who, why and how. Only whilst in the 'adult' state can people tolerate the uncertainty associated with complex business processes.

TA is a substantial branch of psychology that cannot be adequately described within these pages. It offers a means of understanding how childhood experience creates or influences the many needs that were listed earlier. Furthermore, it offers each person an escape from the tyranny of the past by helping people to take control of their lives. Perhaps TQM offers something like this to every company.

TA and personal construct theory make fascinating reading and have helped many people better to understand themselves and others. But this claim could be made equally strongly for other branches of psychology. For example, you might benefit considerably from studying Neuro-Linguistic Programming, or Gestalt Therapy (O'Connor and Seymour, 1990; Perls, 1971).

It is possible that you are, by now, in no mood to study any of the books I have recommended. You may feel that you have endured more psychological theory than is good for you. Perhaps you would really like a more practical method for gaining a better understanding of the people you work with. Perhaps you would prefer to learn from experience rather than theory. If these are your thoughts, I do sympathize. I believe that the best learning results from a blend of theory and experience. Reading the books I have recommended, offers you rapid learning from theory devised by others, but your enhanced knowledge must ultimately face the test of reality that comes with your practical experience.

Unfortunately, your practical study of human behaviour will be made more difficult because many humans do not wish to be studied. The people with whom you live and work may not co-operate fully as you try to discover why they behave as they do. Thus, to accelerate your learning, you need to focus on people who have not yet learned how to hide their feelings. There may not be any such people within your company but they do exist. Schools are full of them. By studying children you may get valuable insights into the behaviour of adults.

Let me suggest, as a working hypothesis, that adults are simply large children who have learned to hide their feelings. I hasten to add, speaking as one large child to another, that this hypothesis does not contain the whole truth, of course. It is a gross over-simplification, but it offers you an alternative route around the congestion of concealment. Next weekend, when you are forced to stay at home, study your children, your grandchildren, your nephews and nieces. Ask yourself if the feelings, so clearly visible in the faces and the utterances of young children, are not also experienced by adults.

Listen carefully to what the children say. Pay particular attention to their words when they become discontented, disputative, disrespectful or simply disruptive. What do they say? Whilst listening to my grandchildren I hear the following phrases repeatedly:

- It's not fair.
- Why can't I do that?
- It's boring.
- Can I come too?

It is clear that young children want fairness, freedom to explore, stimulation, inclusion in social activity and some control over their environment. Furthermore, if these wants or needs are denied, co-operation becomes confrontation. The once happy playroom becomes a battlefield.

Are there not similarities between children at play and adults at work? Do your employees not also want fairness, freedom to learn, stimulation, inclusion in teamwork and some control within their workspace? I believe they do. Of course, they are not going to stamp their feet and say 'It's not fair', because they have learned not to do so, but the pain of unfair treatment may be very real, nonetheless. It is also unlikely that your employees will complain of boredom or powerlessness or rejection. Perhaps they have learned to live with these, or have devised appropriate diversions. How can you tell? Their feelings are concealed.

The need to conceal feelings may not be equally strong at all levels within your company. Perhaps the need is greatest among middle managers. In many large companies, one suspects that a middle manager's career prospects would not be enhanced by openly asking 'What's in it for me?' In many companies, the middle manager is expected to whole-heartedly pursue company objectives, with total disregard of personal or family needs. While few actually do so, all would wish to appear to do so.

Let me bring this somewhat rambling discourse to a clear conclusion. I believe that all human behaviour is motivated by self-interest. All the stakeholders in your company are intent on satisfying their own personal needs. Psychological theory and your own observation can help you to understand the enormous variety of needs people feel and the objectives they pursue. If you ignore these needs you will not obtain the co-operation of all employees that is needed in the pursuit of quality improvement. The alignment of personal objectives with company objectives occurs as a total quality culture is developed. This is a task for all managers. Within a TQM culture everyone is a manager.

1.6 SUMMARY

In subsequent chapters, I will visit companies to discuss quality improvement. Much of this discussion will focus on the tools and techniques that can be used to analyse data. However, you should not lose sight of the fact that this data analysis is not an end in itself. The purpose of analysis is decision and prediction. We analyse data in order to assess how a process has performed in the past. We then make decisions about how the process should be managed in the future and we predict how much better it will perform.

While all of these processes will contain plant and equipment they will also contain people. To obtain the best return on our investment in plant we need to understand how it works. To gain the best return on our investment in people we need to understand how they work. This is best achieved by studying the whole process, of which the people and plant are component parts. It is useful to consider the 'workers' as being within the process and the 'manager' as being outside the process. Thus the manager is in a better position to study the whole process and 'see the big picture', but the manager must also be able to focus on sub-processes and to 'look at the detailed picture'. However, if the manager is to have an accurate picture, he or she will need the co-operation of the 'workers' within the process, for they have knowledge that no one else possesses.

In this chapter I have briefly described the findings of several psychologists. Perhaps you will now be inspired to study their writings in order to gain further understanding of people. Your ability to improve processes will certainly be impaired if you refuse to recognize the uniqueness of each individual and the great variety that exists in any group of people. It is this variety that causes, in part at least, the variation in your products and services. Your customers wish to see a reduction in this variation. We will discuss, in later chapters, many useful techniques but they will prove effective only if you have the co-operation of your people.

Chapter 2

Can we satisfy the customers?

*The consultant makes his first visit to Lubrichem,
which manufactures speciality chemicals. He
meets the Marketing Director and the Quality
Manager. They discuss the ability of Lubrichem to
satisfy customer requirements and how best to
communicate with customers when questions of
capability are raised. Several process capability
indices are introduced and supported by histograms and run charts.*

2.1 INTRODUCTION

Today I am visiting Lubrichem. I am expecting to see Ron Henderson, the
Marketing Director, who contacted me by telephone to arrange the meeting. No doubt there will be one or two other Lubrichem people present, but
I am not sure exactly how many and I do not have an agenda. As I sit in the
train I wonder why the uncertainty surrounding the meeting does not
worry me at all. Perhaps it is because I think I can predict what questions
they will raise.

Lubrichem is smaller than most of my client companies. It manufactures
speciality chemicals, including oil additives which they sell to the major oil
companies. This is potentially a very profitable market, but the products
and the processes are very complex, so the profits are more likely to be
achieved by a company which has invested in the right technology and has
the dedicated, highly trained staff who can manage that technology. It
would not matter whether those people spoke English, German, Japanese
or Urdu. The market for oil additives is truly global.

My experience with similar companies leads me to expect that
Lubrichem will operate batch processes with a cycle time of about four or
five hours, so they probably produce one batch per eight-hour shift, round
the clock. A batch of additive might sell for £20 000 or £30 000. I say
'might', because a batch which fails to meet the customer specification will
be worth much less, and that is why I am visiting Lubrichem. We are going
to discuss the possibility of making every batch right first time – no scrap,
no rework.

2.2 LUBRICHEM AND ITS CUSTOMERS

'Well, Roland, you've seen the plant. What do you think? Can we give the customer what he wants?' The question is put to me by Ron Henderson, the Marketing Director of Lubrichem, as I enter his office. It is true, that I have seen the plant. During the hour since my arrival I have been shown round the site by Dave Smith, the Quality Manager. So I have certainly seen the plant, but I cannot answer the question.

I wonder if Ron really expects me to answer. Surely he does not believe that a consultant, after a short walk round the site, could know enough about the capability of a manufacturing process, to answer 'Yes' or 'No'. Perhaps he does. There is so much mystery surrounding complex processes that some managers believe in magic and they hope that consultants will have extraordinary powers. Ron's facial expression is one of anticipation. I think he would like an answer.

I am aware that Ron Henderson's interest in quality has developed quite recently and that he is from a sales/marketing background. Clearly, he is very extrovert, so he probably speaks before he thinks, just bouncing ideas off people. Perhaps his opening question is simply setting a provisional agenda for our meeting. Well I am certainly very happy to talk about processes and the ability of processes to meet customer requirements, but we will need to use some simple statistical techniques. I am not sure that Ron is prepared for this.

'You've certainly made your people interested in quality', I reply. Obviously this does not constitute a reasonable answer to Ron's opening question, but it certainly reflects what I have seen during my short tour of the site. In the reception area, prominently displayed, is the company mission statement, affirming the commitment of senior management to total quality. In the visitors' waiting room is a list of Philip Crosby's Four Absolutes, announcing to all visitors the views held in Lubrichem:

1. Quality is defined as conformance to requirements.
2. Quality will be achieved by a system of prevention rather than correction.
3. The only acceptable performance standard is zero defects.
4. Any deviation from this standard, or any progress towards the achievement of this standard, will be measured by quantifying the price of non-conformance (PONC).

I have seen it before, in several companies, and been very impressed with the changes that have occurred wherever the Crosby philosophy has been embraced. However, I am also aware of its limitations. In many companies that have been 'Crosbied' there is insufficient understanding of the practical numerical tools that are essential for achieving quality improvement. Thus it is not uncommon for companies to turn from Crosby to Deming, who emphasizes very strongly the need for staff at all levels to have an understanding of variability. This brings my thoughts back to Ron Henderson's question, 'Can we give the customer what he wants?' To answer this question, I will need to talk about process variability, as well as customer requirements.

'Yes, we've made dramatic progress under the new Managing Director', Ron tells me, with more than a little pride in his voice. The first thing he did was to call in Crosby who trained all the senior management team. 'There is absolutely no doubt about our commitment to quality now.' He pauses, then in a more subdued tone continues. 'Much to my surprise, culture change has been quite easy. Achieving improved quality to the customer is another matter. Don't misunderstand me now, . . . all our customers are receiving product in spec, but our PONC estimates have revealed the true cost of achieving this. Rather disturbing, Roland. We're hoping you can help us to get it right first time.'

If Lubrichem management are committed to never-ending process improvement, I can certainly help them. I would like to get down to detail so as to demonstrate what I have to offer. 'Perhaps we could consider one particular product,' I suggest. 'Do you have any data to illustrate what you are producing. We can compare this with the customer's specification.'

2.3 PROCESS VARIABILITY AND PRODUCT SPECIFICATION

Dave Smith, who entered the room with me after the site tour, had been silent up to this point. He produces a sheet of paper from the file he has been carrying and explains that this contains laboratory results for LBC80, an oil additive. This is made by a batch process and he has figures for the viscosity, the calcium content and sediment % of the last 80 batches (Table 2.1).

The silence lasts for many seconds, perhaps even minutes, as all three of us scrutinize the data. I know that we are unlikely to make any progress until this data is presented in pictorial form, but I am reluctant to speak for fear I might stifle some comment from the owners of this process. Finally, it is the more extrovert Ron who breaks the silence. 'Well Roland, you're the expert, what does this tell us about customer satisfaction?'

I feel sure that Ron and Dave have great difficulty drawing conclusions from long columns of numbers. What they do not realize perhaps, is that I also have difficulty, as do most people. 'This data will tell us a great deal more about your production process when we convert it into pictures,' I suggest. 'We can plot some simple graphs by hand, but it will be easier if I type the data into my laptop computer and let my program do the hard work. I use a program called 'Quality Analyst'.'

Dave reads out the numbers and I key them into the computer. This seems to take ages, but it cannot be all that long because Ron only manages two phone calls while we are doing it. Now that the data is in the machine,

Can we satisfy the customers?

Table 2.1 Analytical Results for 80 batches of LBC80

Batch	Viscosity	Batch	Viscosity	Batch	Viscosity	Batch	Viscosity
1	79.1	21	81.4	41	78.2	61	67.9
2	80.5	22	87.2	42	73.6	62	72.7
3	72.7	23	76.9	43	72.1	63	73.0
4	84.1	24	75.0	44	73.0	64	63.9
5	82.0	25	75.6	45	76.7	65	65.2
6	77.6	26	79.9	46	67.9	66	69.1
7	77.4	27	82.0	47	69.2	67	74.7
8	80.5	28	76.5	48	66.7	68	74.7
9	81.1	29	78.4	49	69.3	69	74.8
10	80.8	30	79.6	50	71.3	70	79.8
11	84.5	31	79.8	51	74.0	71	73.5
12	87.9	32	77.9	52	75.8	72	74.6
13	76.1	33	76.2	53	77.1	73	75.9
14	79.9	34	71.2	54	75.5	74	70.9
15	83.5	35	72.7	55	68.0	75	75.4
16	78.6	36	74.9	56	71.9	76	69.7
17	70.9	37	73.9	57	78.5	77	76.6
18	80.5	38	75.3	58	79.2	78	77.6
19	80.6	39	69.1	59	67.3	79	62.7
20	79.7	40	72.3	60	69.8	80	69.4

I can easily produce several very useful diagrams on the screen. Paper copies cannot be produced so quickly, but they are not needed with such a small audience. The first picture I produce is a histogram of the viscosity results (Fig. 2.1).

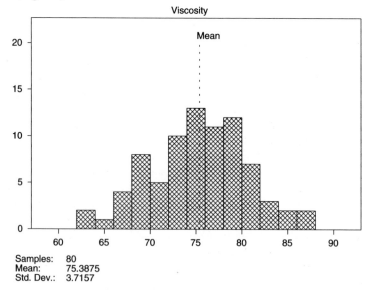

Samples: 80
Mean: 75.3875
Std. Dev.: 3.7157

Fig. 2.1 A histogram of viscosity.

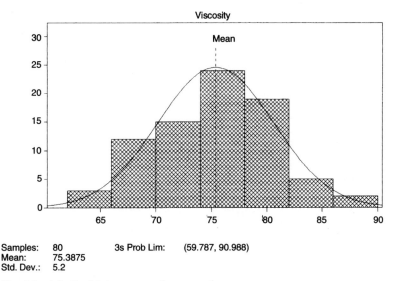

Fig. 2.2   A better histogram and a normal curve.

I realize, of course, that Ron Henderson and Dave Smith will have seen histograms before. Nonetheless, I feel I should say a few words about these very useful diagrams, since they are not as easy to construct as some people imagine. 'To draw a histogram of our viscosity results we first need to put them into groups, so decisions have to be made about what the group boundaries will be. Unfortunately computer programs do not always get this right. In fact, 'Quality Analyst' made some rather poor decisions when it was producing Fig. 2.1 and gave us a histogram with rather narrow groups and hence too many bars. If I tell the computer that I want only seven groups we should get a smoother picture. At the same time, I will ask it to superimpose a normal curve on the histogram.' With a few key strokes I implement these changes (Fig. 2.2).

Ron and Dave agree that the second histogram is a smoother shape, but the new picture has raised several questions. 'How did you know that seven was the right number of groups to ask for? Do you always use seven?', and perhaps more searchingly, 'What exactly is this normal curve that you have introduced?'

The first two questions are easily answered. 'No we don't always use seven groups. The best number of groups to use depends on how much data you have. A man called Sturgess investigated this problem and his recommendations are summarized in Table 2.2.'

I explain to my clients that this rule should not be used rigidly, for that might lead to very awkward group boundaries. With the viscosity data, using seven groups worked well because it gave simple group intervals of

Table 2.2 Sturgess' rule for histograms

No. of observations	4–9	10–24	25–49	50–89	90–189
No. of groups	4	5	6	7	8

62.0–65.9, 66.0–69.9, 70.0–73.9, etc. 'How do you know the computer used exactly 62.0 as the lower boundary of the first group?', asks Dave, who has been closely scrutinizing Fig. 2.2. 'It could be 62.1', he suggests.

I agree that the picture cannot be interpreted with as much precision as I may have implied. However, I am confident of the 62.0 and the 66.0, because I instructed the program to start the lower group at 62 and to use a group width of 4. 'Let us not get bogged down in the detail', I suggest. 'The purpose of the histogram is to give us an overall impression of how the viscosity results are scattered around the average. Notice that the computer uses the word "mean" rather than average, and it marks the mean on the histogram with a vertical line. The mean viscosity is 75.39 cSt.'

The computer also tries to estimate the spread, or scatter of the data by calculating what is known as the standard deviation. The standard deviation of the viscosity data is 5.200 cSt. If the data was more widely spread the standard deviation would be greater. Conversely, the standard deviation would be smaller if the viscosity results were less widely spread, i.e. closer to the mean. The standard deviation would be equal to zero if all the results were equal. An alternative way of assessing the variability, or spread of the data would be to calculate the range. This is much simpler than the standard deviation but it is not so reliable. The range is calculated by subtracting the smallest result from the largest. We can see in Table 2.1 that the highest viscosity was 87.9 cSt and the lowest was 62.7 cSt giving a range of 25.2 cSt.

For a good understanding of statistical process control, you need to delve into standard deviations and ranges in more detail to see how they relate to each other. However, for the purpose of assessing process capability you simply need to remember that a normal curve has a width of approximately six standard deviations. 'Which brings us back to the question that you haven't answered yet', interjects Ron Henderson, 'what exactly is this normal curve?'

I know that in the time available, I cannot produce an explanation that will make Dave Smith and Ron Henderson entirely happy with normal curves, but I offer the following. 'You can regard a normal curve as simply a very smooth histogram. The normal curve in Fig. 2.2 has the same mean and the same standard deviation as the histogram, but you will notice that it is a little wider. Obviously the histogram shows us how the viscosity varied from batch to batch in the past. We can look upon the normal curve as being a prediction of how the viscosity will vary in the future. All things being equal of course.'

'Did you say that the normal curve has a width of six standard deviations?', Ron asks. Before I can reply he continues, 'With a standard deviation of 5.2 cSt, the curve should have a width of 31.2 cSt. Furthermore, it should be centred on the mean viscosity, 75.38 cSt, so we can see how this compares with the specification'.

'Exactly, exactly.' I am delighted that Ron Henderson has seen the relevance of Fig. 2.2 to customer satisfaction. 'If you tell me the specification, I can put it into the computer and the hard work will be done for us', I suggest.

Unfortunately, life is not so simple as I had hoped. Lubrichem has two major customers for LBC80. One customer has agreed a specification of 80.0 ± 12.0 cSt, whilst the other insists on 80.0 ± 10.0 cSt. 'Let us focus on the more difficult customer', Dave insists, 'We may as well face up to the bad news, as soon as possible.' I type into the computer an upper specification limit (USL) of 90.0 cSt and a lower specification limit (LSL) of 70.0 cSt, then I request a further diagram, on which the specification will be included.

Figure 2.3 contains the histogram and the normal curve that we had in Fig. 2.2. To these have been added four vertical lines which from left to right are labelled:

1. −3s This is drawn three standard deviations below the mean.
   $$75.4 - 3 \times 5.2 = 59.8 \text{ cSt}$$
2. LSL This is drawn at the lower specification limit, 70.0 cSt.

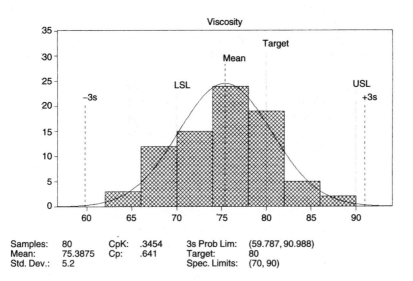

Samples:	80	CpK:	.3454	3s Prob Lim:	(59.787, 90.988)
Mean:	75.3875	Cp:	.641	Target:	80
Std. Dev.:	5.2			Spec. Limits:	(70, 90)

Fig. 2.3 Product variability and customer specification.

3. USL This is drawn at the upper specification limit, 90.0 cSt.
4. +3s   This is drawn three standard deviations above the mean.
      $75.4 + 3 \times 5.2 = 91.0$ cSt.

Note that the whole of the histogram lies within the $\pm 3s$ lines and almost the whole of the normal curve lies within these lines. The important questions are:

- 'Does the histogram lie within the two specification lines, LSL and USL?' If it does, then our 80 batches are within specification.
- 'Does the normal curve lie within the two specification lines?' If it does, then there is a good chance that future production will also satisfy the customer's requirements.

Ron can see that Fig. 2.3 contains some rather bad news. He turns to Dave and fires a whole battery of questions 'Were we aware of this Dave? Have we ever done this sort of analysis? Capability analysis, I suppose you'd call it. Do we produce histograms and compare them with specifications? What about this C_p thing you mentioned earlier?'

Dave does not look too happy. I judge from his facial expression that the true answer to the first three questions is probably 'No'. However, he chooses to focus on the fourth question and he explains to Ron that the C_p is a process capability index which is an alternative to the pictorial analysis we have carried out. He turns to me for confirmation.

2.4 PROCESS CAPABILITY INDICES

For me to tell the Quality Manager that he is wrong, would not be helpful. Of course he is not entirely wrong, for C_p is indeed a name given to one particular type of process capability index. But he is wrong in suggesting that a capability index is an alternative to a graphical analysis of production data. These capability indices are calculated in order to express in one number the ability of the process to meet the specification. The formula used to calculate C_p is:

$$C_p = \frac{USL - LSL}{6s}$$
$$= \frac{90.0 - 70.0}{6 \times 5.2}$$
$$= 0.64$$

I explain to Ron and Dave how the C_p index is calculated and I also point out that '$C_p = 0.64$' is displayed on the screen below the diagram. When we calculate a C_p index we are comparing two lengths on the diagram. 'USL − LSL' is the distance between the specification lines whilst '$6s$' is the distance between the +3s line and the −3s line.

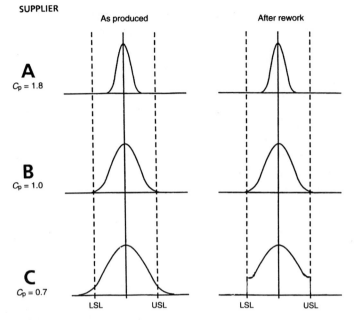

Fig. 2.4 Three competing suppliers.

Ron can see that a C_p of 0.64 is not very good. 'It seems to me that we need a C_p of 1.00, or even higher, if we are to satisfy the customer', he suggests. 'But we are satisfying the customer', Dave insists. 'Don't forget, these are the initial viscosities before we did any blending or re-work. If we had a C_p greater than 1 we wouldn't need the re-work, so we would satisfy the customer at much less cost.'

'That's an important point Dave has made. Your profitability may be less thán that of your competitors if their processes have higher C_p values. Furthermore, your profitability could fall dramatically if the customer insisted on a tighter specification, whilst one of your competitors might be able to accommodate this change without such a loss. Consider the three hypothetical suppliers in Fig. 2.4.'

'Which of the three suppliers is most similar to Lubrichem?', I ask. My hosts agree that supplier C has a similar capability to what we have seen in Fig. 2.3. I hasten to reassure them that I do not have intimate knowledge of their competitors' processes. Figure 2.4 represents three hypothetical suppliers. They could be in any industry.

This diagram clearly speaks volumes to both Ron Henderson and Dave Smith. It is obvious from their comments that they see their company as Supplier C. Furthermore, they appreciate that C is unlikely to survive if it is competing against A in a declining market. I wonder which of my clients will ask the obvious question, 'How can we improve our process so that we become as good as supplier A?'

To my surprise Dave Smith asks a rather different question. 'This C_p index is quite straight forward. What's the snag? Why do people use other indices, which seem much more complex?'

'You're right, Dave. There are other process capability indices and none are as simple as the C_p. You need to know about the others because they arise in discussions between customers and suppliers. Furthermore, you need to have quite a good understanding of C_{pu}, C_{pl} and C_{pk}, or you can easily shoot yourself in the foot.'

I would have expected that the threat of more complex formulae might have dampened Ron Henderson's enthusiasm for further discussion of capability indices. However, he shows an alert interest. Perhaps he was aroused by my mention of feet and shooting. Perhaps he has heard of capability indices in communications with customers or Lubrichem's sales staff. 'Tell us about the C_{pk}', he demands.

I explain that the C_p index is only useful if the average quality is on target, as it is for all three suppliers in Fig. 2.4. Drifting off target does not change the C_p, however, but it will surely change the customers reaction to our product. With the viscosity specification of 80 ± 10 cSt we have a target viscosity of 80 and the C_p index will give a useful indication of our capability if the average viscosity of our product is close to 80. The viscosity data in Table 2.1 has a mean of 75.39 cSt, which is 4.61 cSt off target. This is taken into account when we calculate the upper and lower capability indices:

$$C_{pu} = \frac{USL - mean}{3s} \quad \text{and} \quad C_{pl} = \frac{mean - LSL}{3s}$$

$$= \frac{90.0 - 75.39}{3 \times 5.2} \qquad = \frac{75.39 - 70.0}{3 \times 5.2}$$

$$= 0.94 \qquad\qquad = 0.35$$

Notice that the C_{pu} is larger than the C_{pl}. This is because our average is below the target value. If our mean were above target the C_{pl} would be greater than the C_{pu}. The two indices would be equal if we were on target. An optimist might be inclined to take the larger of the two indices as an indication of process capability, but this would be a foolish self-deception. What we need to do is to discard the larger and focus on the smaller of the two indices. The most widely used index, the C_{pk}, does in fact do exactly that:

$$C_{pk} = \min (C_{pu}, C_{pl})$$

'So, with the viscosity data, the C_{pk} is equal to 0.35', I remind my clients. 'This represents the capability of the process if it is allowed to run off target with a mean viscosity of 75.39 cSt. The C_p of 0.64, that we calculated earlier, indicates how large the C_{pk} would be if we could move the mean viscosity

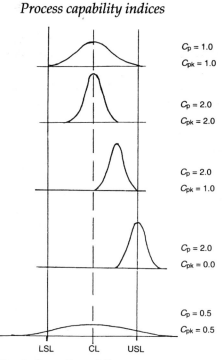

Fig. 2.5 Process capability indices, C_p and C_{pk}.

back on target. Perhaps a diagram will help you to appreciate the difference between the two indices.'

'Getting the process on target might not be too difficult. But then, any further increase in C_{pk} can only be achieved by reducing the variability of the process', suggests Dave Smith.

'Well, there is another way . . .', I start to reply.

'We can change the specification. If we loosen the spec all the process capability indices will increase.' Ron Henderson's forceful interruption of my reply is indicative of the emotion generated by this discussion.

Clearly, the Marketing Director and the Quality Manager of Lubrichem do not want to live with a C_{pk} of 0.35. To increase this capability index they can take three actions:

1. Try to ensure that the mean viscosity of future batches is closer to the target of 80 cSt.
2. Reduce the batch-to-batch variation in viscosity. This will give a smaller standard deviation and hence a larger index.
3. Widen the specification. If (USL – LSL) increases, the index will increase.

At this point I notice that Ron is much happier than Dave. Perhaps Ron is uplifted by his increased understanding of what needs to be done. I suspect Dave is depressed because he has to do it. 'The customers will not allow us to widen the specifications', he asserts. 'In fact, as Roland has said, they are likely to insist on narrowing the specs, sooner or later. Obviously we have to persuade the production people to bring the average viscosity back on target and we have to reduce the batch-to-batch variation. But I don't know exactly how'.

'Well, gentlemen, at this point in time no one knows exactly what needs to be done, but your production people probably have dozens of ideas that need to be taken on board. You must have faith that all variability has causes and that these causes can be identified, if you consistently use the scientific method. Now is the time to start a programme of never-ending process improvement.'

'Can we leave it until after lunch?', Ron asks, with a huge smile. 'We've had a very good session, but now all three of us need a drink.'

'Just one last word', I insist, 'We must carry out further analysis of this data when we return from lunch. There are other diagrams we can produce, and these will shed a different light on the capability of your process. Things may not be as bad as they first appear.'

2.5 VARIABILITY AND CHANGE

We have a drink, then a very good lunch in the Directors' Dining Room. It would be churlish of me to point out that the cultural change achieved under the new MD has not yet embraced single-status dining facilities. I focus instead on impressing my hosts with my knowledge of the chemical and associated industries. I have done consultancy work with several of Lubrichem's customers, with many of its suppliers and even with one of its competitors, when it was part of another group. If I am to have long-term contact with Lubrichem, I need to leave Ron Henderson in no doubt about my competence, my breadth of experience and my willingness to adapt to their particular needs. All companies are different. Indeed, all processes are different, but they will all yield their secrets to those who are prepared to supplement their specific knowledge with an understanding of variability.

'You suggested we take another look at the viscosity data', Ron says as we return to his office.

'First, I have a confession to make', I insist. 'We broke for lunch earlier than I expected. Because we interrupted our analysis at that point, we ran the risk of drawing false conclusions. In fact we broke one of the golden rules of industrial data analysis: **never make use of a histogram without also examining a run chart**. I accept full responsibility, of course, for this misdemeanour, and I will take immediate action to correct any false conclusions we may have drawn.' Having switched on my laptop computer, I need but a few key strokes to bring up on the screen a run chart of the 80 viscosity results.

A run chart is, perhaps, even simpler than a histogram. It shows how the viscosity varied from batch to batch. It is a very useful picture because it

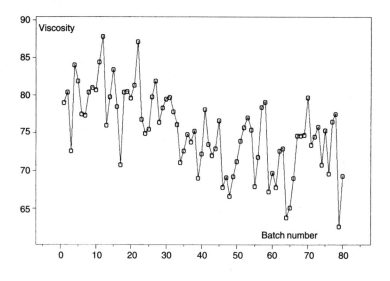

Fig. 2.6 A run chart of 80 viscosity results.

helps us to draw conclusions about the nature of this variability. To illustrate its usefulness in this context I ask my clients, what could well be described as, a leading question: 'When you look at the run chart of the 80 viscosity results, do you see any change?'

I like to think that I have built a good rapport with Ron Henderson and Dave Smith. Nonetheless, they are anxious not to appear foolish or naïve. They consider the run chart for some time before Dave suggests that perhaps the viscosity has decreased. 'Yes', confirms Ron, 'the viscosity dropped quite suddenly after batch 31. I suppose the average viscosity was about 80 then it dropped to about 70.'

'I'm not sure about the sudden drop', says Dave. 'Perhaps the viscosity declined rather gradually from batch 31 to batch 45 or 50.'

'Well, we are all agreed that there was a decrease of about 10 cSt. Perhaps it was sudden. Perhaps it was gradual'. I offer, as a summary of our conclusions. 'Of course you could have answered, quite rightly, that there are 79 changes in the run chart. No batch has the same viscosity as the previous one, as far as I can see.'

My clients seem to be disturbed by this suggestion. Perhaps it implies that they have missed something. Perhaps they now see my original question as unfair. 'Well, I was trying to ignore the wild fluctuations from batch to batch. I thought you wanted us to focus on the underlying trend, the hidden structure, as it were', Dave Smith mutters, rather apologetically.

'Yes Dave, you were right to focus on the underlying trend', I agree. 'If there is a trend of any sort, be it a gradual change or a sudden change, then it is very important to detect it. Furthermore, we must try to detect it as soon as possible, so as to increase our chance of finding the cause. At the same time we cannot ignore what you called "the wild fluctuations" from batch to batch. This is often referred to as random variation.'

At this point I feel the need to restrain myself. Having spent the last 20 years helping managers, scientists and technologists improve their processes, I find it easy to talk about process variability. It is a big subject and we could talk around it for hours. We must return to the run chart and the LBC process, but I will allow myself one more general comment.

'We run a three-day course on statistical process control and two whole days are devoted to control charts. The prime purpose of these control charts is to help us to detect changes in a process. The chart helps us to distinguish between:

- real long-term changes, which we can act upon; and
- random fluctuations, which we must live with, at least in the short term.

As control charting is such a big topic we must stay clear of it today. Let us return to the run chart and see what it tells us about the capability of the process.'

'Do you feel any better about the histogram now that you have seen the run chart?', I ask my clients. The reply indicates an understanding of variability that many managers do not possess.

'The first 30 batches are within the specification', observes Ron Henderson. 'Yes, a histogram of the first 30 batches would be much narrower and would give a much higher value of C_p or C_{pk}', adds Dave Smith. 'If only the process were more stable, it would then be more capable.'

'Gentlemen, you have raised a very important point. If we are to make a reasonable assessment of the potential capability of the process, we need to consider a period when it was stable, such as batches 1–30 or batches 40–80, perhaps. I will produce separate histograms for each of these two periods.'

'Wow! We have improved the process already, and we haven't even got our hands dirty', exclaims Ron Henderson as Fig 2.7 appears on the screen. 'The C_p is now 0.89 and the C_{pk} is 0.86. I guess the production guys must have been almost on target during this period.'

I am sure Ron realizes that we have not improved anything, except our conception of the process capability. By selecting a set of data, which shows the process to be stable and on target, we have obtained an estimate of what this process might achieve in the future. However, it is reasonable to use this estimate, only if we can be confident of keeping the process on target. Obviously the process shifted off target some time between batches 30 and 40, then it remained way off target through to batch 80. These last 40 batches are summarized in Fig. 2.8.

I point out to my clients that the mean viscosity of the last 40 batches was 72.43 cSt. Clearly this is well below the 80 cSt that the customers would

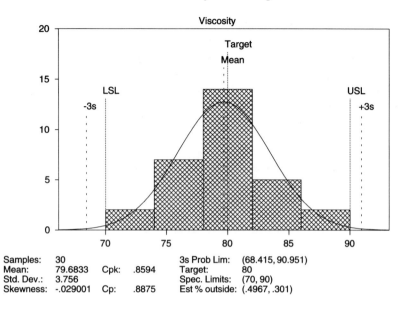

Fig. 2.7 A histogram of the first 30 batches.

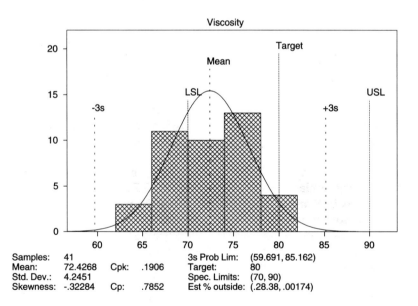

Fig. 2.8 A histogram of the last 40 batches.

wish for. 'That's two weeks' production', Ron Henderson points out. 'How can the production people be so wide of the mark for so long, Dave?'

'I'm sure there must be some explanation', he answers. 'No doubt they would blame the suppliers, or maintenance, or union problems, or . . . I should be able to use our BS5750 traceability system to find out what happened here.'

'Let us look to the future', I suggest. 'If you cannot prevent such large sustained shifts from happening, then you have a process which is unstable and incapable. The C_{pl} for the last 40 batches is only 0.19. I guess that about 30% of those batches must have been out of spec. The good news is that the C_p in Fig. 2.8 is 0.79 and the C_p in Fig. 2.7 is 0.89, compared with 0.64 in Fig. 2.3. These indicate that the process would be much more capable if only you could keep it stable.'

'When you say "stable", do you mean "on-target"?', Dave Smith asks.

The simple answer would be 'No', but such a blunt response might offend. 'A stable process exhibits only random fluctuations, with no shifts in mean and no changes in variability', I reply. 'Figure 2.6 shows that this process was unstable, because a shift in mean viscosity occurred, as you pointed out. If the process suddenly became more variable, or less variable, that would also indicate instability.'

'But the process was stable for the first 30 batches and it was quite capable, if only we could keep it that way. What should we do, Roland?', Ron asks. This is not a rhetorical question. He wants an answer. Lubrichem needs an answer.

'You have two objectives,' I suggest. 'The short-term objective is to keep the process at its best, as it was for the first 30 batches. The long-term objective is to reduce the variability of the process. Statistical process control charts can help you achieve both objectives. Unfortunately, control charting is a very big topic and we don't have time for it today.'

'OK, we'll leave control charts until your next visit, Roland, but I still have some questions about process capability', snaps Dave, anxious that I do not escape before he has the chance to tie up some loose ends.

'We haven't looked at the two other variables, calcium and sediment. The calcium specification is 8.0–8.5% but the sediment spec is one-sided, less than 0.1%. How do you cope with that?'

'Well, I thought *you* might like to cope with it and we could discuss your analysis on my next visit. With a one-sided specification the C_p index is meaningless. We calculate C_{pu} when there is only an upper limit and we calculate C_{pl} when there is only a lower limit.'

Ron's secretary knocks and enters: 'The car is waiting, Mr Caulcutt. You'll need to hurry or you'll miss your train.'

2.6 SUMMARY

Lubrichem experiences increasing pressure from all sides. New competitors enter the market as it becomes truly global. Prices of raw materials are subject to sudden unpredictable increases as political events unfold. Customers make increasing demands for higher quality and/or a more consistent product. In this climate Lubrichem must change. Its staff must accept change as a way of life.

Customers have invited Lubrichem to demonstrate its ability to meet specifications. This dialogue takes place between sales representatives on the one hand and buyers on the other. There is a need for both to understand the content of this chapter.

We have seen how product quality measurements can be presented as histograms and then compared with specifications. The comparison can be quantified by calculating a process capability index, but this is no substitute for a pictorial analysis of the data.

The C_p index gives an indication of the potential capability of the process, but it can be misleading if the mean or average differs substantially from the target value, which is often assumed to be midway between the upper and lower specification limits. The C_{pk} is a more useful index because it takes account of any deviation from target. Furthermore it can be used with a one-sided specification, with which a C_p index would be meaningless.

It is dangerous to draw conclusions from a histogram, without inspecting a run chart of the data. Because a run chart preserves the ordering of the data, it may reveal instability of the process, which would not be evident from a histogram. Instability could take the form of sudden or gradual changes in the mean level. A stable process, by definition, exhibits only random variation.

If we estimate the process capability during a period of stability we will obtain a better indication of its potential capability. Assuming that we can prevent the instability in the future, this estimate will show us how well we can meet the specification. Clearly, it is desirable to have a capability index greater than 1.0. This may be difficult to achieve in the short term, but one of our long-term objectives must be to reduce process variability and thus increase capability, if we are to survive.

I have suggested that you should obtain a standard deviation from a calculator or a computer. This will be OK if you have 'random looking' data from a stable process, but could be misleading if your data contains long-term changes, as we had in Fig. 2.5. I shall have much more to say about standard deviations in later chapters.

Chapter 3

Control charts with high-value products

The consultant makes a second visit to Lubrichem for further discussions with the Quality Manager. He also meets the Plant Manager of the LBC process and they discuss the relative merits of individuals charts and moving mean charts. These control charts are particularly suitable for monitoring and improving such a process which gives one-at-a-time data. The moving range chart is also introduced to distinguish between changes in accuracy and changes in precision.

3.1 INTRODUCTION

Today I am returning to Lubrichem. On this second visit I am travelling by car, because tomorrow I must call on another client who is not so well served by the rail network.

Fortunately, the weather is good and an early start has got me through Leeds before the morning rush hour. If there are no new roadworks on the M1, I could arrive at Lubrichem an hour early. Perhaps I will pass an hour in a motorway service area doing some of the reading I would have done if I had taken the train.

Traffic on the M1 is quite light at this time and most cars in the middle lane are cruising just below the unofficial speed limit of 80 m.p.h. Soon I am lost in thought as my mind focuses on Lubrichem and the manufacturing of oil additives. Since my first visit the Marketing Director, Ron Henderson, and the Quality Manager, Dave Smith, made good progress with the assessment of process capability. Within a week of our meeting, I received from Dave an analysis of their ability to meet the customer specifications for the calcium content and sediment in LBC80. (See Chapter 2.) During that week they had obtained a copy of the computer program, 'Quality Analyst', and used it to produce histograms, run charts and capability indices. On the telephone, I discussed with Dave Smith what conclusions could reasonably be drawn from the computer print-out and I am sure that they are now better equipped to answer any capability questions that their customers might ask.

I am also confident that they are now aware of the need to keep the process on target and reduce process variability, as a means of reducing rework costs. I anticipate that, when I arrive at Lubrichem, Dave and Ron will be ready to discuss control charts, or any other techniques that will help them in their pursuit of quality improvement.

3.2 A SIMPLE CONTROL CHART

'Ron will not be with us today', Dave Smith informs me as we walk from Reception to his office. I am disappointed, but not surprised. Very few senior managers want to become involved in the detail of statistical process control. 'He sends his regards. I know he was very upset that he had to go to London today. We considered asking you to postpone your visit so that he would not lose the thread of our discussions.'

Perhaps I do not look entirely convinced, for Dave continues, 'He is a changed man, you know. He really understood what we were talking about on your first visit and he is now reading the Deming book you recommended. He wants you to help us reach an understanding of variability at all levels throughout the company.'

Now I am more convinced. I am also very interested in the prospect of a large training programme, but I am doubly disappointed that Ron Henderson cannot be with us. Senior management commitment to the use of statistical process control is lacking in many companies. Where it takes root it must be nurtured, lest it wither, for the flower of continuous improvement will not bloom on a weakened root stock.

'I have invited George Grant to join us, Roland. George is Plant Manager on LBC. He has been with us since the first ice age. He has quite a lot of people under him – five shift teams, each with a supervisor and four operators, plus support staff.'

As I was born some time after the last ice age, Dave's description leads me to expect a very old man worn down by the responsibility of managing considerable financial and human resources, probably close to retirement and unlikely to welcome change. When George enters the office, I am pleasantly surprised by his brisk efficiency and cheerfulness.

We shake hands. 'I heard you speak at the Manchester Conference last year', he informs me. 'I am really looking forward to getting cracking with these control charts again. This time we must get it right. I like the ideas you put forward in Manchester on the use of control charts with chemical batch processes.'

It transpires that a previous attempt to introduce control charts on the LBC plant, in the mid-eighties, had been a failure and the conclusion was drawn then that SPC did not work on this type of plant. Obviously, I need to demonstrate that control charts *can* be used with the LBC process. Furthermore, I need to illustrate precisely how they *should* be used and what benefits can be gained.

'Let's not jump the gun, George', Dave Smith pleads, 'I'd like Roland to tell us in the clearest possible terms, what exactly is a control chart. If we are going to sell this throughout the company we need stark simplicity from the outset. You remember how we were bogged down in those special causes and common courses in previous discussions.'

I sympathize with Dave's plea for simplicity and clear definition. I suspect he and/or George have attempted to read books on SPC that do not relate to chemical manufacturing processes. 'There are many types of control chart. Let us focus on those that could be useful with *your* processes and let us start with the simplest', I suggest. 'Do you remember the run chart we looked at on my previous visit?'

I hand each of my clients a copy of the run chart (Fig. 2.6) and recap our conclusions. 'We agreed that the mean viscosity decreased some time between batch 31 and batch 40, but before and after this change we had stable periods. Let us focus on the first 30 batches when the process was not only stable, but also very close to the target viscosity of 80 cSt.' I hand out copies of the histogram for the first 30 batches (Fig. 2.7). During this period the mean viscosity was 79.68 cSt and the standard deviation was 3.756 cSt. The normal curve, superimposed on the histogram, represents what we might reasonably expect if the process continued to perform as it did during this period. Notice that the whole of the histogram and almost all of the normal curve lie between the vertical lines labelled $-3s$ and $+3s$. We can predict that future results will lie between these lines if the process does not change. Let us draw similar lines on the run chart. They will help us to make decisions about whether the process has or has not changed.

The only difference between the run chart (Fig. 2.5) and the control chart (Fig. 3.1) are the three horizontal lines drawn on the latter. The centre line (CL) is drawn through the mean (79.68 cSt). The upper action line (UAL) is drawn at 90.95 cSt and the lower action line (LAL) is drawn at 68.41 cSt. These two values are calculated as follows:

$$\overline{X} \pm 3\sigma$$

where $\overline{X}$ is the mean, and σ is the standard deviation. Many books use the Greek letter σ to represent the standard deviation, though our computer program, 'Quality Analyst', uses the English letter 's'. 'Quality Analyst' places the centre line (CL) at the mean of the data, unless you instruct it to do otherwise. If we were using the chart to monitor future production it might be preferable to place the centre line at the target viscosity, 80.0 cSt. The action lines would then be placed at 'Target $\pm 3\sigma$'.

'So a control chart is simply a run chart with a centre line and two action lines', suggests George, but his tone of voice implies that he is asking a question. 'That is not quite right', I hasten to reply. 'The *individuals chart*

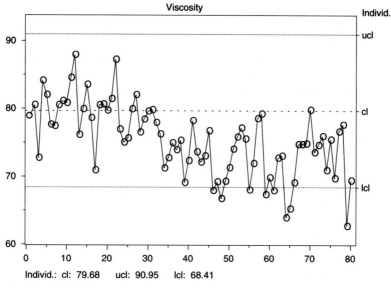

Fig. 3.1 An individuals chart.

(Fig. 3.1) is simply a run chart with action and centre lines. But there are several other types of control chart, on which we do not plot individual values, so they are a little more complex. We will come to them later.'

Dave has been staring at the individuals chart (Fig. 3.1) in disbelief. 'This is ridiculous', he exclaims. 'Why do all the books on SPC discuss rational subgroups and insist that we should plot means and ranges, when all we need is the simple individuals chart?'

'I would like to know where you get this standard deviation', George interrupts. The individuals chart is triggering a deluge of questions, many of which will have to be deferred till later.

'I am sure you haven't read *all* the books on SPC Dave. Perhaps the ones you have read weren't written for you', I suggest. 'Perhaps they refer to processes which are different to yours. Processes with which the individuals chart would not be appropriate. You asked me a simple question, "What is a control chart?" and I have answered by saying that there are several types of control chart and showing you one which could be used with your LBC process. I started with the simplest chart to facilitate the learning process. Later we can discuss other types of chart and we can talk about how we calculate standard deviations but, before we do so, let us make sure that you understand how to use this one. You suggested, during my last visit, that the viscosity decreased some time after batch 30. What does the control chart (Fig. 3.1) tell us?'

'Well, the first point below the lower action line is at batch 46. I suppose the chart is telling us that the viscosity decreased after batch 45', George suggests. He turns to Dave Smith for confirmation.

'Well, the first action point is at batch 46', Dave agrees, 'but I think the decrease occurred much earlier, perhaps batch 34. There is no guarantee that a control chart will indicate a change immediately after it occurs. I suppose it is a matter of luck, with the random fluctuations. You see we almost had an indication at batch 39.'

They look to me, perhaps expecting an authoritative statement on when the change occurred. 'You are right Dave', I concur. 'We use a control chart to detect process changes, but common sense tells us that a large change is likely to be detected quickly, while a small change may persist for some time before it is detected. I think you will understand this better, George, if you imagine the chart being plotted point by point as each new batch is tested.'

To illustrate the concept I lay a sheet of paper over the control chart (Fig. 3.1) and slide the sheet slowly to the right uncovering the points, one by one, so that the control chart grows, as it would if we were plotting the results in real time. As the point for batch 30 is uncovered I ask my clients to stop me as soon as they are convinced that the mean viscosity has changed.

'Stop', Dave shouts as point number 34 is revealed. 'The viscosity has decreased.' He glares at George and then at me, as if challenging us to prove him wrong. 'I am now convinced that the mean viscosity has fallen', he adds.

'Right George, Dave has expressed the opinion that the average viscosity of recent batches is less than 79.68 cSt. What do you think?'

'I think Dave is cheating', George suggests. 'He knows what's under the covering sheet. In practice he would not have that knowledge. At batch 34, I am not yet convinced that the viscosity has fallen. It seems to me that the next few batches could have viscosity above 80 cSt. We haven't yet had a point below the action line, have we? No one can stop Dave from having opinions, but surely, we do not want process operators acting on their opinions. We need clear rules that all 20 operators can follow.'

'My decision was based on the widely accepted rule that the occurrence of seven consecutive points below the centre line indicates a decrease.' Dave makes this statement with the calm assurance of one who has been questioned by someone of lesser competence. He turns to me for confirmation as he adds, 'Surely there is a set of rules laid down by Shewhart, for the interpretation of control charts.'

Asking people to interpret a control chart can be as revealing as giving them a personality test. Some people wish to speak of 'right' and 'wrong'. What are the right rules to use? What are the right decisions? What is the right way to calculate a standard deviation. Other people are less interested in right and wrong, but more concerned with understanding the underlying theory or with having freedom to make their own decisions in their own way. Unfortunately, many users of control charts become so obsessed with rules and/or theory that they forget what they are trying to achieve.

'Let us focus on our objectives', I suggest. 'You want your process operators to plot control charts so that they can detect changes in the process and take timely actions to restore the process to its best performance. Clearly, it is advantageous to use a simple chart with simple rules, so I think you should seriously consider using an individuals chart. However, I would recommend that you put the centre line at 80 cSt, rather than 79.68. Then your action lines would be at 80±3σ. I would also add warning lines at 80±2σ. For interpretation of the chart I recommend the following rules:

1. a change in mean is indicated if one point falls outside the action lines;
2. a change in mean is indicated if two consecutive points fall between a warning line and its neighbouring action line; and
3. a change in mean is indicated if seven consecutive points lie on the same side of the centre line.'

'Shall we do the calculations by hand then draw the lines on to the run chart or shall I use the computer to do the hard work?' There is overwhelming support for the latter so I switch on my laptop computer and quickly obtain Fig. 3.2, with the centre line at 80.00 cSt, the warning lines at 72.49 and 87.51 cSt and the action lines at 68.73 and 91.27 cSt.

'Right gentlemen, let us reinterpret the control chart using the three rules. If we had been plotting the results one by one, at what point would we have concluded that the viscosity had decreased?' Dave is the first to answer, 'Batch 34, as I said earlier. Using rule 3, we find that the point for batch 34 is the seventh in succession below the centre line. Rule 2 doesn't

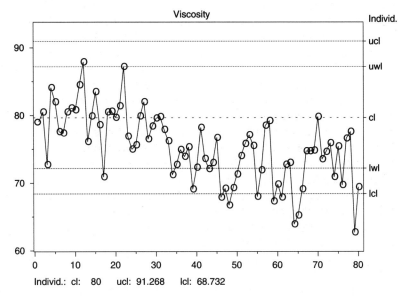

Fig. 3.2 An individuals chart with warning lines.

give a change indication until batch number 47 and rule 1 doesn't give an indication until batch 46.'

George is a little overwhelmed by the speed with which Dave has applied the rules. I recap what Dave has said and help George to come to the same conclusions. 'So the use of rule 3 has helped us to detect the change more quickly than we would have done if we had used only rule 1', he says, in summary.

'That's right George', I concur. 'The purpose of these additional rules is to detect change more quickly. On this occasion, it was rule 3 that indicated change. Next time it might be rule 2, or rule 1. Actually, there are lots of other rules in use in different industries, but we will not concern ourselves with those.'

'I think three rules is enough if we are to expect consistent interpretation of the charts by 20 process operators', George suggests. 'What do you think Dave?'

'Yes, I agree. I like the simplicity of the individuals chart and I don't think we should introduce any more rules beyond the three we already have. But I'm looking for the snag. If the individuals chart is so good, why isn't everyone using it?'

The Quality Manager and the Plant Manager stare at me as if expecting to hear that the individuals chart has some crippling disability, like it can only be used at night or on Sundays, perhaps. 'Well, in many ways the individuals chart is the very best, but there are alternative charts which are superior in one respect. I suggest we have a break, then I will introduce a second type of control chart, then we can compare the relative merits of the two. Do you agree?'

They agree. We head off for the dining room, but as we do so, George reminds me that I have yet to explain where the standard deviation comes from. He also expresses the opinion that detecting changes now seems much easier, but deciding what action to take is still a major problem. 'Will it be possible to obtain agreement among the operators about what action to take when they plot a point outside the action lines?', he asks.

3.3 AN ALTERNATIVE CONTROL CHART

During lunch we talk about British universities, and the national economy, holidays in France, writing, and running. I am happy to talk about these matters rather than statistical process control. When we return to Dave's office, I feel refreshed and ready for further discussion of how control charts can be used to achieve consistent performance of the LBC process. I decide that it would be wise to recap our morning's work before we progress to alternative control charts.

'So far we have focused on the individuals chart. This is simply a run chart on which are drawn a centre line, two warning lines and two action

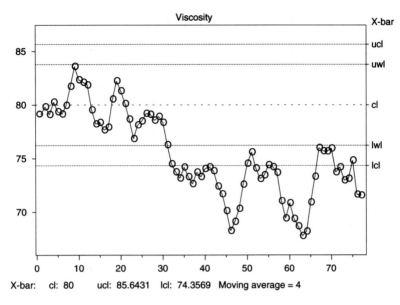

Fig. 3.3 A four-point moving mean chart.

lines. The attraction of the individuals chart lies in its simplicity. In practice it is so easy for the process operators to plot run charts and then for you to introduce the decision lines when the operators are ready to accept them. Unfortunately, the individuals chart is not the best control chart in all respects, so I'd like you to look at an alternative known as the moving mean chart. We can see it on "Quality Analyst" quite easily.'

'On the moving mean chart, we plot means, or averages', I explain. 'The first point plotted (Fig. 3.3) is the mean viscosity of the first four batches. To plot the second point we use the mean viscosity for batches 2, 3, 4 and 5. Then the third point is based on batches 3, 4, 5 and 6, etc. Why don't you work out a few moving averages, George? You can see if your operators will be able to cope with it.'

'Some of the operators are much brighter than George or me', Dave Smith asserts with a smile, but George Grant appears not to hear as he studies the data and the moving mean chart.

'Well, I guess we cannot calculate anything until we have the results for batch 4', George says at last. Then he writes the details of his calculations on the white board:

$$79.1 + 80.5 + 72.7 + 84.1 = 316.4 \text{ Dividing by 4 gives } 79.10$$
$$80.5 + 72.7 + 84.1 + 82.0 = 319.3 \text{ Dividing by 4 gives } 79.83$$
$$72.7 + 84.1 + 82.0 + 77.6 = 316.4 \text{ Dividing by 4 gives } 79.10$$

'You've got it, George', I confirm, 'but it's probably easier if you set it out in a table (Table 3.1).'

Table 3.1 Calculation of moving means

Batch	Viscosity	Moving mean
1	79.1	–
2	80.5	–
3	72.7	–
4	84.1	79.10
5	82.0	79.83
6	77.6	79.10
7	77.4	80.28
8	etc.	etc.

'As you pointed out, George, we cannot calculate a four-point moving mean until we have at least four results. So there is no entry in the right-hand column of Table 3.1 until we reach batch 4, then we put in the mean of the first four results which is 79.10. The second mean, 79.83, is calculated from the viscosity results for batches 2, 3, 4 and 5 and it appears on the same row as the result for batch 5.'

George does not look happy. 'I can understand the calculations', he says, 'but they do not seem to fit in with the chart. Surely, there shouldn't be any means plotted on the chart until we reach 4 on the x-axis?'

'I agree George. It would be better if the plotting of the means started at $x=4$ and ended at $x=80$. "Quality Analyst" has plotted the means starting at $x=1$ and ending at $x=77$. So, when we detect a change, we must add 3 to the x value to find the batch number. There is a further complication: to interpret a moving mean chart we must use slightly different rules to the ones we used with the individuals chart:

1. a change in mean is indicated if one point falls outside the action lines;
2. a change in mean is indicated if three consecutive points fall between a warning line and its neighbouring action line; and
3. a change in mean is indicated if ten consecutive points lie on the same side of the centre line.'

'Note that the action and warning lines on the moving mean chart are not in the same position as those on the individuals chart. The centre line is drawn at 80 cSt and the values for the control lines are calculated as follows.

Action lines at Target $\pm 3\sigma/\sqrt{n}$
Warning lines at Target $\pm 2\sigma/\sqrt{n}$
Where σ is the standard deviation, and $\sigma/\sqrt{n}$ is known as the standard error.'

'With a four-point moving mean chart n is equal to 4. Because of the $\sqrt{n}$ in the formulae the control lines will be closer to the centre line than was the case in the individuals chart. This is appropriate, because means do not fluctuate so wildly as do individual results.'

'Now then, how would you like to use these new rules to interpret the moving mean chart. If we had been plotting these means one by one as the results were obtained, at what point would we have decided that a change in viscosity had occurred?'

I stare at Dave. He takes the hint, and remains silent whilst George carefully applies each rule to Fig. 3.3. 'Well, rule 1 gives an indication at point 33. Rule 2 does not seem to help at all. Rule 3 gives an indication of change at point 31', George concludes. 'We must not forget to add 3 to these numbers. So my final conclusion is that we would have detected a decrease in viscosity at batch number 34.'

Dave nods in agreement. 'How does that compare with the conclusion we reached when we examined the individuals chart?', he asks. George and I answer in one voice, 'It's exactly the same.'

After a rather long silence, during which my clients are probably trying to figure out the advantages of the moving mean chart, I ask the obvious question, 'Well, what do you think of the two charts we have considered so far? Which are you going to use, the individuals chart or the moving mean chart?'

'Obviously the individuals chart is much simpler. In fact I cannot see any advantage whatsoever in using the moving mean chart', George Grant confesses. 'But I've just been racking my brains trying to decide what criteria we should use to select one or the other. Obviously, ease of use must enter into it. What do you think Dave?'

Dave Smith appears to be racking his brain as well. He is certainly in no hurry to answer. 'When in doubt, check your objectives', he says at last. 'We want to use a control chart to detect change in the LBC process. So a good chart is one which is easy to use and which detects changes quickly and reliably. If the moving mean chart does not detect changes more quickly or more reliably than would the individuals chart, then we should not use it. Of course there may be some other advantage beyond my comprehension', he adds, turning to me for verification.

'That's brilliant Dave. You're absolutely right. Choosing a control chart is rather like choosing a new car. You trade off performance against cost when buying a car, and you trade off performance against ease of use when setting up a control chart. Obviously, the individuals chart is easier to use, so let us consider the performance of the two charts. To put it in the words that you used Dave . . . would the moving mean chart detect change more quickly or more reliably than the individuals chart?'

George is clearly struggling to cope with this flood of new ideas, some of which are rather abstract, but he does not intend to drop out of the discussion. 'Surely we have demonstrated that the two charts perform equally well', he insists. 'They both detected the change at batch number 34.'

'Yes, George. With *this* set of data the individuals chart and the moving mean chart performed equally well. But, would their performance be equally good with *other* sets of data?', I ask.

'Good heavens, we could be old men by the time we have answered that question', Dave Smith asserts. 'It has taken us several hours to look at one set of data. How much data would we need to analyse in order to speak with confidence about the performance of the two charts?'

'Well, I looked at 10 000 sets of data using a computer simulation, and I repeated this many times in order to compare several charts. The results are presented in the second edition of my book *Statistics in Research and Development* (Caulcutt, 1991). I am afraid you will have to do some reading if you want the full story, but I can give you a rough comparison of the two charts. The moving mean chart will detect *small* changes more quickly than would the individuals chart, but it offers no advantage with large changes. Both charts would detect large changes more quickly than they would detect small changes, of course.'

'Thanks for sparing us the technical detail, Roland, but can't you be more precise?', George asks in exasperation. 'I'm sure we want to detect large changes in viscosity, but how small are these small changes. If they are not going to take us outside the specification let's ignore these small changes then we won't need the moving mean chart.'

'Right, then let us go back to the data. That will help us keep our feet on the ground', I suggest. 'Both charts have detected a decrease in viscosity. In real life, having detected a decrease we would now need to decide what corrective action to take in order to increase the average viscosity to the target value of 80 cSt. In making this decision it would be useful to know two things':

1. When did the decrease occur?
2. What is the mean viscosity since the decrease?

'Knowing *when* the change occurred may help us to track down the cause of the change. Knowing *how far* the process has deviated from the target may help us to decide how large the correction should be. I would like you to examine the two control charts and decide when the decrease in viscosity occurred and estimate the mean level of viscosity since the decrease. To make this realistic you should cover all points to the right of the point at which the change was detected (i.e. point 34 on the individuals chart and point 31 on the moving mean chart).'

George seizes the individuals chart, leaving the moving mean chart to be interpreted by the Quality Manager, Dave Smith, who has more experience in these matters. I encourage both participants to cover the later points on their respective charts but they appear reluctant to do so. I wait patiently, determined not to interfere.

Dave is the first to speak: 'You know, Roland, with this moving mean chart it is easy to see the changes in the level of viscosity, but it isn't so easy to say exactly when the changes occurred. How are you doing George?'

Perhaps George is encouraged by Dave's lack of success, for he certainly speaks with confidence when he announces his conclusions. 'I think the decrease in viscosity occurred in two stages. There was a small drop in level after batch 22 then a further larger drop after batch 33. But I suspect there is a complication, because the viscosity did not fluctuate so wildly between batches 23 and 46.'

George repeats his findings and I write them on the flip chart. 'Do you agree with what George has said, Dave?', I ask. Dave has already transferred his attention from the moving mean chart to the individuals chart. Then he puts the two charts alongside each other and his eyes dart from one to the other. 'It is very interesting to compare the two charts', he says at last. 'The moving mean chart is useful because it is smoother, but the individuals chart tells you more, because you are closer to the process. Yes, I agree with George's conclusions, but I needed the individuals chart to do so.'

'I am inclined to suggest that we should use the individuals chart', George responds. 'But you have not really explained these large and small changes, Roland. I do not want to reject the moving mean chart prematurely.'

'Right George. You have suggested that viscosity changes occurred at batch 22, batch 33 and batch 45. Let us split the data into four time periods and draw some pictures. We will draw a dotplot for each group of data whilst Dave calculates the mean and standard deviation for each group. Come on George, you read out the viscosity values. If you round them to the nearest whole number, I can plot them very quickly.'

'Well George, for a man who does not understand standard deviations you have done rather well', I suggest. 'It is just as you concluded. The variation in viscosity was less from batch 23 to batch 45. This is clearly

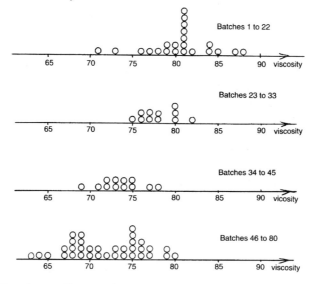

Fig. 3.4 Dotplots to illustrate the changes.

Table 3.2 Summary of viscosity between changes

Batches	Mean	Standard deviation
1–22	80.30	4.007
23–33	77.98	2.169
34–45	73.58	2.460
46–80	72.10	4.418

indicated by the dotplots and by the standard deviations of the four groups of results (Table 3.2). Obviously, 2.169 and 2.460 are less than 4.007 and 4.418. Changes in the variability of the process are very important, of course. Remember that one of our long-term objectives must be to decrease this variability, so as to supply a more consistent product. In fact, we can use an additional control chart, known as a moving range chart, to detect changes in variability – more about that later.'

'How about the changes in mean level? Are they large or small?', George asks impatiently, fearing that I may have forgotten his original question.

'Right George, we will consider each period in turn. For the first 22 batches the mean viscosity is 80.30 which is very close to the target of 80.0 cSt. The deviation from target of 0.30 cSt is very small compared with the random fluctuations and we cannot expect any chart to reliably detect such a small deviation. You may recall that we used a standard deviation of 3.756 cSt when we were setting up the charts. So the deviation from target is only 8% of the standard deviation. I would say that is very small. After batch 22 the mean viscosity drops to 77.98 cSt which is 2.02 cSt below the target. This deviation is 54% of the standard deviation. I would say that a deviation of approximately half a standard deviation is small. After batch 33 the mean viscosity drops further to 73.58 cSt, so the deviation from target is now 6.42 cSt, which is almost two standard deviations below the devised viscosity of 80 cSt. I would describe this as a large deviation.'

'For the sake of simplicity, let us define a small deviation as one which is less than one standard deviation in magnitude and we will define a large deviation as one which is two or more standard deviations in magnitude. So you can now understand my earlier assertion that a moving mean chart can be expected to detect a small change (or deviation from target) more quickly than would an individuals chart. Perhaps you are thinking that the extra complexity of the moving mean chart is a high price to pay for the higher sensitivity. Do not forget that the individuals chart is just as fast, or even faster, in the detection of large changes.'

The Quality Manager and the Plant Manager are in need of a break. I propose that we take one. They readily agree. 'Perhaps we will have time to discuss the moving range chart before I leave. Then I think we should talk about cusums on my next visit', I suggest. 'You will like the cusum chart. It is the most powerful of them all.'

'What's the snag?', asks George. 'It seems there is always a price to pay, for the benefits we get.'

3.4 MONITORING VARIABILITY

As we drink a cup of tea, George points out that I have an annoying tendency to present both sides of any argument. Perhaps this is a characteristic of statisticians I suggest and I risk boring him and Dave by telling them about the small company which placed an advertisement for a one-armed statistician. After the sole applicant was interviewed and offered the post, he asked why two-armed statisticians were not considered. 'We had a two-armed statistician who left quite recently', was the reply. 'Unfortunately, whenever we asked his opinion, he would say, 'Well, on the one hand, . . .'

Dave is not terribly amused by this story and he suggests we take a look at the moving range chart. While George continues to chuckle, I produce a four-point moving range chart on the computer. 'Before we examine the moving range chart, I'd like to make sure you realize why it is used in addition to the moving mean chart. These pictures will clarify the joint requirement.' From my briefcase I extract four diagrams, which show the performance of four people who have each fired six shots at a target (Fig. 3.5).

'Now then, gentlemen, how would you describe the performance of the four riflemen?', I ask. Both Dave and George are eager to answer. Perhaps they know more about shooting than I do. They speak simultaneously.

'Colin is the best shot. He is very precise.'

'So is Alan.'

'Yes, Alan is precise, but he is biased. All his shots are off-target.'

'You would say Dave was biased as well, I suppose. I would say he was inaccurate.'

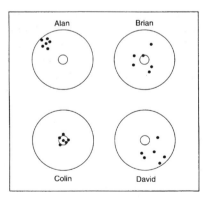

Fig. 3.5 Accuracy and precision.

'So is Brian.'

'No he isn't. Brian is OK on average. So I would say he was accurate.'

'It depends what you mean by accurate, I suppose.'

This lively, but unstructured, debate could continue for some time. Clearly there is great scope for disagreement as the two participants have not defined the key words: precision, bias and accuracy. Dave was an analytical chemist, so he prefers to speak of bias and precision. He would see Colin and Alan as precise and he would say that David and Alan were biased. George, on the other hand, has an engineering background. He would agree that Colin and Alan were precise but he would describe David and Alan as inaccurate, rather than biased.

I prefer Dave's definitions, but I realize that George's terminology is in keeping with that in most texts on SPC. We agree to speak of inaccurate rather than biased and I summarize as follows:

> Alan is precise but he is not accurate.
> Brian is not precise but he is accurate.
> Colin is both precise and accurate.
> David is neither precise nor accurate.

'The distinction between precision and accuracy is important because they require different corrective action', I stress. 'Both Alan and Brian could match Colin's performance if appropriate action were taken. However, whereas an adjustment of sights might be appropriate in Alan's case, an alcoholic treatment might be more effective with Brian. Furthermore, switching the two treatments could make matters worse.'

'Let us now return to the industrial setting', I suggest. 'The most import- ant point illustrated by Fig 3.5 is that a manufacturing process which is performing well (Colin) could deteriorate in two ways. It could go off target (Alan) or it could become more variable (Brian). If we were very unlucky the process might go off target and become more viable, simultaneously (David). It is essential to know which of the two diseases has infected the process, because they respond to different treatments. The individuals chart and the moving mean chart are both intended to be used for detecting deviations from target, i.e. change from Colin to Alan. If we want to detect changes in variability we should use, in addition, a moving range chart. That is what I have just printed out from the computer.'

'This is a four-point moving range chart', I explain. 'On it we plot the range of each group of four results. Thus the first plotted range is 11.4 which is the difference between the lowest and highest viscosities from the first four batches. The second range is based on the results for batches 2, 3, 4 and 5. I will set out the calculations in a table (Table 3.3).'

'It's done it again', George screams in mock horror. 'The computer has started plotting at $x = 1$. The whole picture needs shifting 3 spaces to the right. We must remember to add 3 to these x values if we want batch numbers.'

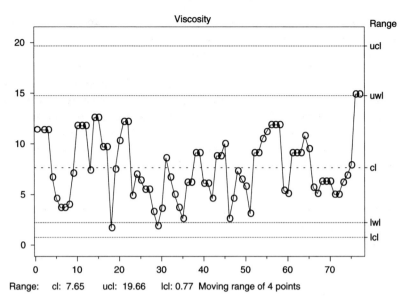

Fig. 3.6 A four-point moving range chart.

'You are right George', I agree, glancing at Dave to see if he has remembered this point, which arose when we first examined the moving mean chart. 'What does the moving range chart tell us about the LBC process? I am afraid I will have to inflict upon you another set of rules:

1. a change in variability is indicated if one point falls outside the action lines; and
2. a change in variability is indicated if five consecutive points lie between a warning line and its neighbouring action line.'

There is a long silence. George needs practice in the interpretation of control charts and Dave is reluctant to dominate the discussion. Eventually Dave breaks the silence: 'I think the moving range chart supports what you

Table 3.3 Calculation of moving ranges

Batch	Viscosity	Moving range
1	79.1	–
2	80.5	–
3	72.7	–
4	84.1	11.4
5	82.0	11.4
6	77.6	11.4
7	77.4	6.7
8	80.5	4.6
etc.	etc.	etc.

said earlier, George. The process was less variable during that middle period from point 23 to point 51, that would be batches 26 to 54. We must try to discover *why* the process was less variable.'

George is happy to be proved right about the reduced variability, but he is not entirely happy with Dave's interpretation. 'Which of the two rules indicates a change?', he asks. Dave explains that the rules cannot encompass all eventualities and it may be necessary to use simple common sense, from time to time. 'I noticed that 23 of the 29 points were below the centre line. Call it Smith's rule if you wish.'

George displays the anxiety of a man sinking in quicksand. He turns to me, hoping I will throw him a life line, but before he can speak, I suggest: 'In this context, it is OK for Dave to invent his own rules but you would not want your operators to enjoy much freedom, would you? You see, this is a post-mortem analysis in which we are drawing general conclusions and reflecting on the usefulness of various charts. With real-time monitoring of the process we would need more discipline. Though I agree with Dave's conclusion about the reduced variability, I must advise caution when interpreting range charts. A long run of points below the centre line is more likely than a similar run above the centre line, because the range chart is not symmetrical like the mean chart. You can see that the two warning lines are not equidistant from the centre line, for example.'

'Yes, I had noticed that', Dave says. 'I suppose the formulae for calculating this warning and action values must be more complex.'

'Well, the calculations are quite straightforward but you need to use four constants taken from a table which is in most text books on SPC (Appendix B). You simply multiply each of the constants by the mean range ($\bar{R}$). This mean range is obtained by putting the data into groups, calculating the range for each group then calculating the mean of the ranges. For the viscosity data the mean range is 7.65. The control lines for a moving range chart are as follows.

- Upper action line = $A\bar{R} = 2.57 \times 7.65 = 19.66$
- Upper warning line = $B\bar{R} = 1.93 \times 7.65 = 14.77$
- Centre line = $\bar{R} = 7.65$
- Lower warning line = $C\bar{R} = 0.29 \times 7.65 = 2.22$
- Lower action line = $D\bar{R} = 0.10 \times 7.65 = 0.77$

where A, B, C, and D are taken from Table A in Appendix B, and R is the mean range.

'The ranges of the subgroups tell us something about the spread of the data. In fact, the mean range can be used to calculate the standard deviation, but there are other methods. The calculation of standard deviations is a controversial topic among some users of control charts. Perhaps we can discuss that on my next visit.'

'Yes, I hope we can Roland', Dave says, 'but we must also plan training courses and you suggested earlier that we should cover cusums. I know that Ron Henderson wants to join us when we discuss training. We will have to fix a date on the phone.'

'Just one last question, before you go Roland', George insists. 'Does anyone use the conventional mean chart and range chart. If they aren't of use to us, how come they are OK for someone else?'

'Lots of people use the conventional mean chart and the conventional range chart. Their processes are different to yours. They make widgets. I am visiting a widget maker tomorrow. He is using mean and range charts but he is having trouble with his standard deviations.'

3.5 SUMMARY

During my second visit to Lubrichem, I have discussed control charts with Dave Smith, the Quality Manager and George Grant, the Plant Manager on the LBC plant. The nature of this manufacturing process is such that it gives us one-at-a-time data. We have, therefore discussed the types of control chart that are appropriate with this type of process.

The **individuals chart** is delightfully simple. If we add a centre line and two action lines to the run chart (which was introduced in Chapter 2) we have an individuals chart. If a point lies outside the action lines we conclude that the process was unstable or that the mean level changed. We can add warning lines and we can use various supplementary rules, to increase the sensitivity of the chart.

The **moving mean chart** is an alternative to the individuals chart, when we have one-at-a-time data. The moving mean chart is obviously more complex, but it can be expected to detect small changes more quickly. When choosing a control chart you must consider ease of use as well as sensitivity or power.

Both the moving mean chart and the individuals chart monitor the accuracy (or bias) of the process. The **moving range chart**, on the other hand, is used to monitor the precision of the process. If a process becomes more variable, or less variable, the moving range chart will detect the change, sooner or later. Clearly a massive change in precision is likely to be detected quickly but a small change may endure for some considerable time before it is detected.

A four-point moving range chart would be used in conjunction with a four-point moving mean chart. With an individuals chart we would use a two-point moving range chart.

In the next chapter we will discuss the conventional mean and range charts which are used with data that falls into natural subgroups. Such data comes from processes which manufacture low-value items, where 100% inspection would be inappropriate.

Chapter 4

Control charts with low-value products

The consultant visits Lancan to discuss the use of control charts with the Production Manager and the Quality Co-ordinator. They have followed the conventional procedure for setting up control charts, but this has not proved successful. A deeper understanding of process variability is required.

4.1 INTRODUCTION

I wake early – much earlier than is necessary, for today I have a rather short journey. I guess it will take just under an hour to reach Lancan and my appointment is not until 11:00, so a 9:45 start would seem reasonable. However, at 9:00 I decide that it is foolish to sit in the hotel worrying about being late, when I could put the journey behind me and sit at the destination. So at 9:15, I am on the rod and I arrive early, of course.

I am expecting to meet Bill Johnson, the Production Manager. I have spoken to him on the telephone and he has told me of his disillusionment. Indeed, he made it very clear to me that he now believes SPC charts just do not work with some of his processes. He has challenged me to prove otherwise.

I look forward to the challenge with some confidence. His comments on the telephone gave me the impression that his people have used the 'standard approach' to SPC charts and found the charts very unhelpful. Bill Johnson may believe that Lancan is the only company to encounter this problem, but I have met the same, or similar, problems in several companies in various industries – hence, my confidence.

It is true that I have little experience in the manufacture of tin cans but I do have experience with other processes that make low-value items, or 'widgets', as they are sometimes called. With widget processes it is normal practice to inspect a small sample, or group, of four or five widgets at regular intervals, perhaps every half hour. It would of course be economic suicide to carry out 100% inspection, though this is normal practice with high-value items.

4.2 WHAT IS A CONTROL CHART?

Bill Johnson takes great care to communicate clearly, whatever the audience, and he expects others to do likewise. He cannot stand slipshod, ill-prepared presentations. Above all, he cannot tolerate waffle. Small wonder, therefore, that he is in such a bad mood when I reach his office. He has just spent two hours in a Weekly Production Review Meeting where every question he asked seemed to trigger a deluge of waffle. He could not elicit a simple answer, no matter how simple his question.

Obviously, Johnson has had enough waffle for one day and he does not intend that I shall subject him to any more. His opening question clearly illustrates this: 'What is a control chart . . . exactly?' The simplicity of the question, the bluntness of his delivery and the emphasis he places on the final word, clearly indicate that he wants a straight answer. I give him one: 'A control chart is a data plot which can help you to decide whether or not a process has changed.'

I pause. Clearly, the answer is inadequate, but at least it is simple and it is not incorrect. Furthermore, I can build upon this initial definition when the questioner is in a more receptive mood. I make a suggestion, 'Look Bill, let me show you one or two pictures which will illustrate how control charts work.' From my briefcase I extract a diagram (Fig. 4.1) and lay it on the desk before him.

'This control chart is from a chemical company', I explain. 'Every time they produce a batch of this particular additive, they measure the viscosity and plot a point on the control chart. As you can see, batch 46 gave a point

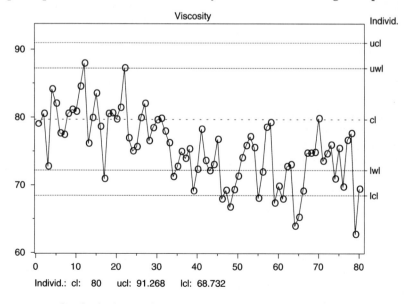

Fig. 4.1 An individuals chart indicating change.

outside the action lines. When this happens they conclude that the process had changed. Prior to batch 46, all the points are between the action lines so no action is required.'

I am reluctant to mention warning lines, or supplementary rules for chart interpretation. I feel that stark simplicity is required with Bill Johnson in his present mood. 'So you are not going to give me any rubbish about common causes and assignable causes?', he asks.

'I would prefer not to speak about causes at all, especially if they upset you', I reassure him. 'It is true that many books on SPC do distinguish between common causes and special causes. Some authors prefer to call them random causes and assignable causes. Furthermore, it is usual to describe a process as being 'in control' when only common causes are present and 'out of control' when one or more special causes act on the process. So these people would say that the process in Fig. 4.1, was in control for the first 30 batches, but later it was out of control.'

'That's just waffle. Don't you agree?', he snaps. Before I can find suitable words with which to express my opinion, he continues, 'How can a control chart know what has caused the process to change? In some cases even the operators and supervisors and engineers don't know the cause.'

'Bill, I agree, to a large extent. Philosophers have discussed cause and effect for thousands of years. Control charts do not possess a wisdom beyond that of Aristotle, but they do offer us a reliable method for detecting process changes. I prefer to talk about variability rather than causes. Thus I would describe the variation in viscosity during the first 30 batches as random variation. This seems a reasonable description as I cannot see any pattern in it. However, somewhere between batch 30 and batch 50, say, there is a sustained decrease in viscosity. This decrease may be due to *one* cause, whereas the random variation is probably the result of *many* causes.'

I pause at this point, wondering how far we can usefully take this discussion of causes. I am relieved to see that Bill Johnson is much more relaxed now and I decide to risk offering further thoughts on this important subject: 'You could argue, Bill, that there are 79 changes in viscosity in Fig. 4.1. Furthermore, you could assert that each of these changes must have a cause or causes. But a practical man, like you or I, can see that it would be futile to attempt to find, and act upon, all these causes. We rely on the control chart to reduce the size of the task to manageable proportions. It does this by telling us when it would be sensible to look for a cause. Thus, Fig. 4.1 is telling us, at batch 46, to look for the cause of a change in viscosity. Of course, the chart cannot tell us what the cause is, or how we should find it.'

'That's what I've been trying to say to my lads, but they go round and round in circles talking about common causes and special causes. I'd like you to explain to them that the sole purpose of a control chart is to detect change. I would like you to tell them that control charts will not help them to improve processes.'

'Oh, but they will', I insist, 'or at least, they can. Especially if they are used wisely by the right people.'

'How?', asks Bill, rather aggressively. 'Can you demonstrate, clearly and simply, how a control chart can help us to reduce the variability of one of our processes?'

'Yes, I think I can. Perhaps the best way to do this would be to show you a video, called 'The Japanese Control Chart'. It runs for about 20 minutes. I think you will enjoy it.'

Bill Johnson leads the way to a training room where I insert the video cassette into the player. We view and listen in silence as we drink our coffee. I sense that my client is impressed with the way that the control chart is being used by a team of Japanese operators, but my feeling is that he is even more impressed with the astute observations of the commentator, Don Wheeler.

'Well, that's a real eye opener', Bill says, as the tape rewinds. 'Where did the tape come from? Is it readily available? How much did it cost?'

'You could have your own copy tomorrow, Bill. Just telephone the British Deming Association, in Salisbury. I think the price is about £125.'

I know, from my own experience, that you need to view the video several times, to pick up all the messages that it conveys, so I attempt to summarize some of the more important points: 'Clearly, a control chart can be used to detect changes. Hopefully, appropriate action will be taken whenever a change is detected. However, as the video demonstrates, each change indication also constitutes a learning opportunity, if we ask questions such as:

- What is the cause of the change?
- What action is appropriate to reverse the change?
- Did the action effectively reverse the change?
- How can the process be modified to prevent the change occurring in the future?

As the operators attempt to answer these questions they should write their comments on the control charts. The result is a permanent record of the changes and their likely causes. As Wheeler says, 'The problems of the past are lessons for the future, only when they are documented and studied." Tell me, Bill, are your operators writing appropriate comments on the control charts?'

'No, they are not', he replies. 'My Quality Manager has pleaded with them to record, in writing, what they have done, but they just don't do it. Obviously, without these comments we won't get the maximum benefit from our charts. What do other companies do, Roland?' I extract from my briefcase a copy of a control chart plotted by process operators in Charter Chemicals. It shows how the melt index of polyethylene varied over a seven-day period (Fig. 4.2). I hand the control chart to Bill Johnson.

'It's certainly not a work of art', he mutters, as he struggles to absorb all the detail of the suspected changes and their possible causes. After a long pause he asks, 'Is this a useful chart? They seem to be taking a lot of action.

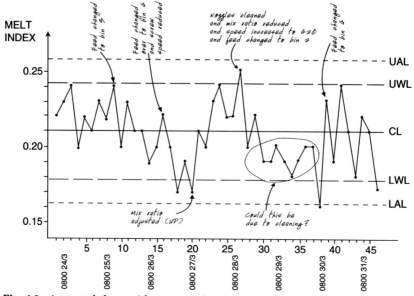

Fig. 4.2 A control chart with operators' comments.

Almost every day they are looking for causes. Surely, that's far too often? We had the same trouble here. Our first charts indicated changes several times a day, so we had to move out the action lines. Is it OK to do that?'

'Well, Bill, that is a very big question. Should we take a break, at this point, then have a detailed examination of what you have been doing?'

4.3 SETTING UP A CONTROL CHART

Bill Johnson had suggested earlier that we would be joined for lunch by Arthur Wilson, the Quality Manager. Unfortunately, Arthur has been called away to attend a meeting at another site, so I am introduced to one of his Quality Co-ordinators, Graham Covey.

'There are three Quality Co-ordinators at this site', Bill informs me. 'The posts were established, eighteen months ago, to help unify the various TQM initiatives within the company. So the Quality Co-ordinators have expertise in teamwork, SPC, training and personal development.' During lunch Graham describes his, very interesting, day-to-day activities and explains how he and his colleagues try to ensure that the quality improvement teams make full use of all available problem-solving tools.

Soon we are talking about motivation and I explain to Bill and Graham how I think it is possible to establish a learning culture, in which all employees have a passion for learning about their processes. The purpose of the learning, of course, is to assist the achievement of quality improvement.

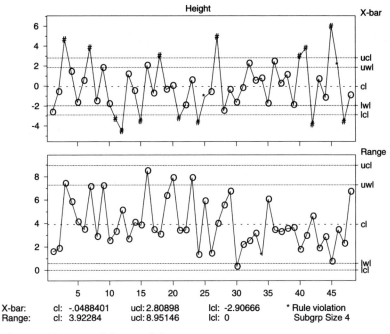

Fig. 4.3 Unsuccessful control charts.

Graham shows considerable interest in my views on how people learn and I recommend that he should read about Deming's 'system of profound knowledge' (Neave, 1990). Bill Johnson, however, has more immediate objectives and suggests that we return to our discussion of control charts. 'Right Graham', he snaps, 'show Roland the charts we were looking at yesterday. Perhaps he can explain what is wrong with them.'

Consultancy certainly becomes easier with practice. If I had been shown Fig. 4.3 20 years ago, I would have had to do some quick thinking in order to retain my credibility. The consultancy process would have involved my asking lots of questions about how the data had been gathered and analysed. I would have found the thinking and questioning quite exhausting. Now, with the benefit of having seen it all before, I probably will not need to do much thinking. Nonetheless, I will still need to ask some questions, just to be sure I do not go down the wrong track.

My questioning reveals that the means and ranges plotted in Fig. 4.3 were calculated from the heights of 192 cans made on one particular day, 15th November. Four cans were sampled every half hour and the height of each can was measured, as a deviation from the standard height. Thus a tall can would have a positive height, a short can would have a negative height and we would expect the mean height to be close to zero.

Both Graham and Bill are noticeably unsettled. I sense that each is anxious to express his opinions about the usefulness, or the correctness, of the charts, but both are hesitant. Perhaps they would like to hear my opinion first. As I am about to ask further questions Bill explodes. 'This mean chart is worse than useless', he insists. 'It gives 14 action indications in one day. If we were using these charts to help us manage the process, we would be running round in circles looking for 14 causes of change. I don't think the process changed at all during this day.'

Bill glowers at Graham, then at me, as if daring us to disagree. I look at Graham. Clearly he does disagree. 'The chart is correct', he insists. 'The mean chart is telling us that the process is out of control. If we cannot identify the causes and take appropriate action, we will not gain control of the process.'

Recalling my earlier conversation with Bill Johnson, I expect him to explode again at this point. He does not. Speaking slowly and carefully, while looking straight at me, he says, 'To cut a long story short, Roland, we have already agreed that the 14 action points in the mean chart probably have only *one* cause, and that is the variation in the steel. We also agree that there is nothing we can do about the steel, because we cannot buy better steel at the right price. Our disagreement is about how to use control charts. Common sense tells me the mean chart should be changed so that the action and warning lines are further from the centre line. What do you think?'

'I would agree that you should change the control chart, if changing it would make it more useful. But I would like to ask Graham how the control charts were set up. I am reluctant to offer any advice until I know how the standard deviation was calculated.'

Graham seems surprised that I should focus attention on the standard deviation. 'Well, if I were doing this by hand', he says, 'I would use the mean range divided by Hartley's constant. But these charts were produced on a computer by a package called "Quality Analyst". I assume the computer program uses the same formula. Doesn't it?'

'Well, it might have used your formula, but it can use other formulae depending on what instructions have been given', I reply. Graham's anxiety appears to rise further as this unforeseen complexity is laid before him. I hasten to reassure him, 'We can probably figure out which formula the program used if you can tell me what data it used. Was the standard deviation calculated from the data displayed in the charts, or had it been calculated previously from some earlier data?' 'Oh, it must have been calculated from this data', Graham asserts with a firmness that belies his falling confidence. However, I feel that he is probably correct, because the program will have followed the 'most reasonable' procedure, unless he instructed otherwise.

At this point, I feel that I should summarize for Bill and Graham, just where we are now and where we are going. 'This is a classic analysis of process stability, Bill', I suggest. 'For this analysis, I would recommend a standard procedure which I call procedure B. It is contained in most SPC books, but it is not always explicitly stated and in some books it has been buried in theory.'

From my briefcase I extract two copies of procedure B to lay before my clients (Appendix A). After allowing them time to read through the procedure, I continue. 'You see that the standard deviation is calculated by dividing the mean range by Hartley's constant. However, there are other ways of calculating a standard deviation. Thus it would be helpful if each formula, or each method, or each result, had a different name. Unfortunately there is no general agreement on what names to use, but I would call this one the **short-term standard deviation**. Can you accept that this is a reasonable name to use, with your can-making data?'

'Absolutely', shouts Bill, excitedly. 'This is what I have been trying to tell them, Roland. The charts are based on this short-term variation, which does not include the variation in the steel. So the action points in the mean chart are just telling us that the steel is changeable. But we know that already. What is more, we know that we have to live with this random variation in the steel. We need a chart that will indicate other changes, which are due to causes we can act upon.'

My respect for Bill Johnson rises even higher as he utters these words. 'Bill, I couldn't have put it better myself. You have reached the heart of the problem without using any statistical jargon. Would you agree with Bill's diagnosis, Graham?', I ask.

'Well . . . yes . . . I must agree', Graham replies very slowly. 'But Bill's description seems to imply that your procedure B has given us an incorrect control chart.'

I make a mental note that Graham is now describing as 'incorrect', the same mean chart that he previously described as 'correct'. I have no desire to draw attention to this change of opinion, but I must comment on his choice of criteria for judging control charts.

'I don't see it as a question of right and wrong, or correct and incorrect. I think you should first clarify your objectives and then use a control chart that will help you to achieve them. If you decide that you must live with the medium-term variation in can heights which results from the random fluctuations in the steel, then procedure B does not give you a useful control chart. The range chart is OK but you need a mean chart with action and warning lines more widely spaced. For such a chart you need to calculate your standard deviation by a different method.'

'So, why do we have a standard procedure that isn't . . . that doesn't work very well?', Graham asks. His words do not come easily. Perhaps he is struggling to avoid 'correct' and 'incorrect'.

'I believe the procedure *does* work well, with many processes. Indeed, some books state that procedure B is the only valid method, and that no deviation from the procedure is permissible. I am sure there are many manufacturing processes with which procedure B will produce very useful control charts. However, with your process it does not work; we need to modify the procedure slightly, so that the standard deviation includes not only the short-term random variability, but also the medium-term random variability, which you suspect is due to variation in the steel.'

'Before we recalculate the standard deviation let me draw your attention to item 9 in procedure B. An individuals chart often complements the mean and range charts, when we are assessing process stability. In some cases it will shed light on what the other charts have revealed and it can help to illustrate the nature of any additional variation. Do you ever plot individual heights, Graham?', I ask.

'Well, no', he replies, slowly. 'I am not sure individuals charts are available on my computer package. In fact, I thought that individuals charts were only used with, what you call, one-at-a-time data.'

'Well, it is true that some people who have one-at-a-time data do use individuals charts to assist process monitoring, whereas people like you, who have naturally grouped data, would almost invariably use a mean chart. Nonetheless, when they are investigating process stability, both groups of people can benefit from plotting an individuals chart, or just a simple run chart. If you switch on your PC, Graham, I will show you how to plot a useful run chart of your can height data.'

Graham is happy to let me use the PC and we soon have the run chart (Fig. 4.4). I am able to obtain the run chart so easily because I have done it before. For Graham to figure out the necessary data manipulation from the manual, would not have been a trivial task.

At this point Bill Johnson appears to regain the energy that he exhibited earlier. 'Marvellous', he shouts. 'Anyone can see it. The variation due to the

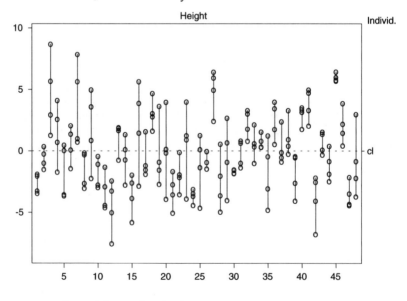

Fig. 4.4 A run chart of the can height data.

steel is so obvious in the run chart. That is one hell of a good picture, Roland. Any fool can see that the variation from group to group is enormous compared with the variation within the groups. How can we get that group-to-group variability into our standard deviation?', he demands to know.

Graham and I are now talking simultaneously. Clearly, Graham is anxious to express immediate agreement with the Production Manager, so I pause to let him do so. I can appreciate that junior staff would not wish to be at odds with Bill Johnson when he is in full flight.

'Well gentlemen', I continue, 'I am glad that you appreciate the run chart. It is so powerful because it reveals *all* of the variation. You see, the mean chart shows only the group-to-group variation and the range chart shows only the within-group variation, but the run chart displays them both, and it allows you to compare one with the other. It is true that the mean and range charts make life simple by separating the two issues, precision and accuracy, but they only work when we have the action lines positioned appropriately. The run chart is always useful, if you are able to interpret it.'

'I agree that the run chart is very revealing, but surely you are not suggesting that we should plot run charts on the shop floor', Graham asks, looking rather puzzled. 'I don't think our operators would appreciate them as we do.'

'No, Graham, the run chart is useful to us here, in this off-line investigation of process stability, but you would be wise to continue with the mean and range charts on the shop floor . . .'

'After we have moved the action lines', Bill interjects. 'Tell us the worst, Roland. I suppose we have to do some really complex calculations to bring this medium-term variation into our standard deviation.'

'Well, we could use a complex statistical technique, known as analysis of variance, but there is a much simpler approach which takes us straight to the standard error. Are you familiar with the term standard error?', I ask. Bill and Graham look at each other in a way that suggests a reminder would not be out of place. 'With an individuals chart we use plus and minus three standard deviations for our action lines. With a mean chart we use plus and minus three standard errors. If we let sigma (σ) represent the standard deviation, then the standard error is equal to sigma over root $n - \sigma/\sqrt{n}$ – where n is the number of results in each group. So with groups of 4 the standard error (SE) is only half as large as the standard deviation (SD). With groups of 9 the SE is only one third of the SD.'

'To calculate, what I call the medium-term standard error, we simply list the group means, put them into pairs, calculate the difference between the two means in each pair, then calculate the mean difference, which we divide by Hartley's constant. For a sample size of 2, Hartley's constant is equal to 1.128.'

At this point I can see a hint of fear, failure and confusion written in the faces of both Bill and Graham. Clearly, I have made the simple procedure

Table 4.1 Calculation of medium-term standard error

Subgroup	Mean	Difference
1	−2.7	2.1
2	−0.6	
3	4.9	3.5
4	1.4	
5	−1.9	2.6
6	0.7	
7	3.9	5.6
8	−1.7	
9	2.0	4.0
10	−2.0	
11	−3.2	1.3
12	−4.5	

appear complex. 'Let us calculate the medium-term standard error by hand', I suggest, 'then you will see how simple it really is. Look, Graham, will you read the means off from the graph? Obviously, you cannot read them very accurately, but you might manage one decimal place.' Graham picks up the mean chart (Fig. 4.3) and examines it most carefully. 'Well I am not so confident about one decimal place but I will try', he says. 'Minus two point seven, minus nought point six, plus four point nine, . . .' As Graham reads off the means from the chart I record them on a sheet of paper. When he has read twelve means, I propose that he stop. 'With only twelve means we can obtain a rough estimate of the medium-term standard error', I suggest. Then I work through the calculation set out in Table 4.1.

'On my calculator, the mean of the six differences is 3.2', I declare. 'Dividing this by 1.128 gives us 2.84 for the medium-term standard error. How does that compare with the standard error used in your mean chart, Graham?'

Graham is studying Fig. 4.3 intently. Nowhere on the computer printout will he find the value of the standard error, but there are at least two ways in which we can calculate the standard error from the information that is printed. 'Well, the mean range is 3.92', Graham informs us. 'Dividing that by Hartley's constant, 2.059, gives a standard deviation of about 1.9. Then, dividing the standard deviation by the square root of 4, gives a standard error of 0.95.'

'Very good, Graham. The short-term standard error is about 0.95', I confirm. 'So three standard errors will be about 2.85. Thus we would expect the upper action line on the mean chart to be about 2.85 above the centre line.'

I pause, to let my clients check out this is indeed the case. Graham is the first to speak. 'The fact that the two calculations check with each other

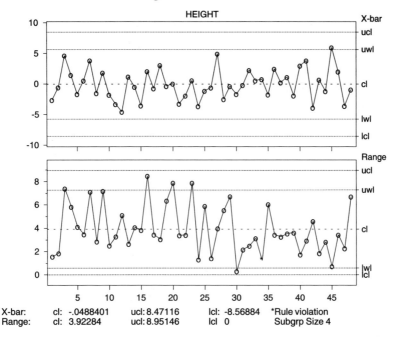

X-bar: cl: -.0488401   ucl: 8.47116   lcl: -8.56884   *Rule violation
Range: cl: 3.92284   ucl: 8.95146   lcl 0   Subgrp Size 4

Fig. 4.5 A revised mean chart.

suggests that the computer program must have calculated the standard deviation from the mean range.' I nod agreement, and Graham appears more relaxed now that he has a more coherent picture. His peace of mind is short-lived, however, as yet another surge of energy from Bill Johnson drags us back to the realities of can-making. 'No wonder my guys are hyperactive', he roars, 'we've been using a standard error of 0.95, when we should have been using 2.84. For goodness sake, Roland, move those action lines out and we'll see what the mean chart tells us then.'

I instruct the computer program that the standard error should be changed from 0.95 to 2.84. Soon we have a new mean chart (Fig. 4.5) in which all 48 points are well within the action lines. I anticipate that Bill Johnson will be pleased. 'There you are', he exclaims. 'The process didn't change. It was stable for the whole day. I bet we would find a similar pattern of variation on most days. So the mean chart is now ignoring the random variation in height caused by the random variation in the steel. If the height has a sustained change, for some other reason, then this revised chart will detect it, I hope.'

4.4 HOW GOOD IS THE CONTROL CHART?

As Bill utters these last two words he looks at me. I nod in agreement, for I share his hopes, but I am well aware that many users of control charts have unrealistic expectations. However, before we discuss Bill Johnson's expectations of performance, I would like to see Graham's reaction to the new mean chart. 'What do you think of the chart now that we have altered it, Graham?', I ask.

'Well, I need to think this through. Moving the action lines opens up a whole new world', he replies rather slowly. 'You say it is not a matter of right and wrong, but that seems to imply that we can put the action and warning lines wherever we want. Are there no guidelines on what is best?'

'I can offer you the same advice that I would offer to any company in any industry. Position the action and warning lines so as best to achieve your objectives. However, I find that many users of control charts have not formulated their objectives very clearly, so I would focus their attention, and your attention, on the following questions:

- Why are you using control charts with this process?
- How would you define a good control chart in this context?'

I pause and wait. I am prepared for the long silence that usually follows when I ask these questions. I am also prepared for the aggression that sometimes emerges when people realize that they do not know why they are doing what they are doing. I am confident that Bill and/or Graham will eventually give me sensible answers, for they are both very capable. However, I find in some companies that control charts are in use simply because someone has attended an SPC course.

Once again it is Bill who breaks the silence. 'Our long-term objective is to improve quality and reduce cost, but our more immediate objective is to detect change in the mean can height. I suppose a good chart is one which detects a change and a bad chart is one which does not.'

Graham is clearly in agreement. 'We certainly hope to detect changes', he adds. 'But I am not sure how we would tell the difference between a good chart and an excellent chart. If both of them detect the change, which is the better chart, Bill?'

'The excellent chart would detect more changes, or the same changes, more quickly, I suppose', Bill replies.

'That's an important point', I suggest with some emphasis. 'If you want to assess, or compare, control charts you need to recognize that there is no perfect system for detecting change. No control chart can be relied upon to detect every change immediately after it occurs. Of course, a good chart will indicate change more quickly than a bad chart. Furthermore, common sense suggests that any control chart is likely to detect large changes more quickly than it will detect small changes.'

'Right then', Graham interjects rather impatiently, 'no control chart is perfect, but can you tell us how quickly a mean chart will detect a change in mean?'

'Yes. Well, I can tell you how long it will take on average', I reply. 'It is possible to describe the speed, or sensitivity, of a control chart in terms of

Table 4.2 Average Run Lengths for Mean Charts with action lines only

Size of change divided by SD	Group size		
	1	4	9
0.0	370	370	370
0.5	155	44	15
1.0	44	6.3	2.0
1.5	15	2.0	1.2
2.0	6.3	1.2	1.00
2.5	3.2	1.02	1.00
3.0	2.0	1.00	1.00

its average run length or ARL. The ARL depends on the size of the change and on the group size, as we can see in Table 4.2.'

'Let me explain this idea of average run length', I suggest. 'It is well worth getting to grips with. Take, for example, that figure of 6.3 in the middle column. That is telling us that we would expect to plot 6 or 7 points on our mean chart before we detected a change of one standard deviation, if we were using a group size of 4. To give a more concrete example let us reconsider Fig. 4.5 in which the group size was 4 and the standard deviation was 5.68. If the mean height suddenly increased by 5.68 we would expect to plot 6 or 7 points before we saw a point outside the action lines. Of course, a mean chart with a group size of 9 would be more sensitive, and it could be expected to detect a change of this size after only 2 points had been plotted.'

'I can see why you don't recommend an individuals chart', Bill exclaims. 'A mean chart based on individual can heights has an average run length of 44 for a change of this size.'

'That's right', I confirm. 'No maker of cans would measure only one can, when it is so easy to measure a group of 4, 5 or 6 cans. The same would be said for most widget processes. Individual's charts are plotted in some industries, but they do not detect small changes very quickly, as you pointed out.'

'With much larger changes the individuals chart seems to be quite good', Graham observes. 'A change of three standard deviations has an average run length of 2. Mind you, three standard deviations would be about 17.1. That's a disaster. We would need to know about it as quickly as possible. I think we will stick to the mean chart. Just a minute, though . . .', he pauses, '. . . perhaps Table 4.1 is misleading us. The title says action lines only, but we also use warning lines. Will they make a difference?'

'Oh yes. The effect of using warning lines is to increase the sensitivity of the chart', I reply. 'You also use the rule about seven points on the same side of the centre line, don't you? That also increases the chart sensitivity. In fact, the more supplementary rules you use, the quicker you are likely to detect a change.'

Table 4.3 Correct and incorrect decisions

	Reality	
Your decision	*The process has changed*	*The process has not changed*
You decide that the process has changed	You have made the correct decision	You have made a wrong decision (Type 1 error)
You decide that the process has not changed	You have made a wrong decision (Type 2 error)	You have made the correct decision

'What's the snag?', Bill asks. 'There is always a price to pay for any benefits you offer us, Roland.'

'Yes, I am afraid there is a price to pay for the increased sensitivity. As you introduce more supplementary rules, you increase the false alarm rate', I inform them. 'A false alarm occurs when the chart indicates a change but, in reality, the process has not changed at all. So there are **two** ways in which the control chart can deceive you: it can tell you that the process has changed when it has not; and it can fail to tell you that the process has changed when it actually has. Thus, there are two possible errors and you run a risk of making either type of error every time you plot a point on the chart.'

I wait patiently whilst Bill Johnson and Graham study Table 4.3 which I have put before them. In the silence, I begin to wonder if they are suffering from an excess of detail, or just too much bad news. They are, of course, experienced users of SPC and much of the complexity I have introduced, has been demanded by their searching questions.

'So these Type 1 errors are what you called false alarms, I suppose?', Bill asks at last. 'Presumably, you can work out what is the chance of getting a false alarm?'

'Yes, and yes', I reply. 'The Type 1 errors are indeed what I referred to as false alarms and it is possible to demonstrate that they will not occur very often. In fact we would expect one false alarm to occur for every 370 points on the mean chart. That's not very often, is it? If you were plotting one point each day you would expect one false alarm each year. You can see the 370 in the top row of Table 4.2.'

Bill is deep in thought, but Graham returns to the previous table where he finds the 370 spread across the top row. 'Aha, yes, I did wonder if a change of 0.0 had any meaning. Of course, it represents zero change and there is a 1 in 370 chance of concluding otherwise. . . .'

'That's every time we plot a point', Bill interrupts. 'As we are plotting a point every half hour, we can expect a false alarm about once a week. But that is if we use only action lines. The false alarms will occur more often if we use warning lines as well. Won't they?'

'Yes, I am afraid that is true gentlemen. Using supplementary rules will also increase the frequency of false alarms. Let me show you another table

Table 4.4 ARLs for mean charts ($n=4$)

Size of change divided by SD	Action lines only	Action lines and warning lines	Western Electric rules
0.0	370	278	92
0.2	200	134	37
0.4	72	43	13
0.6	28	16	6.9
0.8	12	7.4	4.4
1.0	6.3	4.1	3.1
1.2	3.7	2.6	2.4
1.4	2.4	1.9	1.8

to help you assess the risks.'

I fully realize that a large table of numbers can be quite overwhelming, and I can see that my clients are disturbed by this one. To reduce the shock I cover all but the top row of Table 4.4. 'See how the false alarm average run length reduces as we introduce additional rules', I suggest.

'What are the Western Electric rules?', asks Bill Johnson. 'Sounds American. Are they used in Britain?'

'Western Electric is an American Company. I assume that these rules were used in Western Electric at one time. Perhaps they still are. They are certainly used by your computer package, "Quality Analyst", and they are explained in the manual.'

I step across to the flip chart and draw a control chart with action lines, warning lines and additional lines placed only one standard deviation from the centre line (see Fig. 4.6).

'It is easier to describe the Western Electric rules if we label the six zones A, B, C, D, E and F', I explain. 'The rules are as follows. We conclude that the process has changed if we have:

1. 1 point above zone A,
2. 1 point below zone F,
3. 2 out of 3 consecutive points in zone A,
4. 2 out of 3 consecutive points in zone F,
5. 4 out of 5 consecutive points in zone (A+B),
6. 4 out of 5 consecutive points in zone (E+F),

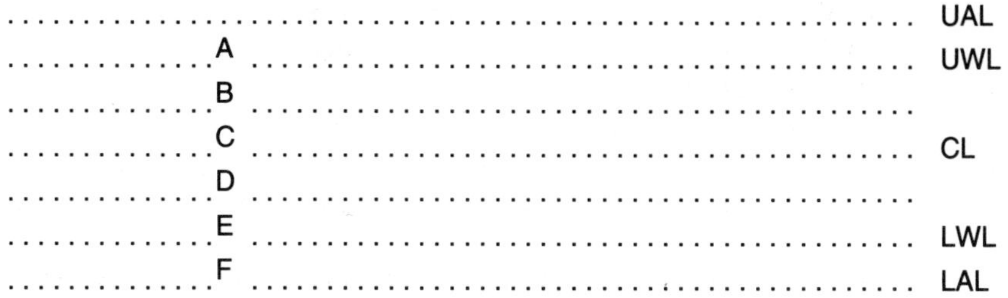

Fig. 4.6 Explaining the Western Electric rules.

7. 8 consecutive points in zone (A+B+C), or
8. 8 consecutive points in zone (D+E+F).

'I guess the rules you use are a little different to these. Is that so?', I ask.

'We certainly use rules 1 and 2. Doesn't everyone?', asks Graham. 'We also use rules 7 and 8 but instead of "8 points on the same side of the centre line" we specify only 7 points. We certainly don't use rules 5 and 6. We do use rules 3 and 4, but without the words "out of 3". So I guess the Western Electric rules are not all that different from the rules we use.'

'It sounds foolish, perhaps', Bill Johnson adds, 'but I thought everyone used the same rules. Obviously not.'

'I am afraid there is a bewildering variety of rules in use, even within the same company. You might even find different rules being used by members of the same work group.' I suggest, rather hesitantly, for I do not want to spend the rest of the day discussing supplementary rules for chart interpretation: 'Shall we return to the ARL table? You can see that we will have a false alarm every 92 samples, on average, if we use the Western Electric rules, compared with one every 370 samples if we use only action lines.'

'So that's the down side', Graham exclaims, 'but we would also expect some advantage from using the rules. Wouldn't we? Slide the sheet down and let us see.'

I slide down the covering sheet to reveal the ARL we would expect with step changes equal to one standard deviation.

'So, the 6.3 reduces to 3.1', Graham says rather slowly. 'That is disappointing. The Western Electric rules seem to offer a bigger payback with smaller changes, say, about half of a standard deviation.'

'Right then, Roland', Bill Johnson says with some emphasis, 'just let me summarize what we have concluded. No control chart is perfect. Whatever chart we use, we run two risks, which you have described very clearly in Table 4.3. The best way to compare the performance of two control charts is by considering their ARLs. Obviously the ARLs depend on the size of change. So one chart might be better at detecting small changes but no better at detecting large changes. The speed with which a chart detects a change will also depend on which supplementary rules we use.'

Yet again I am quite staggered by the way Bill Johnson has grasped the essentials of these rather abstract concepts, then summarized them better than I could have done myself. I suspect that Graham Covey is also impressed. He appears to be about to speak, but before he can do so Bill continues: 'Right then, there is only one more problem to discuss, Roland. Then we can let you get away. How frequently should we sample?'

4.5 SAMPLING FREQUENCY

'You said earlier that you sample four cans every half hour, with this particular process. Why do you sample every half hour and why four cans?

You did say it is a single head process, didn't you?'

'That is right', Bill Johnson confirms. 'It is a single head process. I would like to discuss multihead processes, but that will have to wait until your next visit. As far as I can remember we have always taken four cans every half hour. This was established practice long before we thought of using control charts. Now you have just shown us, with the ARLs (Table 4.2) that it would be foolish to economize by reducing the four cans to only one can, but how about the half hour interval? Would it be safe to take four cans every hour, for example?'

'That is a good question to ask, Bill', I reply, choosing my words carefully, 'but it is important to realize that it is not a statistical question. Surely, it is a social, cultural, political question. The answer is that it would probably not be safe. Any manager who decreed that henceforth sampling will be hourly, would run a risk of being held responsible for any disaster which followed. Thus, in practice, when half-hourly sampling becomes established it may never change, even though no one can remember why the 30-minute interval was chosen.'

I pause to assess the reaction of my clients. They remain silent. Perhaps they are surprised by the direction the discussion is taking. Perhaps they are disappointed that I have not responded to the question with a decisive 'Yes' or 'No', supported by an elegant re-analysis of their data.

'Let us return to basics', I suggest. 'You currently sample four cans every half hour. You subject the four cans to visual inspection and you measure height, bead depth, etc. Now, why do you feel the need to inspect any cans at all?'

'Well, the operator inspects four cans every half hour because he has been told to do so', Graham Covey suggests, 'but, even the laziest operator would not suggest that we stop inspection altogether.'

'Right. So we all agree that we must inspect', Bill Johnson adds rather pensively, 'but that does not answer Roland's question. I suppose we inspect because we do not trust the process. We inspect because we want to see if the process has stopped producing good cans. We inspect to see if anything has gone wrong.'

'Exactly. You have the process working well then, from time to time, you inspect to see if anything has gone wrong. To determine how frequently you should sample you need to ask yourself two questions:

- What could go wrong?
- How quickly do we need to know it has gone wrong?

And it is not helpful to come up with glib answers like "We need to know immediately", because you cannot afford to do 100% inspection.'

Bill Johnson has a reputation, within Lancan, for his anger and aggression. But he has not responded aggressively when I have implied, several times now, that he and his colleagues have not really thought through what they are doing and why. Perhaps it is more acceptable from an outsider.

'Perhaps you should assemble the whole process team and have a brainstorm, focusing on these two questions', I continue. 'You could produce a Pareto chart to show what happens most often. You could draw fishbone diagrams to summarize the possible causes. Of course, it would be invaluable for the team to discuss carefully annotated control charts that had been suitably set up. But you do not yet have them.'

'I accept what you say', Bill Johnson responds. 'Nonetheless, I am surprised that you cannot tell us anything about sampling frequency from the data in the control charts in Figs. 4.3 and 4.5. You were able to draw conclusions about short-term and medium-term variability. Can you not produce a formula which shows how the variability in a set of can heights depends on the length of the time period during which they were made?'

'Yes, I could do something like that if you had suitable data', I reply. 'Let us look back at your original control chart, Fig. 4.3. Several points on your mean chart are outside the action lines. Earlier you expressed the view that these out of control points were due to variation in the steel, and we agreed that they appeared to occur at random. However, if we had much more data we might be able to see that the changes were more gradual. For example, take the third point on the mean chart. It is very different from the second point. What happened in the 30-minute period between the two samples? If you had been taking a sample of 4 cans every 5 minutes, say, the additional points might reveal that there was a gradual increase in can height throughout the 30 minutes. On the other hand, you might find that almost all of the increase in can height for the 30-minute interval, occurred during one of the 5-minute intervals. So, you wonder, what would we find if we took a sample every 30 seconds, say?'

'With any widget process, an inquisitive observer is bound to wonder what you would find if you inspected every widget', Graham suggests, entering into the spirit of this hypothetical investigation. 'So, what would you do with the data if we measured the height of every can?'

'I would run a computer program that would put the data into groups and calculate the average standard deviation within the groups. It would start with very small groups ($n=2$) and then larger and larger groups. It would finally produce a graph to show how the standard deviation increased with the group size.'

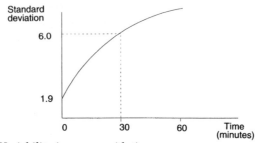

Fig. 4.7 Variability increases with time span.

'And what would the graph look like?', Graham asks impatiently. 'Would the standard deviation increase more and more as the group size increased?'

I approach the flip chart again and draw a smooth curve (Fig. 4.7). 'My experience suggests something like this. With your particular process the very small groups, in other words very short time intervals, would give a standard deviation about 1.9. With a 30-minute time interval the standard deviation would be about 6.0.

'Where did those figures come from?', Bill Johnson demands to know. 'The 1.9 and the 6.0 – did they come from our data?'

'Yes', I reply, 'we calculated them from your data about two and a half hours ago. The 1.9 is a measure of the variability within your samples of 4 cans. We also calculated a measure of the extra random variation that is introduced during 30-minute intervals. That came to 5.7. I have increased that figure to 6.0 to include short-term variation as . . .'

'This is extremely interesting', Graham interrupts in an excited voice, 'but how would we make use of such a diagram? Would it help us to decide how frequently to sample? Do all widget makers have curves like this?'

'You could use it for a variety of purposes', I suggest. 'No, I do not know any widget makers who have produced curves like this. I have certainly produced similar curves for clients in the chemical industry. For example, one client who manufactures polyethylene, measures the melt index of the polymer every five minutes. The plant runs continuously for months, so he has plenty of data. I analysed this data and the resulting curve (similar to Fig. 4.7) is used to decide how he should divide his continuous stream of product into lots. Obviously, the bigger the lots the more variable they will be, and his customers want consistency within lots, above all else. Perhaps you could use your curve rather differently. Suppose, for example, that your specification for can height was so narrow, that you would need a process standard deviation of 4.5 in order to meet it. Clearly you would need to sample more frequently than every 30 minutes. You might decide to sample every 10 minutes. Of course, you would also need to take immediate and appropriate action whenever your 10-minute chart gave an indication.'

I pause at this point. There is a need to halt this stream of speculation. There is a great need to draw together the many threads of our rambling discussions, which have been structured largely by the questions my clients have asked. My hosts did not specify an agenda. I wonder if every item on their unwritten agenda has been covered.

'Clearly, we need to give considerable thought to the variability of our processes', Bill Johnson says in his most authoritative tone of voice. 'I can see now, that the main benefit we will gain from your visit is a realization that we cannot simply follow the prescriptions taught on many SPC courses. Our simplest process, a single head cap maker, has a complex pattern of variability. I have learned a great deal today, Roland. I anticipate learning even more when you come again on the 17th. Then we will discuss multi-head processes.'

Graham Covey flops back in his chair, apparently exhausted. 'I look forward to seeing you again in two weeks', he says. 'You've given us much food for thought.'

4.6 SUMMARY

My first visit to Lancan has involved me in detailed discussion of the variability of one of their processes. Previously, my hosts have tried to use mean and range charts with this process. Their efforts were not very successful. They followed the standard procedure, which is procedure B of Appendix A. It must be emphasized that this procedure has been followed by innumerable people and many have found it to be very useful. However, there exist an unknown number of processes with which this procedure does not produce useful control charts.

To obtain a better mean chart for the tin can process we calculated the standard deviation by a different method. This took account of medium-term variation, in addition to the short-term variation. The larger standard deviation gave action lines further from the centre line so that the mean chart no longer responded to the extra random variation in can height, which Bill Johnson claimed was caused by random variation in the steel.

We discussed the risk of making incorrect decisions whenever you use control charts. There is a risk of concluding that the process has changed when, in reality, it has not. There is a risk of concluding that the process has not changed when, in fact, it has. The size of this second risk will depend on the size of the change. There is little risk of failing to detect a very large change, but a small change may persist for a long time before the chart indicates its existence.

The average run length (ARL) of a chart is the number of points we can expect to plot before a change is detected. The ARL will depend on the size of the change, the type of chart, the sample size and the supplementary rules in use. By comparing ARLs of different charts you can select the one most suited to your purpose. If you do not know why you are using control charts, such comparisons will be meaningless.

Finally, we discussed a graph (Fig. 4.7) which indicated how the variability within a batch of product might increase with the size of the batch. Such graphs have proved useful with continuous chemical processes. If you feel that you need to study the variability of your process in such detail you should contact a consultant.

Chapter 5

Control charts for many heads or short runs

The consultant pays a second visit to Lancan to discuss more complex application of control charts with the Production Manager and a Quality Co-ordinator. Their discussions cover multi-head machines, automatic control systems and processes with short runs of many products.

5.1 INTRODUCTION

As I drive into the visitors' car park at Lancan I have rather mixed feelings. The challenge of trying to explain more complex concepts is always welcome, but I am not sure exactly what complexities will be thrust before me, and I am not sure what sort of mood Bill Johnson will be in.

When we parted company, at the end of my previous visit to Lancan, Bill was in high spirits. I had explained, to his obvious satisfaction, why the standard approach to control charts is not always successful. Furthermore, I had achieved this without speaking of common causes and special causes, as most books do. Bill Johnson held the opinion that control charts display variability and change, but do not tell us anything about causes. I was quite happy to speak of variability rather than causes.

Today, I believe Bill Johnson will wish to discuss the use of control charts with multi-head processes. Lancan has machines which produce many cans simultaneously. They have 12-head machines and 16-head machines. It is very important that they distinguish between variation from can to can from the same head, and variation from head to head within the same impression. If they do not recognize the importance of this distinction they may produce control charts which are as unhelpful as those I saw on my last visit (Chapter 4).

Those charts had action lines which were too close to the centre line. Thus they gave far too many action indications. With multi-head processes you are likely to see the opposite effect; action lines that are too far from the centre line, giving no action indications at all.

Of course, the position of the action lines is entirely dependent on the standard deviation. A successful control chart results from estimating the standard deviation by an appropriate method. The standard method of procedure B (Appendix A) is not always helpful.

5.2 CONTROL CHARTS WITH MULTI-HEAD PROCESSES

'You have met Graham Covey', Bill Johnson bellows as I enter his office. 'He has been doing some good work since your last visit. He has recalculated the control lines using the method you suggested and we now have some useful charts. With multi-head machines we seem to have a different problem. What is wrong with this chart?'

Bill Johnson is very impatient. He has been the Production Manager at Lancan for many years and he has built a reputation for getting things done. He is a man of action. However, I know from previous contact that he is also capable of deep thought and is able to identify the essential elements of a problem. If I can edge him into a thinking mode our discussions will be more productive, certainly more relaxed.

'Hello Graham, nice to see you again', I say rather slowly. 'I am glad you are making progress. Now then Bill, where did this chart (Fig. 5.1) come from? You seem to have a sample size of five. Is there any particular reason for that?'

'A very good reason', Bill Johnson replies, rather tersely. 'This data came from a five-head machine which makes plastic caps. Each point on this mean chart is the mean of five means. From each head we take four caps at 30-minute intervals. We weigh each of the 20 caps and calculate a mean for

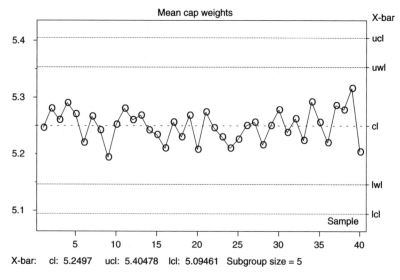

Fig. 5.1 Another unhelpful control chart.

Table 5.1 Mean weight of 4 caps from 5 heads, at 30-minute intervals

Time	Head 1	Head 2	Head 3	Head 4	Head 5
1	5.18	5.24	5.32	5.32	5.17
2	5.20	5.29	5.36	5.33	5.22
3	5.26	5.18	5.33	5.45	5.08
4	5.28	5.21	5.31	5.44	5.21
5	5.22	5.24	5.31	5.39	5.19
6	5.13	5.23	5.35	5.28	5.11
7	5.24	5.27	5.31	5.32	5.19
8	5.15	5.10	5.33	5.40	5.23
9	5.17	5.25	5.21	5.33	5.01
10	5.12	5.21	5.37	5.31	5.25
11	5.19	5.22	5.30	5.53	5.16
12	5.19	5.24	5.31	5.31	5.25
13	5.24	5.24	5.29	5.46	5.11
14	5.18	5.23	5.30	5.35	5.15
15	5.14	5.24	5.29	5.41	5.09
16	5.17	5.21	5.28	5.37	5.02
17	5.25	5.23	5.30	5.42	5.08
18	5.11	5.21	5.27	5.45	5.11
19	5.27	5.21	5.28	5.35	5.23
20	5.26	5.16	5.32	5.36	4.94
21	5.26	5.20	5.38	5.29	5.24
22	5.22	5.22	5.28	5.46	5.05
23	5.09	5.23	5.29	5.42	5.12
24	5.17	5.20	5.21	5.33	5.14
25	5.19	5.19	5.32	5.41	5.02
26	5.19	5.30	5.29	5.41	5.06
27	5.19	5.24	5.29	5.33	5.23
28	5.20	5.21	5.36	5.40	4.91
29	5.19	5.12	5.31	5.48	5.15
30	5.25	5.24	5.23	5.49	5.18
31	5.12	5.23	5.32	5.36	5.16
32	5.23	5.25	5.29	5.43	5.11
33	5.13	5.26	5.17	5.44	5.12
34	5.26	5.21	5.28	5.31	5.40
35	5.22	5.21	5.37	5.26	5.22
36	5.19	5.18	5.40	5.33	5.00
37	5.27	5.21	5.24	5.47	5.24
38	5.29	5.21	5.30	5.35	5.24
39	5.27	5.32	5.23	5.45	5.31
40	5.23	5.10	5.22	5.42	5.05

each head. We can tell which head each cap came from. We feed the five means into "Quality Analyst" and this is the mean chart it gives us. Not a good chart, eh?'

Graham Covey has had little opportunity to speak since I entered the room. He hands me an A4 sheet on which is printed a table of data (Table 5.1). 'Perhaps this will help, Roland', he suggests, then continues to explain, 'Each number is the mean weight of four caps from the same head. Each column represents one head and a new row of data emerges every 30 minutes. So the first point plotted on the mean chart is the mean of the five means in the top row.'

'Exactly', Bill Johnson concurs. 'How was the standard deviation calculated Graham?', he asks.

I glance at Graham Covey. He appears to be quite calm. Clearly, we have made excellent progress. Two weeks ago, when I last visited Lancan, Bill would not have asked such a crucially important question and Graham would not have been able to answer, if he had. Now, one of my clients knows what to ask and the other knows how to answer. Soon they will not need me.

'The computer has calculated the range for each of the 40 groups, then calculated the standard deviation from the mean of the 40 ranges. $\bar{R}/d_n$. Whenever I use a standard deviation from a different formula, or from other data, I print a message on the chart to remind me.'

I am most impressed by Graham's reply. Clearly, he realizes that a control chart cannot be trusted if we do not know how the position of the action lines was determined. 'Thank you, Graham. We can now return to your question, Bill. You asked, what is wrong with this chart? I would suggest that the chart might be more useful if the standard deviation were calculated by a different . . .'

'Not by the method you recommended last time?', Bill Johnson interrupts, with obvious impatience. 'If we took account of the longer-term variations the control lines would be even further from the centre line. Would they not? What trick have you up your sleeve?'

'Before you plot any control charts with this data, you need to take a closer look at the variability in the cap weights', I suggest. 'Let us examine each head separately. It is possible that one head differs from the other four. Do you have the data on "Quality Analyst"?'

The answer to my question is obviously, 'Yes.' Both Bill and Graham turn to a side-table on which a PC is displaying the very chart we have just been looking at. 'May I take a closer look at the data?', I ask. Clearly my hosts are happy for me to take control of the keyboard and explore the data. First, I go into the edit routine to view the data and to check that it matches what Graham has given me. I then instruct the 'Quality Analyst' program to regard the data as if it were five separate variables. Finally I produce, on the screen, a stratified run chart in which the five heads are clearly distinguishable (Fig. 5.2).

'Now then, gentlemen, what does this picture reveal?', I ask. 'What is the specification for the weights of the caps? Are the caps from all five heads meeting the specification?'

I don't often fire questions at my clients with such rapidity, but this chart reveals such a lot about the operation of the process and I don't want any of the indications to go unnoticed.

Graham Covey is the first to speak. 'Well, the specification is 5.2±0.3.

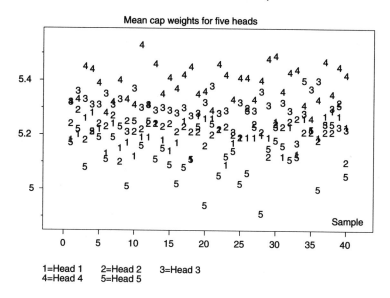

Fig. 5.2 A stratified run chart, showing differences between the heads.

That is 4.9 to 5.5, so it is possible that all of these caps are within specification. But it is obvious that head 4 was producing above target and head 5 was producing below . . .'

'Remember that every point is the mean of four cap weights', Bill Johnson interjects. 'Even if the means are in spec, the individual caps may not be. But what does this run chart (Fig. 5.2) tell us about the position of the control lines in the control chart (Fig. 5.1)?'

'Let us proceed one step at a time', I suggest. 'There are so many questions to answer about the variability, stability and capability of this process. Perhaps we should start by considering this process as **five** processes. Each head is producing a stream of caps. You can identify which caps came from which head so we could investigate the stability and capability of each stream or process. Each column of data (Table 5.1) tells us something about the output from one stream. For example, take the first mean from Head 1, which was 5.18. That is the mean weight of four consecutive caps. The four weights, from which this mean was calculated, could have also been used to calculate a standard deviation. Combining this with the standard deviation of other groups would give us what we could call the short-term standard deviation for Head 1. I guess it would be quite small. Of course we will never know because only the means were recorded.'

I look from Bill Johnson to Graham Covey and back again. Their faces do not register discomfort, impatience or boredom. I will continue: 'We can ask "Quality Analyst" to assess the capability of each head separately. I am sure we will find that Head 4 did not perform so well as Head 1, say.'

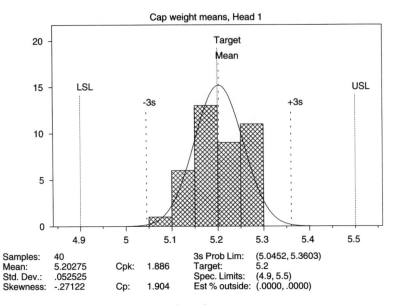

Fig. 5.3 Process capability – Head 1 only.

I call up the process capability routine and select the data from Head 1, only. The screen display shows a histogram of the 40 means from Head 1 (Fig. 5.3). Also displayed are the specification limits (USL and LSL) and the natural limits of the process (−3s and +3s). My clients stare intently at the screen.

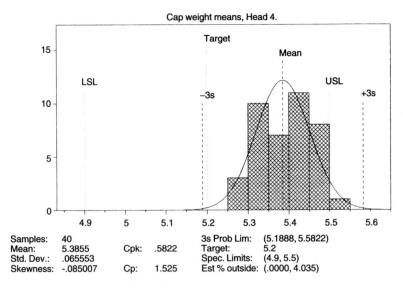

Fig. 5.4 Process capability – Head 4 only.

'Head 1 performed very well during this period', suggests Graham. 'The mean, 5.20275, was very close to target, the C_{pk} is equal to 1.886. That is very satisfactory. Now, give us the bad news, Roland. Show us the histogram for Head 4.'

Bill Johnson does not comment. I assume that he agrees with Graham's suggestion and I go into the process capability routine again, to analyse the data from Head 4. Soon we have a very different picture on the screen (Fig. 5.4).

Bill Johnson howls. 'I have suspected this for years. The engineering guys are responsible for most of the variability. This head is way off target. Look at the mean, 5.3855. Look at the C_{pk}, 0.58. Of course, the true situation is worse than this. Remember Graham, this is a histogram of 40 means. A histogram of the 160 individual cap weights would be even wider.'

'You are absolutely right, Bill', I concur. 'A little of the total variation is missing from this picture, but that is not the most important point. As this diagram clearly shows, Head 4 was biased, off target. If this head were reset to bring its mean back on target we would have a C_{pk} of about 1.8 as we had for Head 1. Let us put the five heads back together and regard all 200 means as coming from one process. We will see what effect the head misalignment has on the overall capability.'

Once again I call up the process capability routine on the computer, but this time I ask the program to analyse all 200 mean weights. The histogram that appears on the screen (Fig. 5.5) is much wider. It includes the variation

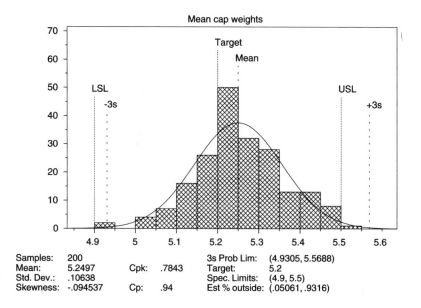

Samples:	200			3s Prob Lim:	(4.9305, 5.5688)
Mean:	5.2497	Cpk:	.7843	Target:	5.2
Std. Dev.:	.10638			Spec. Limits:	(4.9, 5.5)
Skewness:	-.094537	Cp:	.94	Est % outside:	(.05061, .9316)

Fig. 5.5 Process capability – all five heads.

from head to head, in addition to the sort of variation that we have already seen when examining one head in isolation.

'So, that is the overall picture', Bill Johnson mutters rather fiercely. 'Because one or two heads need resetting, a potentially good process is performing like a bad process. As you know, Roland, I hate all this talk of assignable and common causes, but this is a situation in which it is reasonable to use those expressions. The variation in the first two histograms is due to a myriad of common causes, but the **extra** variation in the third histogram (Fig. 5.5) is due to one assignable cause. What is more, I know exactly who is to blame for not removing the assignable cause or correcting its effect.'

Graham Covey seems delighted to hear these words. Clearly he is not the person Bill Johnson has in mind. With a big smile he says, 'Of course, it was not the mean chart (Fig. 5.1) that indicated the presence of this assignable cause – it was the stratified run chart (Fig. 5.2).'

'That is right, Graham. The mean chart is useless, on two counts', Bill concludes. 'First, the assignable variation is lost in the overall means that are plotted in the chart. Head 4 is high, Head 5 is low and the five heads are not too bad on average. Second, the assignable cause inflates the standard deviation. Thus the action lines are too far from the centre line and we will never have any indications. Would the mean chart have been more useful, if the standard deviation had been obtained when all five heads were set on target?'

My clients look to me for an answer. Perhaps they have realized that I have not spoken for some time. I did not need to. Their recent comments have been both pertinent and indicative of real understanding, but now it is my turn.

'Yes, I am sure the mean chart could be more useful if it were set up using data from a period when all five heads were well set. If every head had an overall mean of 5.2 and a standard deviation of means equal to 0.05, then the action lines would be at 5.05 and 5.35. I will move the action lines and the centre line; then you can judge for yourself.'

'Well, we can clearly see (Fig. 5.6) that we were producing high weight items throughout the period', Graham Covey suggests. 'Had we been using this chart, the operators would surely have put the process back on target by reducing the fluid pressure. Yes this is much more . . .'

'It is certainly better', Bill Johnson agrees. 'It would certainly help us to detect any change which affected all five heads, such as a change in fluid pressure or a change in the polymer. Would it detect a change which affected only *one* head? I have my doubts.'

'I share your doubts, Bill. This problem arises with multi-head processes in many industries. Naturally the manager and the people on the process do not want to run a separate mean chart for each head. They would prefer to have just one mean chart for the whole process, but they want a chart that will give an indication if either:

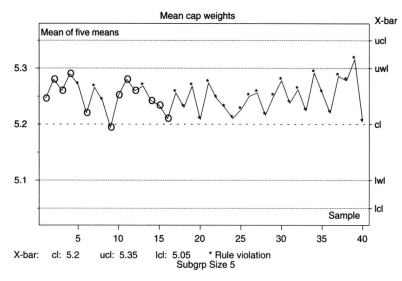

Fig. 5.6 A more helpful control chart.

1. one head changes, but the others continue to operate normally; or
2. all heads change in a similar way, due to one cause which affects them all.'

'Your chart will serve the second purpose, now that we have moved the action lines, but I doubt if it will serve the first purpose very well. A change which affects only one of the five heads will not be easily seen in the mean chart unless the change is enormous. With 12 heads or 16 . . .'

'So, what can we use?', Bill Johnson demands to know. 'This discussion of variation is fascinating, but . . .'

'Could we not use something like the stratified run chart?', Graham asks.

Having interrupted each other, in their impatience, my clients now fall silent and await my answer: 'You must give serious consideration to a chart of that nature, though it requires a lot of extra effort, of course. Instead of weighing all the caps together you have first to sort them, head by head, then make a separate weighing for each head. Because of the extra work you might have to reduce your sampling frequency. Is it better to plot a very useful chart at one-hour intervals or a less useful chart at 20-minute intervals?'

'I think we have to go for the stratified run chart', Graham Covey asserts. 'We can add a centre line at 5.2 and appropriate action lines. We could even use specification lines at 5.5 and 4.9, if we were plotting individual weights.'

'Obviously the heads need to be identified by number, as they were in your picture (Fig. 5.2)', Bill Johnson adds. 'Perhaps, the head numbers need be shown only for the heaviest and the lightest. The important indication comes from the frequent appearance of the same head number at the top, or bottom of the chart.'

Table 5.2 Mean weights of 4 caps

Head	1	2	3	4	5
No. of means	40	40	40	40	40
Overall mean	5.203	5.219	5.298	5.386	5.144
SD of means	0.0525	0.0449	0.0495	0.0656	0.1007

'Where would we put the action lines?', asks Graham, as a lady enters the room carrying a tray. 'I know where I could put a cup of coffee.'

As we drink coffee and nibble biscuits I suggest that the centre line should be drawn at 5.2 with the action lines at $5.2 \pm (3 \times 0.06)$, or perhaps $5.2 \pm (3 \times 0.07)$. 'Remember that the standard deviations for Heads 1 and 4 were 0.053 and 0.066', I remind my clients. 'However, before you add any lines to the stratified run chart you should first check the stability and variability of each head, separately. Let us look at the variability of Heads 2, 3 and 5.'

Using the summary statistics routine on 'Quality Analyst' gives us the mean and standard deviation for each head (Table 5.2). We can see that Head 4 gave a high mean weight, whereas Head 5 was rather low. Heads 2 and 3 were no more variable than Head 1, but Head 5 had a much higher standard deviation. We all agree that the data from Head 5 should be examined more closely.

I instruct the computer program to plot an individuals chart of the 40 means from Head 5 (Fig. 5.7). All three of us study the picture on the screen for some time. No one speaks. Perhaps we are silent because there is no obvious explanation for the excessive variability.

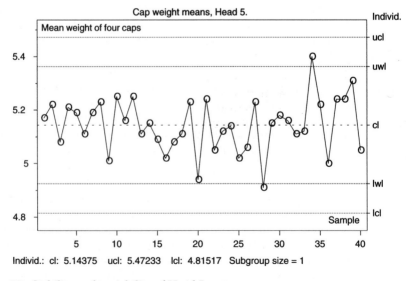

Fig. 5.7 Stability and variability of Head 5.

'I wonder if the last 21 points are more variable than the first 19', Graham says slowly. 'Perhaps there are small changes in mean weight at sample 15 and sample 29.'

Neither Bill nor I greet this speculation with great enthusiasm. I am hoping that my clients will offer physical, chemical, or engineering reasons why one head should be more variable than another. No such reasons are offered, however.

'Can I summarize the conclusions we have reached?', asks Bill Johnson. I am very happy that he should do so and nod my agreement. 'With a multi-head machine we should examine the variability and stability of each head separately before attempting to set up a control chart. We would do that by plotting a run chart or an individuals chart or a mean chart for each head.'

'That is right, Bill', I confirm. 'We would plot a chart like this one (Fig. 5.7) for each head. With 16 heads we should plot 16 charts.'

'If all heads are stable, we would then compare the head means with the target. If one or more are offset, or biased as you say, we should ask why, and we should consider how we can prevent such occurrences in the future. Is it possible for all heads to be closely aligned? Is it possible to keep them aligned for any length of time? Then we should consider the capability of the process. What would be the C_{pk} if all head means were on target? What was the C_{pk} for the data we have analysed? How much could a head mean deviate from target without any out of spec caps being produced?'

While listening to Bill Johnson's rather hesitant, but technically superb summary of our rambling discussions, I realize how lucky I am to work with so many capable people.

'Which leaves only one question', Bill continues, 'what type of control chart should we use to monitor the process? The main objective of using the control chart is to detect as quickly as possible any deviation of a head mean from the target of 5.2. You recommend something like the stratified run chart (Fig. 5.2) with a centre line at 5.2 and action lines at $5.2 \pm 3\sigma$, where σ is the standard deviation for a typical head.'

'Yes, Bill. That is an excellent summary of our conclusions', I confirm, 'provided it is reasonable to speak of "the typical head". That will only be true if all heads exhibit a similar spread of results and all heads are stable.'

'Good', is Bill Johnson's final word. 'Now we can discuss the use of automatic control systems. But first we must have some lunch.'

5.3 AUTOMATIC CONTROL LOOPS

'As you well know, we buy our polymer from companies in the chemical industry', Bill Johnson explains as we stroll to the dining room. 'We would like to establish a close relationship, or partnership, with one supplier but there are obstacles to so doing. Not least of these obstacles is the difficulty of communication. We employ many mechanical engineers and technicians; we do **not** employ chemists. Our suppliers of polymer do employ chemists and chemical engineers, and they want to talk chemistry. We don't – in fact, we can't.'

I cannot describe the pleasure I experience as Bill Johnson utters these words. Many of the companies I visit are suppliers, or customers of other client companies. This gives me a breadth of experience that is very valuable, and helps me to understand that many barriers to progress exist at the interface between companies. Moving towards single sourcing helps companies to focus on these barriers and break them down, but this is only achieved by frequent contact and improved communication. Often this communication must take place across discipline boundaries as well as company boundaries.

I believe these communication problems are important but they are rarely discussed; hence my delight when Bill Johnson puts the issue on the table. Perhaps it is the secret pleasure that comes from having recognized someone else's problem before he or she has.

'It is important for both customer and supplier to realize that the customer may not be able to express his requirements in words that will help the supplier to meet them', I suggest. 'You know that you want your suppliers to deliver polymer that will work in your process. If the stuff they delivered last week produced satisfactory bottle caps for your customers, then you would like the same again. You want consistency. Your supplier knows you want consistency. But, in what chemical and physical characteristics of the polymer do you require consistency? Density, melt index, molecular weight distribution, granule size, granule shape? I suspect that you do not know. Am I right?'

'You are right', Bill Johnson confirms. 'We are not able to put into words exactly what we want from a polymer supplier. Perhaps we have a feeling that the polymer from supplier X does not work so well as that from supplier Y, but we cannot explain why. If we were hellbent on single sourcing we would retain Y and reject X, but we would not be able to explain **why** . . . well, not in terms that would help X to improve.'

Bill Johnson pauses. Perhaps he is thinking of X and Y. He continues in a more forceful tone: 'Big as it may be, this is not the problem I want to raise, Roland. I want your advice on automatic control systems. Our chemical friends tell us we need PID controllers.'

Bill has not asked me a question. However, it is clear that he wishes me to speak about PID controllers. Perhaps he would like me to explain what they are and how they might be used at Lancan. We agree to defer discussion of control systems until we return to Bill's office. First we will enjoy the excellent lunch which is now being served. Graham informs us that he has recently watched Manchester United and we have a relaxed but animated discussion of their outstanding players, past and present. After coffee, we return to Bill Johnson's office and focus our minds on to more serious issues.

'Automatic control systems have facilitated major changes in the chemical industry', I explain. 'For example, I visited in 1982 a major chemical company that I had worked for in 1972. The changes that had occurred during the 10-year period were quite alarming. The number of employees at the site I visited had reduced from 1500 to 500, while the output had increased by 30%. That was made possible by PID controllers. During the 1970s and 1980s the cost of electronic hardware fell sharply while its reliability increased considerably. So it became cost effective to replace much of the people work by automatic control . . .'

'Yes, we have seen the effect of cheaper computers', Graham interrupts, 'but what do P, I and D actually mean?'

'P means proportional, I means integral and D means derivative', I reply. 'With an automatic control system we compare the measured output with the desired output to obtain an error, then we feed back into the process a signal *proportional* to the error. The bigger the error, the bigger the signal. The effect of this feedback is to drive the output towards the desired level, thus reducing the error and the drive. If you studied the performance of a system with proportional feedback, you would find that it did not always perform as you would wish, so you could attempt to improve its performance by feeding back two additional signals – one related to the *integral* of the error and one related to the rate of change (i.e. *derivative*) of the error. A control engineer would aim to get the best performance from your PID control system by attempting to have the three signals into the right proportions, by "tuning the controller", as they say.'

'So they use these PID controllers to control temperatures, pressures, feedrates and such, do they?', Graham Covey asks.

'They do indeed', I reply. 'A process operator in the control room would use a computer keyboard to select the "input pressure", say, then he would key in the required input pressure. They call this a "set point". Two digital indicators on the control panel would show the set point for input pressure and the measured input pressure. The two should agree. Suppose, for example the operator increased a temperature set point from 280 to 300. The change would appear immediately on the temperature set point indicator. The PID control would act so as to increase the actual temperature which would gradually move towards 300. If the control system is well tuned the actual temperature will reach 300 as quickly as possible, without overshooting and without oscillation.'

'Well, that is simple enough', Bill Johnson concludes. 'My new shower controller must work like that. I set the required temperature and an automatic control system attempts to balance the hot and cold feeds so as to give me that temperature. Will it use integral and derivative control signals?'

'I doubt it', Graham interjects with a broad smile, 'but I am no expert on such matters', he adds rather hastily.

I nod agreement, to imply that I am not an expert, either. Then I continue:

'In theory, automatic control systems could replace much more human activity and decision making. With your old shower control, you were an essential component in the feedback loop. Your senses detected the temperature, your brain made decisions about the need for adjustment then your hand made the adjustment. Now, with your new controller the sensing, deciding and adjusting are done automatically by a piece of hardware. It works very well, no doubt. Where the decisions are much more complex, however, it may not be so easy to replace the human being. Or perhaps there will be some losses to offset against the gains.'

Clearly my two clients will not be happy to accept such an assertion unless I illustrate the point with a concrete example. The example will have to come from the chemical industry, but I am sure that the point could be illustrated by reference to any industry, as there is a general principle involved. It concerns the conflict between two options – whether you should try to reduce variability in your process output by:

- reducing variability at the input to your process; or
- compensating, within your process, for the effect of the input variation.

'Consider, for example, a chemical manufacturing process', I continue. 'We know that the impurity in the raw material varies and we know that the viscosity of our product is influenced by the level of impurity. How can we reduce the variation in viscosity that so annoys our customers? We could investigate the impurity variation, paying particular attention to differences between our suppliers. We could reduce the number of suppliers. We could continuously monitor the impurity using appropriate control charts. Alternatively, we could simply accept the variation in impurity, but compensate for its effect by changing the reactor temperature, since the latter also influences product viscosity. To achieve this temperature compensation we would measure the viscosity and correct any deviation from the viscosity target, by making an appropriate adjustment to the reactor temperature. This run chart shows how effective this approach can be.'

I lay on the table a run chart (Fig. 5.8) which shows viscosity variations at the output of the process. 'Well gentlemen, is the temperature compensation effective?', I ask.

My clients stare intently at the run chart for some time. Bill Johnson is the first to speak: 'Well, the output viscosity averaged approximately 80. You say that the target is 80. So the process is getting it right on average, but we have no way of knowing whether this is due to the temperature compensation loop. Perhaps the incoming impurity did not change during this period. Have you any data for the impurity and/or the temperature?'

'Are we all agreed then?', I ask. 'The mean viscosity was close to the target of 80 cSt during this period, but we do not know how this has been achieved. Fortunately, I have a run chart (Fig. 5.9) of the incoming impurity for the same period.'

'The impurity certainly was not constant', asserts Graham Covey. 'There

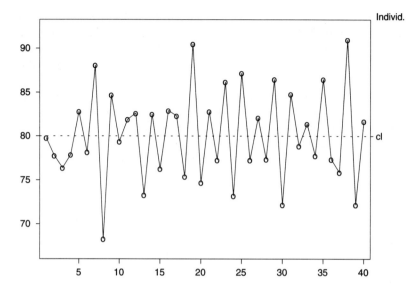

Fig. 5.8 Output viscosity – with temperature compensation.

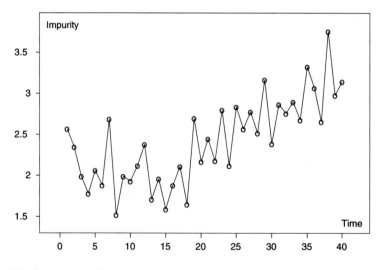

Fig. 5.9 Input impurity.

is random variations plus an obvious upward trend.' He places the two run charts alongside each other, and continues: 'The trend is not present in the viscosity graph. It appears that the temperature control loop has prevented

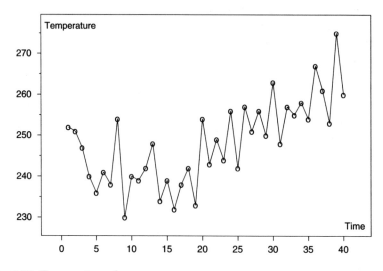

Fig. 5.10 Temperature changes.

the impurity trend at the input, from influencing the viscosity at the output. Perhaps . . .'

'I agree that the input trend does not appear in the output,', Bill Johnson interjects, 'but how do we know that the temperature compensation is responsible?'

'The purpose of the control loop is to prevent changes in impurity at the input from influencing the viscosity of the output', I remind my clients. 'The theory is that an increase in impurity will cause an increase in viscosity. When we detect an increase in viscosity we increase the reactor temperature which should cause a decrease in viscosity, thus compensating for the change due to the impurity. If it is working we should see the temperature change as the impurity changes. I have a run chart of the reactor temperature.'

'That is clear enough', Graham Covey concludes as he examines the temperature run chart (Fig. 5.10). 'Obviously the temperature has been increased by the control loop in an attempt to reduce the viscosity which is being forced up by the increasing impurity. I am convinced, Roland. The control loop is successfully maintaining the mean impurity close to the target of 80.'

Graham and I look to Bill Johnson. Perhaps we are both looking for a sign that Bill is also convinced. 'I would like to see viscosity data for a period when the control loop was switched off and the temperature was held constant', Bill says, slowly. 'We could compare that data with the data that emerged when the loop was working. That is the comparison I would like to make.'

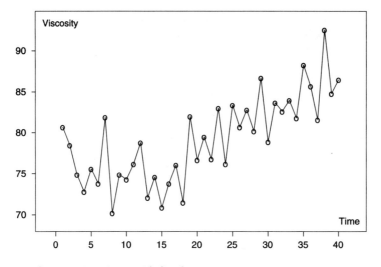

Fig. 5.11 Output viscosity – with fixed temperature.

'Yes, that would be convincing', Graham agrees, 'but we would need to choose a period when the impurity was increasing, as it was in the run chart (Fig. 5.9).'

'No problem, Graham', I reassure him. 'We can run the process again with exactly the same impurity input, but with a constant reactor temperature. We are able to do this because it is not a real process at all. Simply a computer simulation of a process. In fact I have already done what you suggested, and the output viscosity is in this run chart.'

Bill Johnson seizes the latest chart (Fig. 5.11) and places it alongside the viscosity chart we examined earlier (Fig. 5.8). He and Graham study the two charts. 'So, in both of these runs we have the same impurity input. Is that right?', Bill asks. I reassure him that is so: 'In one case the control loop is working (Fig. 5.8). In the other case, we have a fixed reactor temperature of 250 (Fig. 5.11).'

'This is a superb illustration of the strength and the weakness of the automatic control system', Bill suggests. 'Clearly, it has successfully compensated for the drift in impurity, but it has also introduced extra random variation. Do you see that Graham?'

At this point I need to remind myself that Bill Johnson is a Production Manager who started his working life on the shop floor and is now approaching retirement age. It is quite remarkable that he can so quickly draw such sound conclusions from data and ask such probing questions about the origins of the data.

'You are absolutely right, Bill', I concur. 'The increased variation is particularly noticeable in the first 20 results, when the input impurity was stable. During that period there was no impurity drift to compensate. So we derived no benefit from the control loop, but we had the disadvantage of increased variability. Later we do experience a real benefit as the control loop prevents the upward drift in impurity causing an upward drift in viscosity.'

'Tampering with a stable process makes it worse', Graham reminds us. 'Surely that is the first rule of SPC. Do control engineers not know about SPC?'

'Well, some of them do', I reply. 'Especially if they have been on one of my SPC courses. But to be fair to control engineers, it must be said that in many situations the random variations is small whilst the drifts and steps are much larger. So the advantage of the control loop is very clear, but the increased random variation might go unnoticed or be regarded as unimportant.'

'Could I make one more point before we leave this hypothetical process', I continue, somewhat surprised that my clients have tolerated this chemical example for so long. 'It seems to me that no one will be motivated to study the input impurity as long as the control loop appears to be compensating for impurity drifts. Thus the existence of the feedback loop effectively conceals the real problem and hides many learning opportunities. If we did not have the temperature compensation we would be forced to attack the root cause of viscosity variation, which is impurity variation. Reducing the impurity and/or its variation might produce unexpected benefits in other product parameters, in addition to the expected benefit of more consistent viscosity.'

'Can I have one last word on control systems?', Bill Johnson asks, then continues: 'The random variation in the compensated viscosity (Fig. 5.8) is not very random. It bounces. Almost every down is followed by an up, and vice versa. Is this to be expected whenever you use a control loop, or does this control loop simply need tuning, as you called it?'

'You are right again, Bill', I reassure him. 'By reducing the proportion of error that is fed back we would reduce this oscillation during the stable period, but there would be a price to pay. The temperature compensation would not track the trend so well in the later period and the mean viscosity would not be so close to the target of 80. Let me give you some means and standard deviations for the two periods.'

Table 5.3 The effect on viscosity of feedback control

Period		1–20 (stable)	21–40 (drifting)
Input impurity	Mean	2.05	2.80
	SD	0.344	0.390
Output viscosity (fixed temp)	Mean	75.52	82.99
	SD	3.443	3.899
Output viscosity (with feedback)	Mean	79.79	80.49
	SD	5.160	5.380

'Table 5.3 allows you to assess the performance very easily. The feedback loop held the mean viscosity close to the target during the stable period and during the drift, but it gave a standard deviation about 50% greater than achieved with the fixed temperature.'

'Very good. We will be able to have a more meaningful discussion with our suppliers, next time we meet', Bill Johnson adds, with an air of satisfaction. 'The important points to remember Graham, are that the use of automatic control to correct for real changes, may increase variability and will not help to sustain a learning culture. Perhaps we could move on to another topic. How do you use control charts when you only have very short production runs? But we must have some coffee first.'

5.4 SPC WITH SHORT PRODUCTION RUNS

As we drink coffee, I express my surprise that Lancan has processes with short production runs. Obviously bottle-making, can-making and cap-making processes enjoy very long production runs, which last for many days or even weeks, running 24 hours a day, with no scheduled stops. This is in stark contrast to what I find when I visit other clients who produce many different products, or grades, or sizes, from one production line. They experience frequent, planned stoppages for changes to be made. The question they all ask me is: 'Should we keep a separate control chart for each product, or can we use just one chart for the whole process?' I have no doubt that Bill or Graham will be asking the same question.

'We have a subsidiary company, just down the road, Lancoat which makes paints', explains Bill Johnson. 'You will not have heard of them. They make speciality paints which are used in unusual situations, such as corrosive environments, for example. I was hoping that their Quality Manager would be joining us, but that message I received was to tell me that he cannot make it. Most unfortunate. I am sure you would have been able to help him.'

'Does he have a specific problem to discuss?', I ask. 'Are they using control charts?'

'No, they are not using control charts', Bill Johnson replies. 'I believe they are very backward in many ways. They do not seem to get anything right first time. They appear to rework almost every batch. It is quite ironical. Lancoat is the most profitable company in the group and our Group Chairman has suggested more than once that we should be benchmarking against them. Well, I have visited them twice now and I have been most unimpressed each time.'

Bill Johnson obviously cannot understand how a company which manufactures paints rather inefficiently can make a higher percentage profit than a company which manufactures cans and bottles very efficiently. There could be many reasons, but I do not wish to become involved in wild speculation. Nor do I wish to become involved with one of the many initiatives which are currently bringing the word 'benchmarking' into disrepute.

'Can you tell me about their processes?', I ask. 'Unfortunately, I know nothing about paint making. Presumably, many ingredients have to be mixed.'

'Absolutely. The fundamental operation is mixing. Now you have figured that out, you probably know as much about paint making as many people at Lancoat', Bill replies with some bitterness. 'They make about 500 different products, but that number is increasing as they develop new products to meet customer needs. Each product has a sort of production schedule, which is simply a list of ingredients and their quantities with some indication of the order in which they should be added and the mixing time.'

'That sounds quite straightforward. How do they manage to get it wrong?', Graham Covey asks.

'Yes, it sounds straightforward when I describe it', Bill replies, 'but their explanation is not so simple. They use a lot of jargon. Black art stuff, nudge, nudge, wink, wink. Not one of them speaks clearly. I hate them.'

Bill Johnson stops quite abruptly. There is a silence. Perhaps he feels that he has said too much, or revealed feelings that would best be kept hidden. I sympathize. Obviously, Bill tries very hard to communicate clearly, and he does not tolerate people who obfuscate. But in some companies obfuscation is the norm.

'How do they measure the quality of the product?', I ask, hoping that a simple request for information will help my host to recapture the mood of our earlier interaction. 'I suppose colour is important.'

'Surprisingly, colour is not so important. Remember, there are specialist paints for industrial use. The most important parameter is viscosity, and most of the rework is concerned with achieving the right viscosity. It appears that they . . .'

'Don't tell us. Let me guess', Graham interrupts with some excitement in his voice. 'They aim for a high viscosity at the first mixing. Then they reduce it to the desired level by adding more solvent.'

'That is exactly what they do', Bill replies, 'but there is no guarantee that that it will be right at the second attempt. It may take two, three, or more dilutions to produce a viscosity within spec. This can take a very long time, because the measurement of viscosity is a slow job. Meanwhile the paint is sitting there in the mixer waiting for decisions to be made. I could hardly believe my own ears as they described their operations.'

Bill Johnson's voice has risen in volume and pitch as he describes the Lancoat process and its management. Much of what he has said has revealed the narrowness of his experience, which has been confined to one company. What can I say that will restore his equilibrium and help our discussion to draw on his strengths rather than his weaknesses?

'If you are to derive any benefit from mutual benchmarking you need to focus on the things they do better than you', I suggest. 'Furthermore, you need to bear in mind that they operate in a different business environment. Lancoat and Lancan are not competitors. Perhaps it would be impossible for Lancan to match the profitability of Lancoat. Perhaps their great strength lies in their product development.'

Bill Johnson speaks more calmly as he returns to the item on the agenda: 'Yes, perhaps they can learn from us how to use SPC to make their operations more efficient. As their Quality Manager has not shown up we will have to operate with some hypothetical data.'

He steps across to the flip chart and writes four column headings, Batch, Product, Aim and Actual. Then somewhat hesitantly he lists product letters, aim values and actual values. Soon we have a set of data that will serve as a very useful focus for discussion (Table 5.4).

'How would you use control charts with data like that?', Bill Johnson asks, when he can fit no more batches on the flip chart. 'Would you plot a separate chart for each product?'

'If they make 500 products and months elapse between consecutive campaigns for the same product, then it would be crazy to have a separate chart for each product. But I notice that products A and C both have two campaigns in the data you have put on the flip chart. If one or two products are made frequently it might be useful to have a chart for each, but I would prefer to focus on the process, not the products. Let us put this data into my laptop then we can explore various possibilities.'

Table 5.4 Initial viscosity

Batch	Product	Aim	Actual
1	A	150	141
2	A	150	163
3	B	70	75
4	C	105	103
5	C	105	115
6	C	105	97
7	C	105	108
8	D	100	95
9	D	100	107
10	E	180	190
11	A	150	132
12	A	150	138
13	F	105	90
14	F	105	100
15	F	105	97
16	G	100	106
17	H	150	171
18	H	150	160
19	C	105	119
20	C	105	105
21	C	105	110

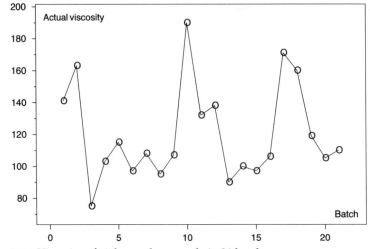

Fig. 5.12 Viscosity of eight products made in 21 batches.

Soon I have keyed in the data and we are ready to go. 'Let us start with a simple run chart', I suggest. 'Now then what does that tell us?'

'Figure 5.12 tells us, what we already know, that the process is not in control', Graham Covey replies. 'There are assignable causes of variation. But we know that these are due to product changes.'

'In fact, it would have been amazing if we had found only random variation, when we know that there were so many deliberate changes', Bill Johnson adds.

'So, it would be pointless to add action lines to the run chart as it stands. What we must first do is to remove the effect of the product changes. The easiest way to do this would be to ask "Quality Analyst" to calculate values for a new variable: the difference between the actual viscosity and the aim. Then we can plot a run chart or a control chart, of these differences.'

I instruct the computer program to calculate the differences for each batch and then to plot an individuals chart of the 21 differences. I request that the centre line be drawn at zero and the computer places the action lines at ±28.45. It has calculated the standard deviation from the differences, of course, not from the original data.

'We appear to have a process which is in control', Graham concludes, after examining the individuals chart (Fig. 5.13). 'Does this chart have a special name?'

'Some people call it a difference chart, but I am not sure that name would be accepted by everyone. Do you think this type of chart could be used at Lancoat, Bill?', I ask.

'It looks promising,', Bill Johnson concedes, as he subjects the difference chart to further scrutiny. 'I am not so sure that the process is in control. There are five consecutive points below the centre line then six above the centre line. I wonder if these changes coincide with product changes?'

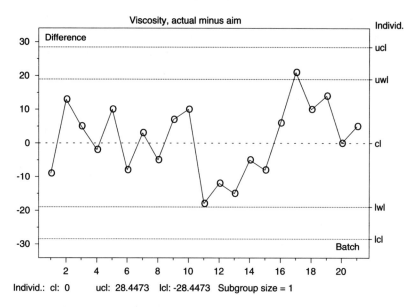

Fig. 5.13 A difference chart for the viscosity of 21 batches.

'Let us write the product letter next to each point', I suggest. Graham reads out the product letters (Table 5.4) and I label each point. As I do so it becomes clear that the apparent changes in the difference chart do coincide with product changes (Fig. 5.14).

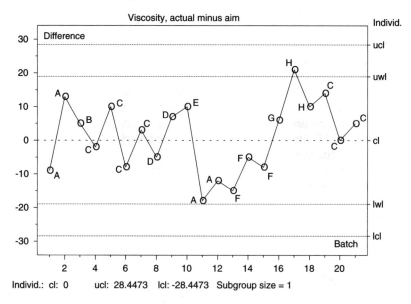

Fig. 5.14 A difference chart showing product letters.

'The five points below the line are for products A and F', Bill observes. 'Are they low viscosity products? It did occur to me that the products with lower viscosity might give smaller differences and hence points closer to the centre line.'

'With so few points and so many product changes we could talk ourselves into conclusions which will not stand up to further testing', I caution.

'Perhaps we have seen too many charts today', Graham says as he flops back into his chair. 'But I wonder if that is an important point you were making Bill. Surely it is often true that larger values tend to have larger errors. You must have a view on that, Roland.'

'Yes it is a very good point. You could reasonably suggest that, if a run of batches with an aim of 100 had a standard deviation of 5.0, say, then a run of batches with an aim of 200 might have a standard deviation of 10.0. So the percentage standard deviation would be 5% for both runs. With many processes this is found to be the case. To prove it were true with this process we would need much more data.'

'How would you attempt to prove it?', Bill asks. 'And if you found it to be true, what sort of chart would you use?'

Bill Johnson's tone of voice suggests that he is no longer preoccupied with his experiences at Lancoat. He is again asking penetrating questions. I must supply convincing answers.

'Perhaps the best approach would be to extract the results for each run of two or more batches with the same product, and calculate the mean and standard deviation for each run. We have only seven such runs in this data; it could be nice to have at least 20. Then we would plot a scatter diagram of the standard deviation against the mean. If the points lay close to a straight line which had a positive slope, that would support the hypothesis that the variability was proportional to the mean. If we were convinced that this was true, we would then abandon the difference chart and plot an alternative. A chart recommended in many books is the z chart, in which you plot z values, with the centre line at zero and the action lines at ±3.

I write on the flip chart

$$z = \frac{(actual - aim)}{SD}$$

then pause to allow my clients to seek clarification, should they so wish. Experience has shown me that, near the end of the day, an exhausted client will appear to accept something that he or she would have questioned in the mid-morning. Clearly, Bill is not yet exhausted.

'Where would the standard deviation come from?', he asks.

'The standard deviations, note the plural, would come from past data. For each product we would need an aim and a standard deviation. So a lot of data would be needed. On the other hand if we were prepared to make assumptions about the variability, we would need less data. For example, if we assumed that the standard deviation were constant, we could use the difference chart. If we assumed that the standard deviation were proportional to the level, then we could obtain it from the scatter diagram I mentioned. For the scatter diagram we would need data for many products but not all.'

'I can assure you, Roland, that those guys at Lancoat could not cope with this heavy data analysis. Is there no simple alternative?' Bill Johnson asks.

'If simplicity is an essential requirement you should consider the percentage difference chart as an alternative to the difference chart', I suggest. Rising from my seat I write on the flip chart:

$$\text{percentage difference} = \frac{\text{actual} - \text{aim}}{\text{aim}} \times 100$$

'So you would be expressing the difference as a percentage of the aim', Graham says. 'I suppose you could do that quite easily on "Quality Analyst", with this data.'

'It is almost identical', says Graham Covey, when the two control charts (Figs. 5.13 and 5.15) are placed alongside each other. 'So the percentage difference chart does not appear to offer anything extra from the difference chart. So there would be little point in using the more complex chart. Is that right?'

'That is a reasonable conclusion to draw from this very limited set of data', I concur. 'Of course, with a much larger set of real Lancoat data you might find that the percentage difference chart gave much more reliable indication of real process changes, without responding to the product changes.'

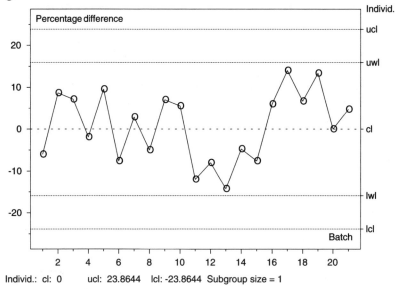

Individ.: cl: 0   ucl: 23.8644   lcl: -23.8644   Subgroup size = 1

Fig. 5.15 A percentage difference chart.

'Yes, that summarizes their requirement rather well', Bill Johnson suggests. 'They need a chart that will help them to control and improve the mixing process. This chart should not respond to random variation or to product changes, but it should ring a bell whenever there is some other change. I believe their greatest need is for a simple strategy which produces an accurate record of what has happened I think a difference chart or a percentage difference chart could play an important role in that strategy.'

Bill Johnson sits back in his chair. He seems to be more relaxed and rather satisfied with our progress. It becomes clear that our day's work is over, as he rises and starts to pack piles of papers into his briefcase. 'This has been a very useful discussion, Roland. Very useful indeed. You should put all this wisdom into a book.'

As I walk to the car park I reflect on what we have achieved during my two visits to Lancan. Perhaps Bill is right. Perhaps I should write a book. But it might be impossible to produce a book that would satisfy the needs of people like Bill Johnson and the needs of his colleagues at Lancan.

5.5 SUMMARY

My two visits to Lancan have focused attention on processes which do not display a simple pattern of variation, even when they are in control or stable. You may recall, from Chapter 4, a can-making process which had medium-term random variation in addition to the short-term random variation. Thus, when judged against the short-term variation, this process would never be in control, in the strictest sense. To cope with the additional random variation we calculated the standard deviation by a different method, which gave more useful action lines further from the centre line.

In this chapter we studied the output from a multi-head process making bottle caps. Use of the conventional approach with such a process can lead to an unsatisfactory control chart. It is important to distinguish between the two sources of variation:

- head-to-head variation, and
- piece-to-piece variation, within heads

In order to achieve satisfactory control and/or meet customer requirements it may be necessary greatly to reduce the head-to-head variation. A control chart can assist the systematic monitoring and study of the process, but care must be taken in placing the action lines. The chart will be much more useful if it indicates which heads produced the items with extreme values.

The benefits of automatic control systems were discussed in this chapter. It is possible to use feedback control to compensate for gradual drift or sudden change in raw materials. Such systems are now cheap and reliable. It appears not to be widely realized, however, that any system which corrects for bias will also increase random variation. Furthermore, an automatic control system does not establish the root cause of the variation and may distract attention from one of the twin objectives of process management, which are:

- to maintain the average as close to target as possible, and
- to reduce variation about the average.

Finally in this chapter we looked at yet another non-standard application of control charts, with a process that produced many products in short runs. It is obviously not sensible to keep a separate chart for each product. We must monitor the process performance by plotting one chart, which does not respond to the product changes. To set up such a chart may require the analysis of a substantial data set.

After discussing the difficulty of applying SPC techniques to non-standard processes, it may be timely to remind you that many people have considerable success using the standard procedure referred to in Chapters 3 and 4 (procedure B in Appendix A). This relatively simple procedure has passed the test of time. If it gives you a control chart that helps you to monitor and improve your process, do not spend too much time worrying about Bill Johnson's problems.

Chapter 6

Cusums and training

The consultant pays a third visit to Lubrichem where he explains the use of the cusum technique to the Quality Manager and the Assistant Plant Manager. He then discusses training requirements with the Quality Director and the Training Officer.

6.1 INTRODUCTION

This is my third visit to Lubrichem. I am due to arrive at 10:00 and I expect to leave by 16:30 at the latest. Many people would be envious of such a short working day, but I have an hour's drive before I can start my day's work and a similar journey afterwards. I will be paid my one-day consultancy fee, of course, as I was on the two previous occasions, but I suspect that this will be my last consultancy visit.

I hope that the next time I drive down to Lubrichem, I will be accompanied by a colleague and that we will be staying for three days, running a course in statistical process control (SPC). I further hope that this course will prove to be the first of several such courses, but it is foolish to count your chickens before they are hatched. The customer will decide how many courses there will be and how long each course will last. I will listen carefully as the customer outlines his requirements and then make a proposal.

The discussion of training courses is scheduled to take place after lunch. My first appointment is with Dave Smith, the Quality Manager, and I believe we will be joined later by George Grant the LBC Plant Manager. I had lengthy discussions with Dave and George on my second visit, of course. It will be interesting to see what conclusions George Grant has reached about the use of control charts on the LBC process.

'Unfortunately George will not be able to join us today', Dave Smith informs me, when I reach his office. 'This is Roger Hunter, who is George's right-hand man on LBC.'

We exchange pleasantries. Roger Hunter is just as friendly as all the other people I have met at Lubrichem. I am reflecting on how fortunate I am to spend my working life discussing such interesting problems and helping such pleasant people, when Dave suggests that we start without delay. He reminds me that we are meeting the Quality Director, Ron Henderson, for lunch at 12:30. He also reminds me that I promised to reveal the strengths and weaknesses of the cusum technique.

6.2 CUSUM POST-MORTEM ANALYSIS

'Cusum is an abbreviation of cumulative sum', I explain. 'The calculation of a cusum is remarkably simple. In fact, you may find it hard to believe that such a simple technique can be useful, but it is actually very powerful. When you have seen this power, you may wonder how such a useful technique could be so simple.'

I feel at this point, that I am about to drift into a deeply philosophical monologue. To do so would be utterly inappropriate. If my clients are to appreciate both the power and the simplicity of the cusum technique, I must focus their attention on to a specific example, using Lubrichem data. 'Let us have a look at a cusum chart of your viscosity data', I suggest. 'You remember the 80 viscosity results we examined using an individuals chart (Fig. 3.2) and a moving mean chart (Fig. 3.3). I have produced a cusum chart (Fig. 6.1) of the same data.'

'Now, I must impress upon you from the start', I caution, 'that a cusum chart should not be interpreted as if it were a run chart. A cusum chart is quite different and it must be interpreted differently. With a cusum chart we are only interested in the slope of the graph and we are especially

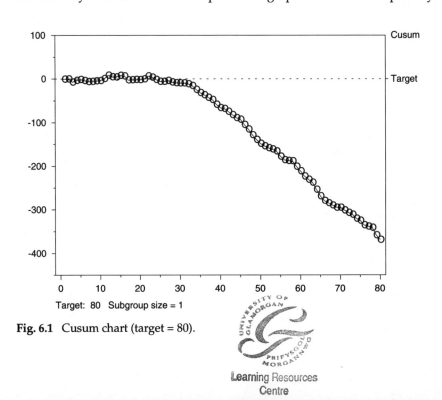

Target: 80   Subgroup size = 1

Fig. 6.1 Cusum chart (target = 80).

Learning Resources Centre

interested in changes in slope. What can you tell me about the slope, or slopes, of this cusum?'

After quite a long pause, Dave Smith suggests: 'Well, the graph is obviously sloping downwards after batch 30. But, I suspect you are looking for a more subtle answer than that.'

'No, no, subtlety is not required at this point', I assure him. 'So the cusum has a downward, or negative, slope from batch 30 onwards. That is telling us that the mean viscosity was *below* 80 during that period. A negative slope on the cusum chart implies that the mean of the data was below the target value, and I used a target of 80 when calculating the cusum.'

'The cusum graph is horizontal for the first 30 batches', Dave continues. 'What does that tell us? Does it mean that the viscosity was on target?'

'It does indeed, Dave. Zero slope in the cusum implies that the data is on target. In other words the horizontal cusum tells us that the mean viscosity was about 80 for the first 30 batches. If we had a positive slope in the cusum that would inform us that the viscosity was above 80. So, *slopes* are important, when we interpret a cusum, and *changes in slope* are extremely important because they indicate changes in mean level. The five rules for interpreting slopes must not be forgotten so I have listed them for you.'

1. A positive slope on the cusum chart indicates that the mean of the data is above the target value.
2. A negative slope on the cusum chart indicates that the mean of the data is below the target value.
3. Zero slope on the cusum chart indicates that the mean of the data is approximately equal to the target value.
4. A change in slope indicates a change in the mean of the data.
5. The actual value of the cusum at any point in time tells you nothing about the mean of the data.

'When I explain to you how the cusum is calculated these rules may seem more reasonable', I reassure my clients. 'However, whether they seem reasonable or not, you must observe these rules, especially Rule 4, about slope changes. In practice, you must attempt to locate slope changes as accurately as possible. Do you agree that the change occurred at batch 30, Roger?'

'Well, I am not so sure', Roger Hunter replies, rather hesitantly. 'I do not know much about statistics, but I reckon my eyesight is better than Dave's. I think the downward slope starts at batch 22, then becomes steeper at batch 32. Would that mean there were two changes in the mean viscosity?'

'Yes it would', I confirm. 'Every change in slope on the cusum graph indicates a change in the mean level of viscosity. It is very interesting that you spotted two changes, Roger. Two weeks ago, when we last looked at this data, George Grant made a similar suggestion. On that occasion we were looking at an individuals chart (Fig. 3.2). Do you remember, Dave?'

Dave's face lights up as he recalls our discussion. 'Yes, that's right', he says. 'If I remember rightly, George suggested that the first decrease occurred after batch 22 and the second after batch 33. Then you calculated the means and we agreed that the second change was about twice as big as the first. (The means are in Table 3.2.) I suppose you can see in the cusum graph that the second change is bigger than the first.'

'Well, I am not sure it would be obvious to everyone, Dave', I caution. 'You can certainly estimate means from the cusum chart. Then from these means you can calculate the size of the change. Let us do it. What is the value of the cusum at point 33 and at point 80? Can you estimate them roughly from Fig. 6.1?'

'Very roughly', Dave Smith replies. 'At point 33 the cusum is approximately −20 and at point 80 it is approximately −370. But these are very much rough estimates.'

'Yes, but they are sufficiently accurate, Dave', I reassure him. 'The cusum has changed by (370 − 20 =) 350 during a 47-batch period. Dividing 350 by 47 gives a slope of 7.4. This is telling us that the mean viscosity is 7.4 cSt below the target of 80 cSt. So we estimate the mean for these 47 batches to be 72.6 cSt. I think you will find that it is very close to the mean I calculated two weeks ago (Table 3.2).'

'Let us estimate the mean viscosity for batches 22 to 32,' Dave Smith suggests, with some enthusiasm. 'I reckon the cusum changes from +10 to −20 for these 10 batches. That gives a slope of 3.0, which gives a mean of 77.0 cSt. I suspect that the mean you calculated from the data was more like 78.0 cSt, was it not?'

'Yes, you are right, Dave', I confirm. 'Of course it is not easy to estimate such a small slope over such a small number of batches. I prefer to calculate the means from the data. In practice, I use the cusum chart to discover *when* the changes occurred, then I return to the run chart, before drawing any conclusions. The run chart brings you closer to the data. Now then, Roger, perhaps Dave and I are galloping ahead too quickly. We have seen this data before, of course.'

'Well, I follow what you have been saying', Roger replies rather slowly, 'but I would feel much better if I knew how the cusum was calculated. You did say it was very simple, didn't you?'

'Yes, it is simple. You will have no difficulty understanding the calculation', I promise. 'I have a listing of your data, somewhere. Let me set out the calculation in a table.'

'In Table 6.1 I have listed the viscosity results in column 2, then subtracted 80 from each to calculate the deviations in column 3. The cusum, in column 4, is just a running total of the deviations. That's it', I declare, with a flourish. 'Notice that some of the deviations are positive and some are negative, so the cusum column in Table 6.1 stays small. Later batches have lower viscosity and will give mainly negative deviations, so the cusum will become more and more negative after batch 22.'

Table 6.1 Calculation of a cusum

Batch	Viscosity	Viscosity minus target	Cusum
1	79.1	−0.9	−0.9
2	80.5	0.5	−0.4
3	72.7	−7.3	−7.7
4	84.1	4.1	−3.6
5	82.0	2.0	−1.6
6	77.6	−2.4	−4.0
7	77.4	−2.6	−6.6
8	80.5	0.5	−6.1
9	81.1	1.1	−5.0
10	80.8	0.8	−4.2
11	84.5	4.5	0.3
12	87.9	7.9	8.2
13	76.1	−3.9	4.3
etc.	etc.	etc.	etc.

'Well, it is certainly simple', Roger Hunter admits, 'but I don't feel that I am an expert on cusums, yet. Why did you use a target value of 80? What would the cusum look like if we used some other target?'

'I chose 80 as the target value because 80 cSt is the mid-point of the specification. I used the manufacturing target as the cusum target. Of course, I could have used any number that entered my head. Very often in a post-mortem analysis we use the mean of the data as the target value. Let us do that on my laptop computer, then you will see how the cusum changes in appearance if we change the target value.'

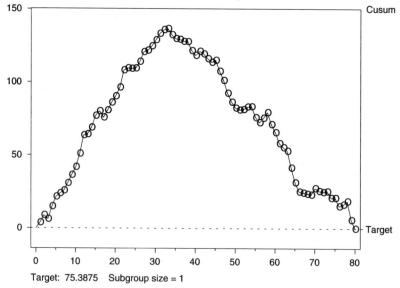

Fig. 6.2 A cusum chart using the mean as target.

It is a simple matter to change the target value from 80 to the mean of the data, which is 75.3875 cSt. Soon we have the revised cusum on the screen.

'Figure 6.2 is a cusum of the same data, but with a different target. Notice that this cusum starts at zero, as all cusums do, but it also returns to zero. This return to zero always occurs when we use the mean of the data as the target value. Now, what conclusions would you draw from this cusum?', I ask.

'At first sight it is completely different', Roger Hunter suggests, 'but the big change in slope is at batch 33 again. For the first 33 batches it is going up, then it is going down.'

'What exactly do you mean when you say "it is going up", Roger?', I ask with some concern. 'Do you mean the viscosity is going up?'

'No. I mean that the cusum is going up', he replies, 'which tells us that the viscosity is above the target value of 75 point something. Later the cusum is going down, which implies that the mean viscosity is below the target. Thus at batch 33 the viscosity must have suddenly decreased.'

While Roger has been practising his cusum interpretation skills, Dave Smith has been studying the new cusum in silence. 'It is almost impossible to see the change in slope at batch 22', he asserts, 'but I can now see a clear change at batch 66, which was not noticeable in the first cusum. A change from negative slope to zero slope, must indicate an increase in viscosity. I wonder if that would be visible in the run chart (Fig. 2.6, Fig. 3.1 or Fig. 3.2).'

'Yes, batches 67 to 78 have higher viscosity', continues Dave Smith pointing at the run chart (Fig. 2.6). 'That is something we had not spotted before. The cusum chart is certainly a powerful tool for detecting changes. I must say, though, I am rather concerned about the arbitrary nature of the way we are going about it. The number of changes we detect seems to depend on how carefully we inspect the charts. Is there no objective criterion we can use, like the action lines on a control chart?'

'Yes there is, Dave', I reply, with some relief, for he has unwittingly introduced a cue for a natural break. 'We use a device known as a V-mask, but I think we should discuss that after we have had some coffee, if you don't mind.'

6.3 THE V-MASK AND DECISION INTERVAL CHARTS

'Let us pick up the point that Dave raised before we broke for coffee', I suggest, looking at Roger Hunter and fearing that perhaps he had not fully understood Dave's concern for more objectivity. 'On my previous visits we discussed run charts and control charts. Obviously you could make decisions about the state of the process using only a run chart, but this would be rather subjective. Indeed, on my first visit, we examined a run chart (Fig. 2.6) and decided that the process had not been stable. On my second visit,

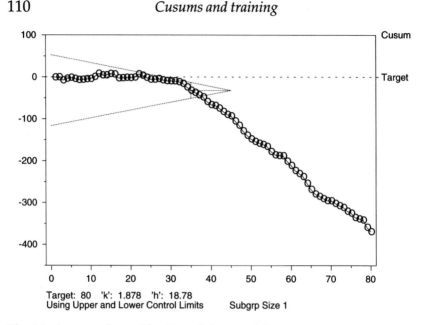

Target: 80   'k': 1.878   'h': 18.78
Using Upper and Lower Control Limits   Subgrp Size 1

Fig. 6.3 A cusum chart with a V-mask (target = 80).

we repeated the exercise using an individuals chart (Fig. 3.1) and a moving mean chart (Fig. 3.3). The second analysis was less subjective because we had action lines, warning lines and supplementary rules to aid our decision making. However, for a truly systematic and objective assessment of process stability, I would recommend that you follow what I call, procedure B' (Appendix A).

I offer copies of procedure B to Roger and Dave. They read through the rather lengthy document with occasional nods and grunts, as I ponder the difficulties associated with describing a V-mask. 'Adding a V-mask to a cusum chart is like adding action and warning lines to a run chart. The V-mask helps us to make decisions more objectively. Let us return to our first cusum, with a target value of 80, and I will instruct the computer to add a V-mask.'

'The cusum chart in Fig. 6.3 is exactly like the first cusum (Fig. 6.1) except that I have added a V-mask which is placed on point 35', I explain. 'I am going to cover the picture to the right of point 35, because I want you to imagine that this is an ongoing process monitoring exercise. Imagine that we have just received the viscosity result for batch 35. We subtract 80 from the result and add the deviation to our previous cusum value to calculate the new cusum, which we plot. Then we place the V-mask on the point we have just plotted.'

I pause to check that Dave Smith and Roger Hunter are visualizing the process monitoring exercise, then I continue: 'Now then, we use the V-mask to help us reach a decision about the state of the process. We ask ourselves

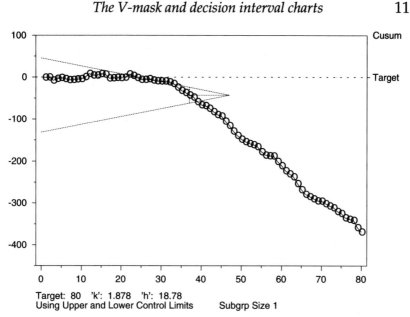

Fig. 6.4 The V-mask indicates a change.

the question "Is the cusum plot within the arms of the V-mask?" Clearly the answer is "Yes", so we are unable to conclude that the process mean has deviated from the target value of 80.'

'But even at this point, there is strong evidence in the cusum chart that the mean viscosity *has* decreased', Dave Smith asserts.

'That's right', Roger concurs. 'The cusum plot has been going down since the point for batch 23 was plotted.'

'I agree, gentlemen. Since batch 23 we have been accumulating evidence of a process change. But at batch 35 this evidence is not yet conclusive. Clearly, if the decreased viscosity persists we will find, after a few more batches that part of the cusum plot lies outside the V-mask. Remember, we always place the mask on the point we have just plotted. In fact, if I instruct the computer to put the V-mask on point 37 (Fig. 6.4), I think we will then see an action indication.'

'Oh yes', exclaims Roger. 'When you place the V-mask on point number 37, there are several points outside the mask. Batch 22, batch 27, batches 30 to 33 all have points outside the V-mask. Does that imply that the change occurred at batch 22?'

'With this data, Roger', I reply, 'it is not obvious when the change occurred. Perhaps there are two changes as you suggested earlier. However, regardless of when the lower level of viscosity started, we do not prove its existence until we plot the point for batch 37. Of course the cusum chart is not suggesting that the decrease started at batch 37.'

'So, the cusum chart does not detect a change immediately', Roger says, speaking rather slowly. Perhaps he is hoping I will interrupt, contradict or prove him wrong in some way. However, before I can formulate an appropriate response, Dave Smith explains: 'We discussed this point on Roland's last visit. He demonstrated that certain charts detect changes more quickly than others.' Turning to me, he asks: 'How does the cusum chart compare with an individuals chart or a moving mean chart?'

'Probably the best way to assess the relative ability of different charts to detect changes, is to compare their average run lengths (ARLs)', I suggest. I am always reluctant to thrust upon my clients this concept of ARL, because it is rather abstract. However, it seems that Dave Smith would like to take our discussion of control chart performance beyond the point we reached on my last visit. So here goes. 'Let us suppose that the change in viscosity really did start at batch 22. We will never know for sure, of course, but let us imagine that the mean viscosity decreased by some unknown amount immediately after batch 22. We did not detect the change until batch 37, so the run length is 15 (i.e. 37 minus 22). With a larger change we would expect a smaller run length. With a smaller change we would expect a larger run length. If we had several changes of the same size, we would be unlikely to get the same run length with each, so we speak of *average* run length (ARL). Let me show you a table which compares the average run lengths of different charts'.

'Let me add a little detail to Table 6.2', I suggest. 'The three control charts being compared are an individuals chart with action lines only, a moving mean chart with action lines only, and a cusum chart of individuals using the standard V-mark. Many people would regard this as a fair comparison because the ARLs in the top row are approximately equal. Obviously you can add warning lines to an individuals chart or a moving mean chart. If you did so the ARLs would reduce. You could also use a narrower V-mask to reduce the ARLs. However, Table 6.3 helps us to make a fair comparison of the three charts. Which do you prefer?'

'The cusum chart is very impressive', Roger Hunter concedes, 'but I cannot see our process operators coping with it. I am reluctant to reject a chart which is four times as fast, but the simplicity of the individuals chart is a very important factor.'

Table 6.2 Average run lengths of three control charts

Size of change divided by SD	Individuals chart	Moving mean chart	Cusum chart
0.0	370	370	440
0.5	155	56	34
1.0	44	13	11
1.5	15	4.9	6.1
2.0	6.3	3.2	4.1
2.5	3.2	2.3	3.2
3.0	2.0	2.0	2.5

'Of course, we discussed some of these issues with George Grant on your last visit', Dave reminds me. 'He certainly prefers the individuals chart to the moving mean chart, but he has yet to see the cusum. What do people use in other companies, Roland?'

'You name it, someone uses it', I reply, with an expansive gesture. 'Different companies use different charts. One of my clients in the chemical industry makes extensive use of moving mean and moving range charts. Another certainly uses individuals charts. It is also true that many managers use the cusum technique in problem solving and post-mortem analyses, but, I must admit, that I do not find widespread use of V-masks.'

'Are these people plotting charts by hand, or are they using computers?' Roger Hunter asks.

'I would say the majority are plotted by hand. But in one of the companies I visit, the process operators refused to plot graphs by hand. *They* wanted the charts plotted on the console screens. Of course, they were highly computer literate people driving the latest technology. Clearly, there are advantages in using computers, but the big disadvantage is that the operators cannot write notes on the charts, to record the action they have taken or the causes they have investigated. So when a manager or a team attempt to use the chart for performance review, it tells them a lot about effects, but nothing about causes.'

'What we want is the power of the cusum, with the simplicity of the individuals chart', Dave Smith suggests. 'I suppose that is what everyone wants.'

'Well, one advantage of using computers is that you can use several charts', I continue. 'For example, you could display an individuals chart on the screen, whilst in the background running a cusum. If the cusum detects a change, this can be indicated by a flashing point on the individuals chart.'

Roger Hunter appears to be deep in thought as I am speaking. The nature of his thoughts is revealed as he asks, 'Can we return to the cusum? Perhaps we should give it further consideration, Dave. Obviously, it must be possible to draw a V-mask on acetate sheet, Roland. How would you do it?'

I take a sheet of paper and draw a V-mask (Fig. 6.5). I explain that the line ABCDE is the V-mask, but the additional line FCG helps us to align the mask correctly. FCG should be parallel with the time axis when the V-mask is placed on a point.

'Yes, yes. But how about the dimensions?', asks Roger. 'How long is line BC, for example?'

'Well, you cannot draw your V-mask, until after you have marked off your scales on the time axis and then the cusum axis', I reply. 'If you use inappropriate scales your cusum plot will either be very cramped or it will run off the page. A useful guide is to let *one* time unit on the x-axis be approximately equal to *two* standard deviations on the y-axis. So you need to have an estimate of the process standard deviation, before you start.'

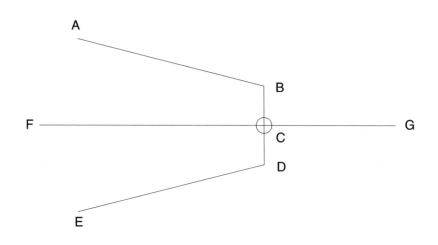

Fig. 6.5 A V-mask.

'Can you remember the standard deviation we used when we set up the individuals chart and the moving mean chart?', I ask. Roger Hunter looks at Dave who shuffles through his notes. 'Yes. Here it is', he replies. 'You calculated the standard deviation from the first 30 results. It was 3.756 cSt. Do you not remember, George asked you how this was calculated, and you said you would explain on your next visit.'

'That's right, Dave', I confirm. 'Well, if the standard deviation is 3.756, two standard deviations will be equal to 7.512. So, if you let 1 cm equal one time unit on the *x*-axis, you need to let 1 cm equal about 7.5 on the *y*-axis. If that gives an awkward scale, you could let 1 cm equal 5 or 10. To keep the discussion simple, let us say that you use 1 cm equals one batch on the *x*-axis and 1 cm = 10 cSt on the *y*-axis.'

'Right then', I continue. 'Now you have marked the scales on your two axes you can draw your own V-mask (Fig. 6.5). Line BC should be *five* standard deviations long. Line AB should have a slope of *half* a standard deviation per time unit.'

'Why five standard deviations and half of a standard deviation?' asks Roger Hunter.

'Those are the rules for creating a "standard" V-mask. BC is known as the "decision interval" and is equal to five standard deviations. The slope of line AB is known as the "decision slope" or the "reference value" and is equal to half a standard deviation. The easy way to draw the slope correctly is to mark off 10 time units along CF, then make HJ equal to ten standard deviations (Fig. 6.6).'

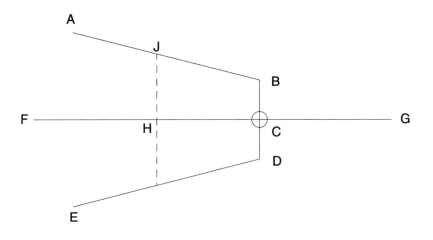

Fig. 6.6 The standard V-mask.

$$(BC = 5\sigma, HJ = 10\sigma, HC = 10 \text{ time units})$$

'Obviously you could draw a V-mask that had a different decision interval or a different reference value. A narrower V-mask would detect changes more quickly and a wider V-mask would detect changes more slowly. I call this V-mask the "standard" V-mask because it is the one used by "Quality Analyst", unless you specify otherwise. Furthermore this "standard" V-mask gives the ARL in Table 6.2.'

'Well gentlemen, what do you think?' I ask. 'Can you see your process operators using V-masks?'

There is no immediate reply. Dave and Roger appear to be deep in thought. 'I like cusums', Roger says, 'but I see a lot of snags with the V-mask. We could not expect the process operators to design their own V-masks, could we Dave? But I am not sure we could ask them to use V-masks, either.

'Is there no other way?', Dave asks. 'Can we not draw action lines on the cusum, or something simple like that?'

'Well, in effect the V-mask is very similar to a pair of action lines', I suggest. 'There is in fact an alternative type of cusum chart available from "Quality Analyst". Some people call it a "decision interval chart." It involves twice as much effort to do the calculations, because we calculate two cusums – an upper cusum and lower cusum. But the interpretation is simpler because it does use fixed action lines rather than a moving V-mask.'

Dave Smith looks at his watch. 'We must join Ron Henderson for lunch at 12:30. Can you show us this decision interval chart in 10 minutes, Roland?'

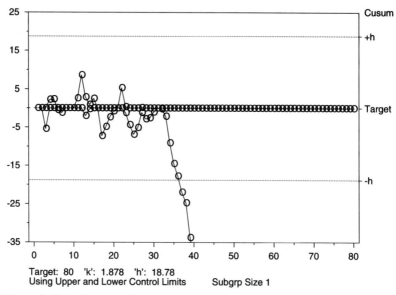

Target: 80   'k': 1.878   'h': 18.78
Using Upper and Lower Control Limits   Subgrp Size 1

Fig. 6.7 A decision interval chart.

'In 10 seconds', I reply as I send the package into its change routine. The decision interval chart (Fig. 6.7) soon appears on the screen.

'Let's see if I can explain this decision interval chart in the nine minutes remaining', I suggest. 'The centre line is labelled "Target", while the upper and lower action lines are labelled $+h$ and $-h$. A process change is indicated by the cusum plot going outside the action lines. That seems to . . .'

'It happens at batch 37', Roger Hunter interrupts. 'Just as it did with the V-mask. Will the normal cusum and the decision interval chart always agree?'

'Yes, they will, provided they both use the same decision interval and the same reference value. Unless you specify otherwise, "Quality Analyst" will use 5σ for the decision interval and 0.5σ for the reference value, whichever chart you request. Remember, the standard deviation was 3.756 cSt so the decision interval will be 18.78 cSt and the reference value will be 1.878 cSt. They are on the screen. The decision interval is h and the reference value is k. I just have time to show you the calculations for the decision interval chart.'

'For a decision interval chart (Table 6.3) we calculate two cusums', I explain. 'The upper cusum is a running total of the deviations from the upper target. The lower cusum is a running total of the deviations from the lower target. You recall that we used a target of 80 cSt for the normal cusum. Our targets for the decision interval chart are 80 ± 1.9, where the 1.9 is our reference value, rounded to one decimal place. There is just one other complication. We set the upper cusum to zero whenever it becomes negative and we set the lower cusum to zero whenever it becomes positive.'

Table 6.3 Calculations for a decision interval chart

Batch	Viscosity	Viscosity minus 81.9	Upper cusum	Viscosity minus 78.1	Lower cusum
1	79.1	−2.8	0	1.0	0
2	80.5	−1.4	0	2.4	0
3	72.7	−9.2	0	−5.4	−5.4
4	84.1	2.2	2.2	6.0	0
5	82.0	0.1	2.3	3.9	0
6	77.6	−4.3	0	−0.5	−0.5
7	77.4	−4.5	0	−0.7	−1.2
etc					

Dave Smith is walking towards the door. 'That's very interesting', he says. 'The decision interval chart is much more complex to calculate but so easy to interpret. We will have to go. Ron Henderson will be on his second gin and tonic.'

'Fascinating', adds Roger Hunter, as we walk towards the dining room. 'Perhaps we could have a decision interval chart and an individuals chart on adjacent screens. I must talk to the operators and supervisors.'

6.4 TRAINING FOR QUALITY IMPROVEMENT

Ron Henderson has lost none of his enthusiasm for total quality management, since I last spoke to him. It is a pleasure to listen as he describes the companies he has visited and the conferences he has attended and the books he has read, in the past four weeks. All things seem possible, as he outlines his plans for removing the barriers which hinder quality improvement.

We enjoy a good lunch as Ron tells us about the conversations he has had recently with quality specialists in other chemical companies. Clearly he is anxious to benefit from the experience of those who have already travelled further down the path of TQM. He is now aware that other companies have wasted money on blanket training and he does not want to make the same mistake.

Though Ron Henderson does not say so, I suspect that the directors of Lubrichem must now believe that their initial investment in TQM training has not yet yielded the expected benefits. I have no doubt that future spending on training will have to be more carefully planned, managed and justified.

'It seems to me', Ron says in a lower voice, as if he is about to confide a secret, 'that a TQM programme needs to be balanced. Perhaps, last year we put too much emphasis on motivation, with insufficient attention to tools and techniques. Have other companies followed this route, Roland?'

'Yes, I know of two large chemical companies that have done exactly the same, but they are now correcting the imbalance with appropriate training. On the other hand, I know of companies in which tools and techniques have received due attention, but managers have not created a quality culture which empowered their people to make best use of these tools. I agree wholeheartedly that balance is essential. In fact, I am speaking at a conference in the USA in May, and I will put forward the thesis that TQM failure often results from an unbalanced approach.'

'Is that the ASQC annual quality congress in Boston?', Ron asks excitedly.

'Yes it is. Will you be there, Ron?'

'Well, I am hoping to attend, but it is dependent on my being able to arrange a visit to our subsidiary company in New Jersey. I hope you will not be using Lubrichem as an example of a company that failed to implement TQM?', he asks, with some concern in his voice.

'No, no. The paper is already written and no company names are mentioned', I reassure him.

Dave Smith has said little throughout the meal. Perhaps he prefers to play a supporting role when his Quality Director, Ron Henderson, is present. However, as we drain our coffee cups Dave reminds us that we are due to meet with Alan Braithwaite in five minutes.

Alan Braithwaite is the company Training Officer. He is surprisingly young for such a post, but he does appear to have had considerable and varied experience. Furthermore, he does seem to have a good understanding of TQM and an acute awareness that TQM training will be prominent amongst his objectives in the coming year. Alan has drawn up an agenda for the meeting and item one is 'Lubrichem's training needs'.

'We fully appreciate that TQM is for everyone in the company', Ron Henderson assures me, 'but we are anxious not to waste money on blanket training, in which everybody receives the same course, regardless of his or her needs.'

I sympathize with Ron's objective, and I would like to suggest a variety of courses, that will meet the needs of Lubrichem employees at all levels. However, before I can reply, Alan Braithwaite issues a further warning that the era of profligate spending is over for Lubrichem. 'In the present climate we must plan carefully and spend wisely. We would like to establish a long-term partnership with someone like yourself, so that we have courses tailored to our needs and you are assured of a fair return for the time you spend in planning and preparation. Do you have such agreements with other companies?'

'Well, yes and no, Alan', I reply, rather hesitantly. 'I do not have any formal contracts, but I do have unwritten agreements with several companies. I believe these companies trust me. They know that I am serving their long-term objectives. These informal agreements do not offer me any security, of course, but who can enjoy security in the present climate? In every one of these companies the trust has grown, but it started in every case with me running one three-day course in statistical process control (SPC).'

'So you would be happy to run your standard SPC course just once. Then, when we had evaluated its effectiveness, you would adapt subsequent courses to our needs. Is that right?' Alan asks.

'I am sure I can do better than that, gentlemen', I reply. 'The first course will be tailored to your requirements, as I now perceive them, but further courses may be even better, as we respond to your feedback. Furthermore, all of the courses will focus on your data. Might I also suggest that each course should be followed, after about six weeks, with a follow-up session in which I discuss the findings of quality improvement teams which have been engaged in group projects.'

Alan Braithwaite appears to be impressed with what I am offering. However, it is his responsibility to manage the training budget, so I am not surprised when he questions the cost of my services. 'Would the follow-up session be included in the cost of the three-day course, or would there be an additional charge?' he asks.

'You already know our fees for a three-day course. To that you should add the cost of a one-day consultancy to cover the follow-up session. Plus travel expenses, plus VAT, of course. However, we would make no charge for analysing your data and preparing special material. I am already familiar with some of your processes so I would not need to make any visits to your sites before the first course.'

'And the content?', asks Alan Braithwaite, rather brusquely. 'What would you include in the first course?'

Far from being dismayed by Alan's aggressive questioning, I take it as an indication that he will be asking me to run one or more courses. I suspect that he knows Ron Henderson is in favour of engaging me and Alan is simply taking this last opportunity to assert himself before giving me the good news. But I must not appear to be taking anything for granted.

'I would start the course by defining quality and discussing your customer's requirements. We would then go on to talk about your ability to meet these requirements and to calculate process capability indices from your data. In most companies, process capability arouses a lot of interest and it is a relatively simple topic with which to start the course.' I am trying hard not to sound stilted or formal, but it is difficult to appear fresh and spontaneous when repeating well worn phrases.

'Of course', I continue, 'there are dangers associated with capability indices, so this is a topic we will return to after discussing process stability. We introduce a clearly defined procedure for assessing process stability and the course members will use this to examine the stability of your processes, for which we have data.'

'By now we must be into the second day,' Alan Braithwaite suggests. 'You make it sound very easy, Roland, but there are some rather tricky concepts underlying process capability and stability.'

'Well, I am a complete beginner in statistics', interjects Ron Henderson, 'but I reckon I got a good grasp of process capability when Roland explained it to me. Carry on, Roland. What comes next? How deep do you normally go with chemists and engineers and managers in a company like ours?'

'Well, what I have described so far, takes us to the end of the first day. We usually set some "homework" questions so that people can consolidate, if they wish. I always stress that this work is optional and, of course, not everyone can find the time to do it. On day two we re-visit process capability indices, pointing out the practical difficulties and showing how to make best use of existing data, even if it was gathered when the process was unstable. We also discuss ways of estimating how much of the variability in the product is due to different causes. For example, some of the batch to batch variation in viscosity with LBC80, must be due to variation in raw materials. But some must be due to the test method and some must be caused by the operators, etc. If you wish to make a more consistent product you need to work on those causes which contribute a substantial part of the variability. Thus, it is just not efficient to spend a fortune on new analytical equipment, if the current test method has more than adequate precision, for example. It might be much more effective to improve the operating procedures, say.'

Dave Smith, the Quality Manager, becomes quite energized at this point and breaks his long silence. 'So, decisions on capital expenditure [capex] could be made on statistical grounds', he suggests. 'The capex budget would no longer be shared out among those who shout loudest. The money would go to those managers who could demonstrate potential for quality improvement.'

I wonder, at this point, if Dave might have been wise to continue his silence. Perhaps Ron Henderson would not approve of this jaundiced outburst.

'No doubt, we will enjoy more co-operation and less competition as we go deeper into TQM', Ron says hopefully. 'It will take some time for Dr Deming's views to spread to all corners of the company. Do continue, Roland.'

'Yes. I propose that the remainder of the day should be devoted to statistical process control charts. We will demonstrate the use of the types of chart that are particularly useful in the chemical industry, such as individuals charts and moving mean charts. We would also spend a little time on charts for attributes.'

'Would you not include cusum charts?', asks Dave Smith with some surprise.

'Cusums will be covered on the third day, followed by the seven basic tools for quality improvement. Then we are all set for the grand finale, which is based on a case study. The course members work as teams to analyse data and present their recommendations for quality improvement.'

Alan Braithwaite has scribbled copious notes as I have described the course I would like to run at Lubrichem. 'It sounds like a rather full three days. Are you ever asked to reduce the content and run it as a two-day course?' he asks.

I name some of the chemical companies in which I have presented three-day courses and two-day courses and one-day courses. Then in summary I make a proposal. 'Gentlemen, I am at your service. I will run any length of course you request, and I guarantee that your people will benefit greatly. However, if I run a two-day course, many of the course members will tell you, in the feedback, that it should have been extended to three days, especially if we use computers.'

'You must introduce "Quality Analyst" in the course. It will have to be three days Alan', Ron Henderson asserts.

There is no dissenting voice. We agree dates for the three-day course and for the follow-up session. We further agree that we will review the situation after we have seen the feedback from the people who attend the first course. However, on the assumption that this feedback will be favourable, we pencil in dates for two more three-day courses.

6.5 SUMMARY

My third visit to Lubrichem has ended with an agreement to run at least one three-day course in Statistical Process Control. This course has been designed to meet the needs of chemists, engineers and middle managers in production and support services. Throughout the course various techniques will be illustrated with reference to Lubrichem data.

Prior to my meeting with the Training Officer and the Quality Director, I discussed the cusum technique with the Quality Manager and the Assistant Plant Manager. They could see, very clearly, the power of cusums to detect process changes, but were concerned about the technical detail underlying the construction of the V-mask. This is quite natural. When used in its post-mortem role the cusum chart has a basic simplicity which is surprising, when one considers the obvious power of the technique. Introducing the V-mask, or switching to the decision interval chart, reduces the subjectivity of the change detection process but also introduces greater complexity. Thus the cusum chart is more widely used as a post-mortem tool than as an aid to process monitoring.

Chapter 7

Company culture and techniques for improvement

The consultant pays a fourth, unexpected visit to Lubrichem to explain the differences between statistical quality control (SQC) and statistical process control (SPC) to the Quality Director, the Quality Manager and the Plant Manager. He demonstrates how various tools and techniques can be used to achieve quality improvement, then discusses the need for a learning culture in which the tools can be used effectively.

7.1 INTRODUCTION

Today I am at Lubrichem for a fourth visit. Two weeks ago, when I departed from Lubrichem, leaving my clients in good heart, and having agreed dates for the first of a series of courses, I did not anticipate further consultancy visits. However, three days later I received a telephone call from Ron Henderson, the Marketing Director, suggesting that we hastily reappraise our strategy. So we scoured our diaries for the earliest possible date, and I have returned.

Ron Henderson also informed me, during our telephone conversation, that he was to relinquish some of his sales and marketing responsibilities in order to devote more time to the Total Quality Initiative. Thus he confirmed the rumour that had been circulating during my previous visit. I offered my congratulations and expressed my confidence in his ability to give additional momentum to the quality movement within Lubrichem. However, I wondered if his request for a reappraisal was an expression of no confidence in my ability to guide his company in the best direction.

On the telephone Ron explained that he had attended yet another quality conference which had raised some doubts in his mind. It now appeared to him that I was advocating a policy of statistical quality control (SQC) rather than statistical process control (SPC). He was anxious to ensure that the planned courses would help his people to get inside the process and improve it. 'Could I guarantee that this would occur?', was the question he wished me to answer. Furthermore, this question was so important that Ron Henderson would like an answer before the first course was run.

So here I am again at Lubrichem. My client is rapidly acquiring a greater understanding of the philosophy of quality improvement and showing a healthy disrespect for the advice given by consultants. As my taxi stops at the gates of Lubrichem I wonder which of my competitors have been here since my last visit. Soon, however, I am in Ron Henderson's office and the warmth of his welcome makes me feel a twinge of guilt about some of the thoughts that have passed through my mind during the journey. 'Perhaps, Ron is not entirely convinced of my competence or my sincerity', I tell myself. Today's challenge is to convince him of both.

7.2 SQC AND SPC

'Am I right to make the distinction between statistical quality control and statistical process control?', Ron Henderson asks as we take our seats around one end of his oval table. Also present are Dave Smith, the Quality Manager, and George Grant who is Plant Manager on LBC. I have met Dave and George on previous visits, of course.

'Yes, it is a distinction many people do make', I reply. 'Though I must say that there is some scope for confusion if SQC and SPC are not clearly defined.'

'But the essential difference between the two is that SQC controls the product whereas SPC controls the process. Is that not so?', Ron asks.

Both Dave Smith and George Grant nod their heads rather emphatically as if to imply that the answer must be an unqualified yes. I gain the impression that Ron, Dave and George have been through this discussion already and have reached agreement. It may be difficult to change their opinions.

'Well, I am reluctant to answer the question before we have agreed a definition of the word "process". Perhaps I can persuade you to adopt my definition. This picture will help', I reply, as I extract a diagram from my briefcase (Fig. 7.1).

'As I see it, the outputs from your process are deliveries of LBC80 to your customers', I explain. 'Now, I would suggest that the inputs to your process include raw materials, personnel, procedures, the plant, delivery tankers, storage tanks, analytical methods, . . . and many other elements which do not immediately come to mind. Any variation in the quality of your product must result from variation in one or more of these inputs.'

I pause at this point to gauge the reaction of my clients. It can come as a shock to have this rather abstract view of a process thrust upon you, especially if you have recently invested £300M in a chemical plant. To be reminded that the latest technology produces nothing without the co-op-eration of your process operators, can be very sobering.

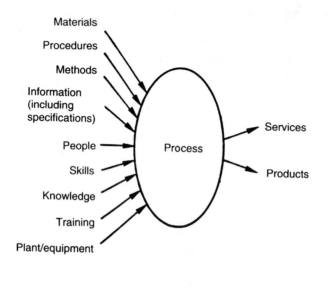

Fig. 7.1 A process.

'So you would not regard the LBC plant in isolation, as a process?', asks George Grant, speaking rather slowly.

'No, I would not, because it is not useful to do so', I reply. 'You can draw the process boundaries wherever you like. You can define the process in many ways, but some will be more useful than others. The process definition I have offered you is rather vague, I must admit, but it is useful. Furthermore, you should bear in mind that any process can be considered as part of a larger process, and it can be said to contain lots of sub-processes. We need to define the process so as to help us improve the quality of the product it delivers to your customer. I think the definition should include raw materials, people, etc.'

'This is very interesting, Roland', Ron Henderson interjects. 'It seems obvious that we should define what we meant by "process" before we talk about statistical process control. Why did we not discuss processes in this way during your *first* visit?'

'I suppose the agenda was largely determined by the questions you asked. This discussion could have occurred during any one of my earlier visits but it was just pushed out by other, more urgent, topics. The process model certainly features very strongly in all our SPC courses. One topic we cover is flowcharting and we suggest that every process investigation should start with the question "Have we got a process flowchart?" Perhaps I should have asked you that very question on my first visit. What do you think?'

'Well, perhaps we would have resented you asking that question on your first visit', Ron Henderson concedes.

'For the obvious reason that we have never drawn a flowchart', adds George Grant, somewhat amused by the trend of the discussion, 'but we do have written procedures so it would not be too difficult to draw a flowchart, I suppose.'

'Well, the written procedures would help but it can prove surprisingly difficult to flowchart a process, especially a non-manufacturing process which spans several departments', I suggest, recalling the frustration, and subsequent elation, experienced by a group of people who I helped to draw a flowchart of an invoicing process. 'This is part of a flowchart', I add, as I extract another diagram from my briefcase.

'I expect you have seen flowcharts before', I continue. 'The rectangular boxes contain actions and the diamond shaped boxes contain decisions. Using these two basic building blocks we can represent the logical flow of action and decision which results in your customer receiving a quality product. It is basically very simple, but the flowchart of a manufacturing process is sure to be very large and very detailed. None the less, the time and effort spent in creating a flowchart can often pay a handsome dividend.'

'So you think we should have drawn a flowchart before we discussed SPC? Does everyone start by drawing a flowchart?, asks George Grant.

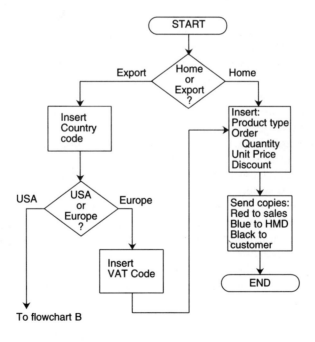

Fig. 7.2 A flow chart of an invoicing process.

'The importance of the flowchart depends on the process', I suggest. 'If you were attempting to improve your invoicing process, or your order reception process, or your expense claims process, I would strongly recommend that you start by drawing a flowchart. With your LBC manufacturing process, many of your staff must have a rough flowchart in mind already, but it would have been useful if you had attempted to draw a flowchart after my first visit, say. I apologise for not having suggested it.'

'My experience with flowcharting suggests that we might not have finished it by the time you arrived for your second visit', George Grant interjects, reflecting the jocular mood that he seems to be in today. 'Very time-consuming, and it really requires a team effort.'

'Let us get back to my original question', Ron Henderson insists. 'You recommended that we should measure the viscosity of our finished product, plot the results on a control chart and take appropriate action whenever the chart indicated a change. Now, is that SQC or SPC?'

The most remarkable aspect of Ron Henderson's question is that he was not present at the second meeting when I discussed control charts with Dave Smith and George Grant. Clearly there has been communication between the three, and the fact that the Marketing Director could ask such a question testifies to the effectiveness of that communication.

'Many people would describe that as statistical quality control', I reply. 'Furthermore, their tone of voice might imply that SQC is a second-rate activity. However, I maintain that you would benefit from doing what I advised. Plotting the data would be a big step forward from simply recording it. If the operators did the plotting, as I suggested, then they would become more involved. They would discuss variability and change. They would put forward suggestions for better procedures. They might even draw a flowchart.'

'This SQC sounds perfect, Roland. Why would we need SPC?', Dave Smith asks, rather bluntly. These are the first words Dave has uttered during the discussion. I have noted before that he does not seem as friendly when Ron Henderson is present.

'I prefer not to make a distinction between SQC and SPC', I reply. 'What I have recommended, which you want to describe as SQC, would get you off to a good start. But sooner or later you might suspect that there were further benefits to be gained by better control of process variables during the batch reaction. Many people would call that SPC.' I pause to check that all three clients are still on board as we change tack. I suspect that further progress in this discussion is dependent on us getting down to more detail. George Grant is clearly the person best equipped to supply that detail.

'George, could you list some of the process variables that might influence the product quality?', I ask.

'How many do you want?', asks George Grant. 'Two, ten, a hundred ... ?'

'Well, just give us half a dozen, that readily come to mind and please spare us the detailed chemistry', I suggest.

'Obviously the input materials will influence the LBC80 viscosity. These include the LBC10 from the upstream plant, the lime, the sulphur, the dispersant, the foam inhibitor, etc. Then the timings are important. We can vary the reaction time and the time when we introduce the lime and when we introduce the carbon dioxide. We can also change various temperatures, pressures and feedrates. Is that enough?', George asks.

'Thank you, George', I reply. 'No doubt other variables would occur to you, if you had more time to think of them. In the statistical profession, we refer to these process variables as independent variables, while the quality and quantity of the product would be known as dependent variables or response variables. Obviously the viscosity and the calcium content and the sediment in the LBC80 are dependent variables. Can I ask you an embarrassing question, George. Do you know precisely what effect each of the independent variables has on the dependent variables?'

George Grant does not appear to be at all embarrassed as he replies: 'In a word, no. This is a very complex reaction and we cannot claim to understand all of the relationships, but we do have some knowledge of some of the relationships. For example, increasing the quantity of lime will increase the calcium content of the LBC80, but it is not a linear relationship. What is more, the effect of changing the lime quantity may depend on the reaction time or on changes in the upstream plant.'

'So you are not in the ideal position for using so-called SPC', I suggest, rather forcefully. 'You have a lot of learning to do and so-called SQC can help you.'

I am conscious that Ron Henderson has been silent for some time as George Grant and I have mixed elementary chemistry with more advanced statistical concepts. I wonder if Ron appreciates the complexity of the process and the learning culture that is required if such processes are to be effectively managed. Perhaps I can help Ron to focus on what is important if I offer further thoughts on SQC and SPC.

'The distinction between SQC and SPC is rather artificial', I continue. 'If you are measuring the calcium content of your product with a view to controlling it you call that SQC, because calcium content is a process output. If, on the other hand, you are measuring the reactor temperature with a view to controlling that, then you call that SPC because the temperature is a process input. But both variables can be viewed as process outputs. The reactor temperature is an output of the heat control process, which is a sub-process of the main process. So, rather than quibble about SQC and SPC, we should attempt to measure those variables which will best help us to control and improve the quality of our products.'

'So, as we make progress we will focus on smaller and smaller sub-processes, achieving tighter control of their outputs', George Grant suggests. 'If each variable we measure is at the output of a process we can say we are doing SQC. But each variable can be seen as being within a larger process, so we are always doing SPC.'

'So, the distinction between SQC and SPC is rather unimportant', I add, in confirmation. 'But I must warn you of the danger of focusing on smaller processes. If you take a large process and break it down into many sub-processes, then optimize each sub-process, you will not have optimized the large process. The same can be said about departments. Most large companies are arranged in departments for administrative purposes, but large processes often span several departments. Thus it is possible to manage each department very well while failing to manage the process which supplies the customer. Deming warns us of the danger of sub-optimizing. I would advise every manager to "get the big picture", by focusing on the largest process he or she is allowed to manage, and studying it over the largest possible time span. Obviously, the manager will also need to attend to short-term problems and local difficulties. Flexibility is called for.'

'The question is, Roland', Ron Henderson asks in a slow, controlled, voice, 'will the control charts you recommended, help us to gain a better understanding of our process?'

'Yes, they will', I reply. 'Provided you involve the operators in plotting the charts and you create a learning culture in which all your people want a better understanding of their processes and you give them the tools to do the job. They need all of the seven tools, not just control charts. We have already discussed histograms, run charts, control charts and flowcharts. They also need to be familiar with Pareto charts, cause and effect diagrams, scatter diagrams, stratification and check sheets.'

'To name but nine, of the seven tools', interjects George Grant with a huge smile. Ron and Dave turn to me as if expecting a hasty correction of an obvious numerical error. No correction is forthcoming, but an explanation is called for.

'Yes, I have mentioned nine basic tools', I confess. 'I have added run charts and flowcharts to Ishikawa's original list of what he called "the seven indispensable tools for quality improvement". Ishikawa maintained that everyone in Japanese industry understood the seven tools. Perhaps that was an exaggeration, but they do teach the seven tools in Japanese schools, you know.'

The expression on my clients' faces, suggest to me that they did not know. I reflect that, in truth, I am simply repeating what I have been told by a colleague who has actually worked in Japan, though I doubt if my colleague opened many classroom doors during his two-year stay.

My thoughts are interrupted by a welcome suggestion from Ron Henderson that we take a break and have some coffee, before we discuss the other five tools.

Table 7.1 The 'seven' basic tools for quality improvement

1.	Check sheet
2.	Histogram
3.	Run chart
4.	Control chart
5.	Flow chart
6.	Scatter diagram
7.	Stratification
8.	Pareto chart
9.	Cause and effect diagram

7.3 TOOLS FOR QUALITY IMPROVEMENT

'What is stratification?' asks Dave Smith when we resume our discussion. He is pointing at Table 7.1 – the list of quality improvement tools, I have placed on the table. Perhaps stratification is the only technique on the list with which Dave is not familiar. It certainly does not appear in every published list of 'seven tools', but it was included in Ishikawa's recommended tool kit.

'It is difficult to explain stratification in isolation', I reply. 'It can be used to increase the power of histograms, run charts or scatter diagrams. So, I would like to look at scatter diagrams first, if you don't mind.'

'Certainly', says Ron Henderson, nodding agreement. George Grant also nods, but Dave Smith stares at the list looking very unhappy. Perhaps, as Quality Manager, he feels that he should be familiar with every quality technique that is labelled 'basic'. Now he has to sit through a description of scatter diagrams before I reveal the secrets of the stratifying fraternity.

From my briefcase I extract a scatter diagram (Fig. 7.3). 'This is a scatter diagram which we often use on SPC courses', I explain. 'Course members

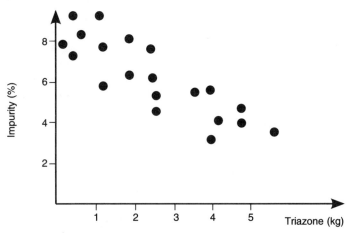

Fig. 7.3 A scatter diagram.

work in groups on a small case study, drawing conclusions from the data and identifying opportunities for process improvement. The 42 points in the scatter diagram represent 42 batches of digozo blue pigment. For each batch we know the percentage impurity in the pigment and the weight of triazone that has been added during the reaction. Note that the independent variable triazone, is on the horizontal axis while the dependent variable, impurity, is on the vertical axis. That is a convention that most people adhere to. What conclusion would you draw from this simple diagram?'

'Well, it is pretty obvious', Ron Henderson asserts. 'The more triazone they use the lower the impurity. But you would not need a picture to tell you that. You would be able to see it by inspection of the data.'

'I don't think you would', George Grant insists. 'I find that a picture like this is much more powerful than two columns of numbers. The trouble is that I have no time to draw pictures. What worries me about this data is the way that the triazone varies so much from batch to batch. Didn't the operators have any procedures?'

'They have *now*, George, but they had no procedure for inserting the triazone when this data was gathered', I explain. 'The triazone was introduced as a panic measure to reduce the impurity, but it is very expensive stuff, so the operators were asked not to use too much.'

'So, the scatter diagram has told us nothing we did not already know', interjects Dave Smith with a sneering tone. 'They introduced triazone because they knew it would reduce impurity. Now the scatter diagram tells us that adding triazone reduces impurity. Big deal.'

'I agree, Dave, that the scatter diagram has confirmed, what they already knew, that the triazone would reduce impurity', I reply, speaking in a conciliatory tone and hoping that this might help Dave Smith to switch to a more positive mood, 'but the diagram can help us to quantify the benefit. If we drew the "best straight line" on the diagram using a ruler, it would indicate that the addition of one unit of triazone reduces the impurity by about 2%.'

George Grant seizes the ruler on Ron Henderson's desk and draws, in pencil, a straight line on the graph. 'Yes, you're right', he says. 'About 2% decrease in impurity could be expected for an input of one unit of triazone.'

'The line does not fit the data very well', Dave Smith comments rather bluntly.

'Yes. That is worrying me', adds Ron Henderson. 'Some of the points are a long way from the line. Why is that, Roland?'

'That is due to other causes of variation', I reply. 'The variation in impurity from batch to batch is caused by many factors. *Some* of the variation in impurity is caused by the changes in triazone but the remainder is caused by other factors such as raw materials, people, testing error, etc. Let me show you a stratified scatter diagram (Fig. 7.4) which will help us to see the people variation.'

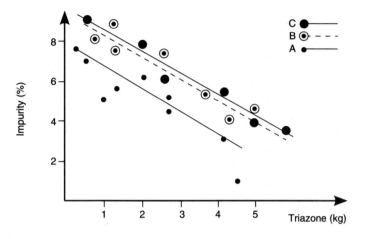

Fig. 7.4 A stratified scatter diagram

From my briefcase I extract a second scatter diagram which has been stratified. Different symbols have been used to indicate which shift team produced each batch (Figure 7.4). I lay the stratified scatter diagram on the table, anticipating that my clients will be delightfully surprised.

The initial response is certainly favourable. 'Good Heavens' says Ron Henderson, searching for words to describe what he sees. Clearly, he senses intuitively, that the stratified scatter diagram is telling us something important.

'The points for shift team A are lower. They are producing lower impurity' suggests Dave Smith.

'And they are using less triazone' adds George Grant. 'Any fool can produce lower impurity by adding more triazone, but team A are producing lower impurity whilst using less of the expensive additive.'

Ron Henderson nods agreement, pleased that others are finding the words which eluded him. Dave and George have the benefit of a scientific education, of course. To further clarify our conclusions I ask. 'How much less impurity would we get from team A if all three teams were using the same level of triazone in every batch? Suppose, for example, that all three teams used 1.5 units of triazone in future batches, what level of impurity would you expect from each?'

George Grant demonstrates pencil power as he pulls the scatter diagram towards him and draws a vertical line through a triazone value of 1.5. Before he can speak, however, Dave Smith has seized the initiative. Turning the diagram around on the table, Dave announces: 'About 2% impurity from team A, but 4% from teams B and C.'

Ron Henderson now takes up the scatter diagram and studies it carefully. With an expression of amazement, or is it disbelief, he attempts to summarize what we have concluded. 'The scatter diagram shows that team A have produced batches of digozo with 2% less impurity than teams B and C. But we only discovered this by stratifying the diagram. So people who don't know about stratification could be missing out.'

'That is right Ron', I reply, 'Ishikawa included stratification in his list of seven indispensable tools. Obviously it is very useful. But stratification has only helped us to discover the effect. We have not yet identified the cause. The manager of the digozo plant must find out how team A are achieving this success. Do the operators in team A know that they are achieving so well and how they are doing it? Will team A be prepared to share their secret with teams B and C? This is where we need a culture of openness, in a learning organization.'

At this point I realize that I am in danger of getting carried away. I just love to talk about learning and culture and winning the commitment of people on the shop floor. Perhaps I have a vested interest. Fortunately, I am prevented from riding my hobby-horse by a suggestion from Ron Henderson. 'We must go to lunch now', he says, 'but I must admit I can hardly wait for you to reveal the power of the other three tools.'

As we walk towards the dining room Dave Smith appears to be deep in thought. Perhaps he is checking Ron's arithmetic.

During lunch we discuss the nature of quality management in other industries. Ron Henderson has much to say about the conferences he has recently attended and the quality problems raised, which seem to vary enormously from one industry to another. Clearly Ron is relishing the novelty and the challenge of his new appointment.

7.4 MORE TOOLS FOR QUALITY IMPROVEMENT

'Let us start with check sheets', I suggest when we return to Ron Henderson's office. I hope that my tone of voice is not apologetic, but I always feel a little embarrassed when talking about check sheets, because they are almost trivial. But they are important.

'This is a simple check sheet', I continue, taking another sheet of paper from my briefcase (Table 7.2) 'It was produced by process operators at another chemical company. They placed a mark in the tally column whenever a batch was rejected. Obviously, the totals in the final column were obtained by counting the number of tally marks in each row.'

My three clients are examining the check sheet. Feeling that this task does not require great concentration I take the liberty of talking while they do so. 'The totals tell us how many batches were rejected for each of the ten reasons listed. We can see that a high proportion of the failed batches were rejected because of insolubles or low viscosity. Obviously, there is nothing very impressive about check sheets, but it is desirable to have such a data recording sheet if many people are involved in the data collection.'

Table 7.2

Reason	Tally	Total
Contamination	1111	5
High moisture content	1111 1111	10
Black speck	11	2
Insolubles	1111 1111 1111 1111	20
Low viscosity	1111 1111 1111 1111 1111 111	28
Excess triazone	11	2
High viscosity	1111 11	7
Unreacted naphtha	1	1
Melting point	1111	4
High copper content	1	1
		80

'It is essential', confirms George Grant, 'and it is highly desirable that everyone clearly understands the categories, or reasons for rejection as they are called in this case.

Dave Smith and Ron Henderson do not offer any comments on the check sheet. I gain the impression that they were much more impressed with the stratified scatter diagram that the check sheet. 'Well, I guess you are quite underwhelmed by the trivial nature of the check sheet', I suggest, 'but it was on Ishikawa's original list of seven tools. Shall we look at the Pareto chart?'

There is clearly no desire to study the check sheet any longer, so I place on the table a Pareto chart, which is simply a pictorial representation of the totals in the check sheet (Figure 7.5).

'This is very simple', exclaims George Grant. 'I am sure I have seen Pareto charts that were much more complicated than this. Yes, that's right, they contained percentage frequencies and cumulative percentage frequencies and percentage costs.

'I see no reason for complexity. The Pareto chart conveys a simple message in a simple format', I reply. 'We can see at a glance how many batches were rejected for each reason, with the most frequent on the left and the least frequent on the right. It helps us to focus on the important few (i.e. low viscosity and insolubles) and to disregard the trivial many (i.e. the other eight). The height of each bar in the Pareto chart is determined by the total, or frequency, in the check sheet (Table 7.2). We could convert these frequencies into percentage frequencies by dividing each by 80 then multiplying by 100. We could then let the Pareto bars have heights equal to the percentages, but the chart would have exactly the same shape and lead us to exactly the same conclusions. Some people like to add up the percentages to obtain cumulative percentages and then draw a cumulative percentage line on the chart. I have never found any use for this line, so I leave it out.

'How about costs?', asks Ron Henderson. 'The chart you have produced is OK. It tells us how often things happened but it does not tell us what it

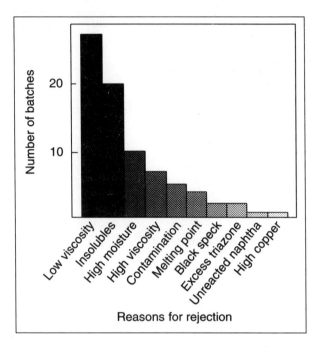

Fig. 7.5 A Pareto chart showing frequency of occurrence.

cost to put things right. If these process operators want management action they must talk money.'

'And they did talk money, Ron', I reply, with some enthusiasm. 'With the help of their supervisor they tabulated the costs associated with each type of failure. Then they drew a second Pareto chart based on the total costs for each type.'

Table 7.3 Cost of failure

Reason	No. of batches	Cost per batch(£)	Total costs (£)
Contamination	5	40 000	200 000
High moisture content	10	4000	40 000
Black speck	2	5000	10 000
Insolubles	20	700	14 000
Low viscosity	28	500	14 000
Excess triazone	2	2500	5000
High viscosity	7	4000	28 000
Unreacted naphtha	1	900	900
Melting point	4	35 000	140 000
High copper content	1	10 000	10 000

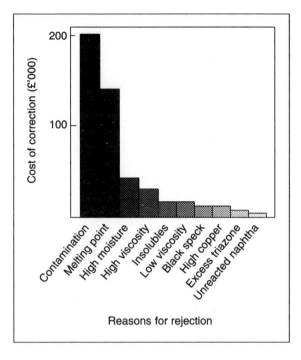

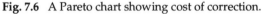

Fig. 7.6 A Pareto chart showing cost of correction.

I place on the table two more sheets (Table 7.3 and Fig. 7.6), and attempt to explain how they were developed. 'The costs per batch in the table are estimates of what it cost the company each time a failure of this type occurred. You see that it cost only £500 to correct low viscosity, but contaminated batches had to be disposed of at a cost of £40 000. Multiplying the number of batches by the cost per batch gives the total costs in the final column. These total costs were used to draw a second Pareto chart.'

'This second Pareto chart looks very similar to the first', suggests George Grant. 'I wonder . . .'

'Look at it carefully, George', interjects Ron Henderson. 'It has a similar shape, but it indicates very different priorities for action. They should concentrate on contamination and melting point if they want to reduce the costs of scrap and re-work. Low viscosity and insolubles have slipped way down the list of priorities.'

Once again I am very impressed with the way Ron Henderson, an ex-marketing man, has grasped the essentials of a production problem and shown empathy with the concerns of the shop floor. I am even more impressed as he continues. 'Perhaps *both* of these Pareto charts are important, Roland. If we are to become a total quality company, then managers must pay attention to reducing the operator frustration, displayed in the first chart, as well as the costs in the second chart.'

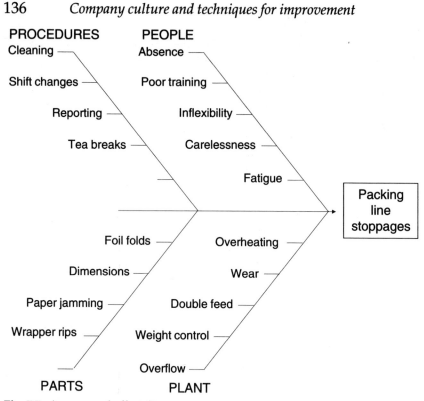

Fig. 7.7 A cause and effect diagram.

George Grant nods his agreement. I guess George is also very impressed with the man who is now driving the Lubrichem quality initiative.

'Yes indeed', I reply. 'In some companies, the Pareto chart is regarded as the most important tool for quality improvement. Shop floor people produce Pareto charts quite spontaneously. But very few of those companies have a culture that allows a process operator to suggest that the reduction of his frustration should be a management objective.'

Ron Henderson looks at his watch and suggests we move on, to the last of the seven tools, the cause and effect diagram. 'I know that Dave has to leave us at four o'clock and I am sure George has things to do at the plant', he says rather deliberately.

'As always', George Grant replies with a nod and a smile. Dave Smith appears preoccupied. 'The cause and effect diagram is also known as the fishbone diagram or the Ishikawa diagram', I explain, as I search my briefcase for a suitable example. 'Ah, here we are. This fishbone diagram was drawn by a team of operators in a chocolate factory. It summarizes the results of a brainstorm they carried out in order to identify possible causes of the stoppages in a packing line. Demand for this particular chocolate bar could not be met because of the frequent stoppages.'

'You notice that the possible causes are grouped under four headings: procedures, people, parts and plant', I continue. 'Many people prefer the four Ms: methods, men, materials and machines. Obviously, you can use any headings you wish. They do not have to have the same initial letter.'

'It's very terse,' observes George Grant. 'A few more words would have made the diagram much more meaningful. Still, it was not produced for us, was it? I suppose Willy Wonka and his mates would understand it, easily enough.'

George has a way of saying something important in a light-hearted manner. The result seems to be that Dave Smith and Ron Henderson ignore much of what he says. This is unfortunate.

'Yes, George', I confirm, 'the diagram was not produced for outsiders. But, as you imply, it is very important that everyone in the quality improvement team fully understands what each word means.'

'That's that then', says Ron Henderson, in summary. 'We have covered all nine of the seven tools, I think.'

'Only eight and a half', I reply. 'For the sake of completeness, I must show you a reverse fishbone diagram. This is a sequel to the first diagram. It shows the possible consequences of implementing a potential solution.'

'Having produced the first fishbone diagram', I explain, 'the quality improvement team then discussed possible solutions to the problem of frequent packing line stoppages. One rather radical proposal, that the technicians should work on the line as process operators, was discussed at some length. The arguments for and against were summarized in the reverse fishbone diagram (Fig. 7.8), which displays the imagined consequences of implementing the proposal.'

My clients do not greet the reverse fishbone diagram with the enthusiasm they showed for the stratified scatter diagram before lunch. It occurs to me that Ron, Dave and George have been somewhat disinterested throughout our discussion of both cause and effect diagrams and Pareto charts. The meeting seems to be drifting to a close. Perhaps I should attempt to recapture some of the earlier excitement by summarizing all nine tools.

'We like to include all nine tools in a three-day SPC course, whatever company or industry. Of course, certain tools are more likely to be put to use with certain types of process. Which tools do you see as being most useful in Lubrichem?'

'Scatter diagrams, run charts and stratification', answers George Grant, 'but we have to put them into the hands of the operators. The training implications are enormous and I can predict, right now, that success will only occur where the plant superintendents are committed.'

'We will use histograms and run charts', adds Ron Henderson, 'in our discussions of process capability with customers. There's another big training expense for all the business people. I think we will need many short, familiarization courses, but we can discuss that after you have run the first three-day course.'

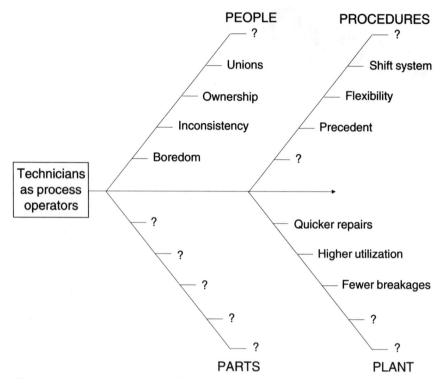

Fig. 7.8 A reverse cause and effect diagram.

Ron has risen to his feet while speaking, as if to imply that our meeting has ended. However, I am not the first person to leave. Dave Smith mutters a hurried good-bye and is out of the door with unseemly haste. George Grant, cheerful as ever, informs me that urgent problems at the plant demand his immediate attention and he follows.

'Good', says my senior client. 'Let us have some coffee. I would like to talk to you about *learning* before you go.'

7.5 A LEARNING CULTURE

I am always happy to talk about learning. What could be more interesting than discussing a process which plays a crucial role in our physical and economic survival?

For many years I have read books on educational psychology and learning theory, as a leisure time interest and as a way of turning potentially tedious train journeys into useful and stimulating experiences. This reading has not made me a professional psychologist, but it has helped me to appreciate what an important contribution psychology can make to the practice of TQM.

Fig. 7.9 Learning for survival.

⌈'In my conversations with you, Roland, and with other quality experts, I have the feeling that one major difference between good companies and bad companies, is the attitude of people towards learning. In progressive and successful companies, people at all levels are more than willing to learn. Learning is seen as a long-term investment, and managers speak of a learning culture.'⌋

Ron Henderson's words are like music in my ear. Much of my working life is spent in helping people to learn about their processes, and I have often expressed the view that learning is a prerequisite for quality improvement. 'Let me show you one of my favourite slides', I suggest. 'I use it in my introduction to SPC courses. You need to read it from the bottom upwards (Fig. 7.9).'

'Three groups of people benefit from quality improvement: customers, shareholders and employees', I explain. 'But quality improvement and/or cost reduction can only result from process improvement and this, in turn, must be the result of one or more employees learning something about the process. No learning, no improvement. I believe this slide is entirely compatible with the Deming philosophy. Have you read much of Deming?'

'I have read *Out of the Crisis*', Ron Henderson replies, 'but it left me with very mixed feelings. He offers a lot of good advice for managers, which is surprising when you consider that he does not seem to have real management experience, like other gurus. But the wisdom is mixed in with very glib remarks and sneering comments.'

'I know exactly what you mean, Ron. I have read *Out of the Crisis* time and time again. Not from cover to cover, just dipping into it and then becoming engrossed. The wisdom is in there, all right, but it is contaminated with rather silly remarks. It is like a mixture of real gold nuggets with chunks of fool's gold. At first reading, I thought, well there is no problem, I will take the gold and leave the pyrites, but when I read some parts for a second time I realized that I had made some bad decisions. Some of what I first thought of as false, now appeared to be real gold wisdom. So, I am now very reluctant to reject any of Deming's philosophy, but I refuse to worship Dr Deming as some of his disciples do.'

'Yes, I have heard that the tone of Deming's meetings is very religious', Ron adds. 'Have you read Deming's new book? Is that written in the same style?'

'Well, it is a shorter book with a different focus. *Out of the Crisis* was built around the 14 points, the six deadly diseases and the obstacles to change. Obviously, several of the 14 points are relevant to the learning culture that you seek to create. Constancy of purpose, for example, and driving out fear and instituting a programme of self-improvement. But Deming's new book, *The New Economics* has even more to say about learning and culture. Its focus is Deming's theory of profound knowledge which has four elements:

1. appreciation for a system,
2. some knowledge of theory of variation,
3. a theory of knowledge, and
4. some knowledge of psychology.'

'Those four elements seem, at first sight, to be very different from Deming's 14 points. Are the two books contradictory, in any way? Does Deming still hate managers, or has he moderated his views?'

'Well, I see no sign of moderation, Ron. He is still very critical of managers. To win Deming's full approval, a manager would need to pass all four tests for profound knowledge. He or she would need some knowledge of psychology, to understand how to harness every employee's creative potential. He or she would need an understanding of the theory of knowledge, in order to create a learning culture. He or she would need to have studied the theory of variation, in order to distinguish between special causes and common causes and to appreciate how the basic tools can be used to achieve quality improvement. Any manager who overcame these three hurdles would also need to acquire an appreciation of systems or processes, in which there are feedback loops and interactions between components, so as to understand that quality problems are rarely due to the behaviour of individual people and can only be prevented by management action to improve the system.'

'We have some good managers in Lubrichem', says Ron Henderson, with a sigh, 'but they are not that good. Deming seems to offer a vision of how the company might be, at some time in the future, probably long after I have retired.'

'Well he does not promise anyone an easy ride, that's for sure, but his vision is based on what he experienced in Japan. I am beginning to wish I had not mentioned Deming's theory of profound knowledge. Can I tell you how people learn, or how I believe people learn?'

'Please do, Roland. It cannot be so threatening as the full diet of systems, variability and psychology. Surely philosophers have been studying learning for centuries', Ron suggests.

'I am sure they have. There is certainly a vast literature on the subject. What I have read leads me to believe that people learn in only three ways:

1. We can learn by accepting what we are told or shown. Our willingness to accept will depend on the authority and/or the credibility of the source.
2. We can learn from experience. This is usually active or participative. Perhaps the most reliable experience is that which can be quantified.
3. We can learn from theory. This is less active, requiring contemplation which results in the prediction or projection into the future, or into situations not actually experienced.'

'That is very interesting, Roland. It is not quite what I expected. I must admit that I cannot immediately see the implications for our training programme or for the way we set about quality improvement. Which method of learning do you recommend?', Ron Henderson asks.

'Well, I would say that each method has its advantages, but each method can let you down badly, if used in isolation. Learning by accepting offers, perhaps, the fastest route to greater understanding and is obviously very important during childhood, when we can progress rapidly by accepting what we are told by teachers, parents and television. But, sooner or later, we suspect that these sources are not entirely reliable and we have to put our trust in other methods. Many adults, especially managers, place great value on learning by experience. But this can also be misleading if it is not tempered by theory. I believe that the best learning does not come from experience, but from thinking about experience, and thinking is grossly undervalued by managers, by workers and certainly by students.'

Ron Henderson is greatly amused. He laughs loudly as he pours a second cup of coffee. 'You have just been talking about my two daughters', he explains. 'As children they were marvellous. Even television programmes did not undermine my credibility or authority. Then in their early teens they became monsters, but very different monsters. The only thing they had in common was that they were reluctant to accept anything I or my wife said to them. Deborah, the elder girl, devoted her life to a frantic search for experience, but she did not seem to anticipate the disasters that this experience would lead to. On the other hand, Jane became morose. She seemed to be in permanent contemplation and was clearly aware of the dangers her sister could not foresee. But we digress. I'm sorry.'

'No, no, Ron. We do not digress', I suggest. 'Obviously it is easy to oversimplify the problems of growing up, but it is possible that each of your

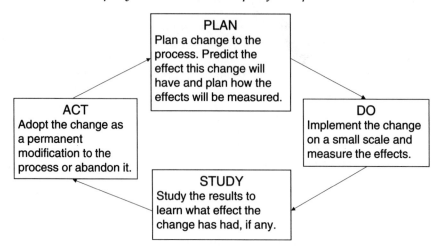

Fig. 7.10 The Deming cycle, or PDSA cycle.

daughters placed undue reliance on one mode of learning. I would recommend a balance of experience and theory. That is what we have in the Deming cycle. Let me show you a diagram (Fig. 7.10).'

'At every quality conference I have attended, someone has mentioned the Deming cycle', Ron asserts. 'Obviously it is important, but I am not sure that I can see why it is so useful.'

'Let us start at the top', I suggest. 'We wish to gain a better understanding of a process so we plan an investigation. This may involve deliberate changes to the independent variables or it may be more passive. During the planning stage we decide what should be measured and we predict the outcome. Our predictions are based on theory. No theory, no plan, no investigation. The 'do' stage should be easy if we have planned well. Unfortunately, we tend to plan rather badly, perhaps because of an obsession with action, so we end up re-planning and re-doing, whilst the Japanese pass on smoothly to the 'study' stage, in which the data is analysed. We learn about the process as we compare the actual outcome (i.e. the data) with the predicted outcome.'

'How does the "act" stage differ from the "do" stage?', asks Ron Henderson. 'They sound very similar. I am sure many people confuse the two.'

'Well they differ fundamentally. At the "do" stage we carry out the planned investigation. At the "act" stage we might not do anything at all, depending on what we have learned at the "study" stage. However, if we have learned something that will help us to improve the process we may decide to implement a permanent change at the "act" stage. This will not be a trivial step, of course, as it may involve changing procedures and training staff. Obviously many people carried out investigations in this way before Deming spoke of PDSA. In fact, Deming does not call it the Deming

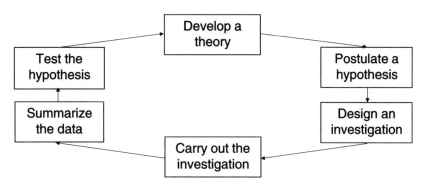

Fig. 7.11 The scientific method (hypothetico-deductive method).

cycle, he calls it the Shewhart cycle. You could argue that this cycle is simply a variation of the scientific method or hypothetico-deductive method (Fig. 7.11), which has been with us for centuries and is largely responsible for our incredible progress in science and technology.'

'I sometimes regret not having had a scientific education', Ron admits, speaking in a low voice as if sharing a secret. 'But I suspect that my thinking is just as scientific as that of many chemists and engineers.'

'I am sure that's true, Ron', I hasten to agree. 'You seem to grasp the essentials of statistical thinking more quickly than most scientists and engineers who attend my courses.'

'Well, I am hoping to sit in on the first course. I am quite looking forward to it', Ron Henderson informs me as we walk from his office to Reception. 'By the way, Dave Smith will have left by then. He is moving to our Distribution Centre.'

7.6 SUMMARY

Six months ago Ron Henderson's working life was focused on marketing, as it had been for 20 years. Now, though he still has the title of Marketing Director, he must focus on quality and he must try to make sense of the conflicting advice which assails him from all quarters. At a recent conference he was advised that statistical quality control (SQC) would not yield the improvement in quality that is experienced by users of statistical process control (SPC). Naturally, he was concerned, as the training package he had just bought appeared to offer only SQC.

We have seen in this chapter that the distinction between SQC and SPC is rather arbitrary and depends upon how you define your processes and sub-processes.

I would advise managers to focus on large processes. Of course, the word 'large' has different shades of meaning at different levels within the organization. What appears large to a junior manager will appear small to a senior manager who has a larger span of control.

Having chosen a process, it is important to define the process and, particularly, its boundaries. This is, perhaps, best achieved by drawing a flowchart of the process. Managers from a technical background need to keep in mind that it is not very useful to regard a piece of hardware as a process. All of the processes I have worked with contain people and procedures in addition to the plant. I believe that many companies fail to achieve the best return on the capital they have invested in plant and equipment, because they fail to obtain the best out of their people, who could contribute much more to the improvement of the process, of which the plant is only a part.

Quality improvement can be achieved by the use of appropriate control charts on which you plot data from appropriate points in the process. You may plot the quality of the final product or you might plot some measurement from upstream within the process. If these charts are plotted by operators and regularly reviewed by managers, they will almost certainly facilitate improvement.

Control charts were listed by Ishikawa in his 'seven basic tools for quality improvement'. I have added run charts and flow charts to the list. A familiarity with all nine tools is strongly recommended. We have seen in this and earlier chapters the usefulness of run charts, histograms and scatter diagrams in the chemical industry. Clearly these techniques can be effective with any process in any company, especially when used in conjunction with stratification. The power of check sheets, Pareto charts and Ishikawa diagrams should not be underestimated.

Ron Henderson, who has responsibility for quality at Lubrichem, can now see that staff at all levels must develop an obsession with learning about their processes. He is not alone in coming to this realization. In the last decade of the twentieth century, many companies are giving serious consideration to the development of a 'learning culture'. Deming's 14 points, listed in *Out of the Crisis* (1986), are entirely consistent with this learning movement and he offers further support by using 'a theory of knowledge' as one of the four pillars of his system of profound knowledge in *The New Economics* (1993). In this chapter I offer some thoughts on the ways that people learn and strongly recommend the Deming cycle or the scientific method, as an approach to process learning. This philosophy will feature strongly in a later chapter devoted to the use of planned experiments for process improvement.

Reducing variability

The consultant visits Middshire Water Ltd to discuss process capability and the benefits of reducing variability with the Quality Manager and an analytical chemist from the laboratory. They explore techniques that will help them cope with skewed distributions and with random variation that is coming from many sources. They also discuss inter-laboratory trials that are carried out to assess the precision of test methods or measurement processes.

8.1 INTRODUCTION

I am driving down a rather narrow and very leafy lane, through some of the most beautiful countryside in Britain. I am driving slowly and looking for a small sign that will direct me to Beach Grove. The person I am going to see, sent me a detailed map and warned me to drive carefully, lest I miss the turning, but he did not warn me that I would be distracted by the glorious rolling landscape bathed in sunshine. As I round a bend I am wondering if my host appreciates that very few quality managers are privileged to work in such beautiful surroundings.

The sign appears and I turn right. A further 200 yards and I should see my next landmark, which is a large blue sign instructing me to turn left into the Beach Grove Sewage Treatment Works. Here it is. I turn. I have arrived.

As I park my car I make use of my nostrils to monitor the environment. All is well. I can look forward to a pleasant day discussing sewage treatment with my host Tony Walters, who is the Quality Manager of Middshire Water Ltd. I have spoken to Tony recently on the telephone, when he reminded me that we had met at a conference, some years ago. I am unlikely to recognize him, though he may well spot me, especially if I make no attempt to hide the fact that I am unsure which way to go.

I follow a sign to Reception where I am greeted by a tall, smartly dressed man with grey hair and a dark beard. 'Roland Caulcutt?', he asks. 'I am Tony Walters. I drove in just ahead of you. Did you have a good journey?'

'Yes, very pleasant', I reply. 'Thank you for sending the map. It was very useful.'

It is true that I found the map useful, but I think I could have managed without it as I had already located the sewage treatment works on the Ordnance Survey map. It is very difficult to hide a sewage treatment works, or a reservoir.

'I have booked us into Meeting Room 3', explains Tony Walters. 'We should be joined later by Edward Sutherland, but he is coming from Central Laboratory and will not be here until 11:00 or 11:30. When he arrives we can discuss our analytical test methods, but before then I would like you to advise me on how we can reduce our energy consumption.'

8.2 QUALITY IMPROVEMENT AND COST REDUCTION

As we walk to Meeting Room 3 Tony Walters tells me that he has recently spoken to Richard Britain of Central Water and that Richard sends his regards. I have run several SPC courses for Central Water, training some 80 to 90 managers, engineers and scientists. Richard Britain attended the first of these courses and has since run many half-day courses for operators and technicians.

'Your courses seem to have been very successful', Tony informs me. 'Richard is certainly very proud of the progress they have made. Mind you, I was able to show him one or two initiatives here, that we are very proud of. Teamwork, for example.'

I am pleased to hear that people in different water companies are now talking to each other more openly. Though they do not compete against each other for customers, since privatization, each wishes to appear at least as good as the others. Clearly my experience with Central Water is very transferable, but I would be unwilling to act as consultant to any water company that was at war with Central.

'We are not as large as Central Water', Tony Walters informs me when we are seated in MR3, 'but we do have about 200 sewage treatment sites. Some are very small, of course, but the larger ones are very similar to the ones you have seen in Central. We discharge our final effluent to rivers and there are limits imposed, by the National Rivers Authority, on the quality of these discharges.'

'The limits are referred to as "consents" or "concessions", if I remember rightly. Presumably, you measure ammonia content, suspended solids, and biochemical oxygen demand, or BOD.' My statement is based on what I have seen elsewhere and upon my telephone conversation with Tony.

'That is right', replies Tony Walters. 'Each of the three variables should be less than the consent figure for at least 95% of the time. Have you looked at the data I sent you?'

'I have analysed part of your data', I reply. 'As you know I have now advised four water companies and each one has overwhelmed me with data. There is no data drought, even in the south east. Figure 8.1 shows a histogram of the first 60 BOD results.'

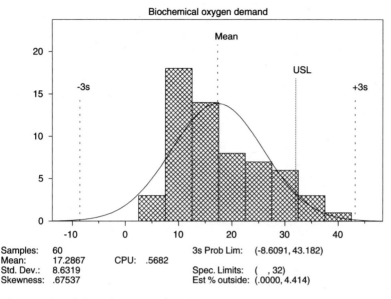

Samples: 60
Mean: 17.2867   CPU: .5682
Std. Dev.: 8.6319
Skewness: .67537

3s Prob Lim: (-8.6091, 43.182)

Spec. Limits: (, 32)
Est % outside: (.0000, 4.414)

Fig. 8.1 Capability of meeting the BOD consent.

Tony Walters studies the histogram for some time. 'Obviously this picture was produced by a computer. Which package do you use?' he asks.

'This was produced by "Quality Analyst". I do use other statistical packages, but I find QA the best for assessing process capability and stability. Of course, there are hundreds of computer packages available. How could one select the best? By the time you tried them all, there would be dozens more. Do you use an SPC package?'

'We have just started thinking about SPC', Tony Walters replies, 'though we have dabbled with TQM for three years now. We are certainly lagging behind Central Water. They are probably leading the field, you know. There is so much to do and so little time. I now have full responsibility for the quality programme and I answer directly to John Greenfield, the Operations Director. So the board are really taking quality seriously, now. To return to your question, no I have no SPC package, but I can clearly see the need for one. I had to draw a histogram by hand. My histogram was like yours. Its upper tail protruded beyond the consent value of 32 and the lower tail went down to almost zero.'

'I saw similar histograms in Central Water, three years ago', I offer in consolation. 'Their histograms are now much narrower and the upper tail is just inside the consent. Even though the National Rivers Authority permit 5% of the histogram to protrude beyond the consent, Central have opted for a more stringent internal specification, with no protrusion.'

'As you obviously appreciate, Roland, we could reduce energy costs considerably by eliminating the lower half of this histogram. The longer we process the sewage the lower we can get. Those low values of BOD are the result of over-processing.'

'Or measurement error, or both', I suggest. I am acutely aware, at this point, that it would be unethical for me to reveal to Tony Walters exactly how Central Water had managed to reduce the day-to-day variation in the biochemical oxygen demand of their discharges. However, I am entirely free to discuss the general principles of process improvement.

'That is why Edward Sutherland is joining us later to discuss the precision of our test methods. How much of the spread in the histogram is due to measurement error? How narrow would the histogram be if we had a perfect analytical method?', Tony Walters asks.

'And how could you control the process better, if you could obtain your test results more quickly?', I add, in order to widen the discussion. 'The conventional method for determining BOD takes about three days, does it not?'

'Yes, it does', Tony Walters admits. 'There is a danger that information will be obtained when it is already too late to do anything about it. A quicker test method, that could be used by the operators, would be very useful, provided it were equally precise. I believe that is what Edward will want to discuss, when he arrives. In the meantime, perhaps you could tell me about process capability indices. I believe they can be used to quantify a histogram.'

'There are many ways to describe a histogram quantitatively', I suggest. 'For example, you can calculate the mean and the standard deviation. Quality Analyst has printed these below the histogram. They have practical implications, in terms of quality and cost. If you could reduce the standard deviation, by making the process less variable, then you could save energy by increasing the mean. Notice that the computer has also printed $C_{pu} = 0.5682$. This is a process capability index. It is calculated from the consent limit, the mean and the standard deviation as follows:

$$C_{pu} = \frac{\text{consent limit} - \text{mean}}{3 \times \text{SD}}$$

$$= \frac{32 - 17.2867}{3 \times 8.6319} = 0.5682$$

The fact that the C_{pu} is less than 1.0 implies that you may be discharging effluent which is outside the consent limit.'

'So, if all of the histogram had been to the left of 32, would the C_{pu} have been greater than 1.0?', asks Tony Walters.

'Not necessarily', I reply. 'You will see that the computer has drawn a normal distribution curve, which has the same mean and standard deviation as the histogram. If the whole of the normal curve lay to the left of 32 then the C_{pu} would be greater than 1.0.'

'I am amazed to hear you say that, Roland', Tony Walters asserts with obvious surprise. 'The tails of a normal curve go on for ever, do they not?'

'Strictly speaking you are right, Tony', I reply. 'The tails are infinitely long, but we often pretend that they stop at plus or minus three standard deviations. Note the two vertical lines, labelled $+3s$ and $-3s$ (Figure 8.1). Let me revise my earlier statement. If the $+3s$ line is to the left of the USL line, then the C_{pu} will be greater than 1.0.'

'So, the capability index is based on the normal curve and not on the histogram. If the normal curve and the histogram had very different shapes, then, the capability index could be misleading. Couldn't it?', Tony asks.

'Yes, indeed', I agree, most emphatically. 'That is why it is dangerous to interpret a capability index without examining a histogram. You will notice that this histogram is not symmetrical. One tail is longer than the other. We describe a histogram as **skewed** if it is not symmetrical. The computer prints out a skewness coefficient below the histogram. It is equal to 0.67537 which is significantly different from zero. You would have a skewness of zero with a symmetrical histogram.'

'So, what do we do?' asks Tony Walters. 'Should we use a different formula to calculate the capability index, when the histogram is skewed?'

'One of the good features of "Quality Analyst" is that you can ask it to abandon the normal curve and fit a skewed distribution curve. Then it will automatically change the way it calculates the capability index. However, it would be unwise to pursue that course of action immediately, until we have checked the stability of the process. The first rule of statistics tells us **never** to calculate a capability index without drawing a histogram. The second rule tells us **never** to interpret a histogram without looking at a run chart.'

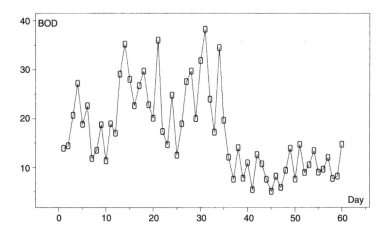

Fig. 8.2 A run chart of the 60 BOD results.

Table 8.1 Summary of BOD results during three stable periods

Days	Mean	SD
1–12	17.40	4.720
13–35	25.26	7.147
36–60	9.90	2.901

'This is a run chart of the 60 BOD results', I announce, placing the chart on the table (Fig. 8.2). 'Clearly the process was not stable during this two-month period. In my opinion there were two distinct changes. So I have split the data into three groups (Table 8.1) and calculated the mean and standard deviations of each.'

'This run chart is fascinating', Tony Walters exclaims. 'What was that rule, "Never use a histogram without first checking the run chart"? How very wise. I can see in the run chart that there is enormous potential for energy savings. From day 36 to day 60 the variability is much reduced. If we could retain that consistency while increasing the mean we could reduce electricity consumption considerably.'

I am delighted that Tony Walters can see the potential of using simple statistical techniques supported by histograms and run charts. I recall a similar awakening at Central Water, when I first advised them. Later, I realized that many managers in the water companies come from a civil engineering background, and are, therefore, more experienced in project control than process management. They were certainly not avid plotters of run charts.

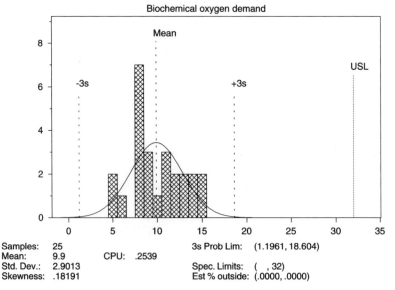

Biochemical oxygen demand

Samples: 25
Mean: 9.9
Std. Dev.: 2.9013
Skewness: .18191

CPU: .2539

3s Prob Lim: (1.1961, 18.604)
Spec. Limits: (, 32)
Est % outside: (.0000, .0000)

Fig. 8.3 Process performance, samples 36 to 60.

'I have produced a histogram (Fig. 8.3) for days 36 to 60', I announce, selecting another sheet from the small pile of diagrams in my file.

Tony studies the histogram for some time and appears to be thinking aloud as he reads the print-out below the histogram. 'The mean BOD for these 25 days was only 9.9 and the standard deviation was only 2.9. The C_{pu} has shot up to 2.539. That is very good, I suppose, but it must have cost us dearly. The electricity consumption needed to bring the mean BOD down to 9.9 does not bear thinking about.'

'That is right, Tony', I concur. 'You could plan to operate at a much higher mean, if you could be confident that the standard deviation would be so small. That C_{pu} of 2.539 is good news for the National Rivers Authority, who are receiving the discharge, but it is bad news for your shareholders. You could increase the mean to about 27 and the whole of the histogram would still be within the consent limit of 32. A C_{pu} of 1.0 would be more than adequate, provided your histogram had a normal shape.'

'Would you say the histogram looks normal?' Tony Walters asks. 'I was just thinking that this histogram (Fig. 8.3) was not very good. It would be more helpful if it had the same scale as the first histogram (Fig. 8.1). The two would be more comparable.'

With a smile I select another diagram from my file. 'Does this meet your requirements?', I ask, laying before him a third histogram (Fig. 8.4). 'A computer program will not always give you exactly what you would like. But a good program will allow you to make changes. With "Quality Analyst" you can use a "change option" to specify the group width and the scales that you require.'

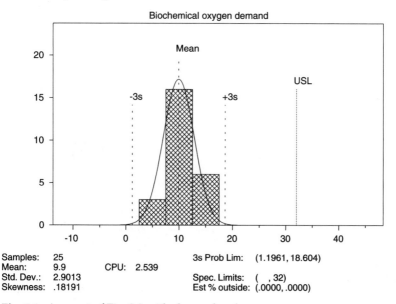

Samples:	25		3s Prob Lim:	(1.1961, 18.604)
Mean:	9.9	CPU: 2.539		
Std. Dev.:	2.9013		Spec. Limits:	(, 32)
Skewness:	.18191		Est % outside:	(.0000, .0000)

Fig. 8.4 A repeat of Fig. 8.3 with changed scales.

Tony Walters aligns the two histograms (Figs 8.1 and 8.4) before him on the table, to facilitate the comparison. 'It seems to me that the skewness in the first histogram is simply misleading. Perhaps we are witnessing a normal distribution which has shifted once or twice, with the result that we have an overall impression of skewness.'

'I must agree, Tony. The histogram can be misleading when the process is unstable. The run chart reveals that the level has changed twice and the standard deviation also appears to have changed. (The changes are summarized in Table 8.1). It is quite possible that BOD results from a period of stable operation would have a normal distribution. It is also possible that the process could be managed so that the mean BOD was, say, 25 and at least 95% of the results were less than 32', I suggest. 'Of course, to achieve this you would need to know **why** the changes in this data occurred and **how** you could prevent such changes in the future.'

'It seems to me that we could make considerable cost savings if our managers had a feel for this process capability analysis', Tony Walters says pensively. 'Did you look at the ammonia and the suspended solids?'

'Yes, I have produced a few pictures of the ammonia results. Now here you really do have a skewed distribution. You will need to take extra care when assessing your ability to meet the ammonia consent figure.'

8.3 SKEWED VARIABILITY

'Which do you want first, Tony?', I ask. 'Do you want a histogram of the 60 ammonia results or do you want to see the run chart?'

'I think I would like to see the run chart', Tony Walters replies, with only the slightest hesitation. 'I feel that the run chart will tell me more than the histogram.'

'A wise choice', I suggest. 'If the process was not stable during these 60 days, the sooner we know about this the better. Furthermore, you may be able to guess what the histogram would look like as you inspect the run chart, but you cannot get a feel for the run chart from the histogram. Can you see the skewness in the run chart?'

My host pulls the run chart (Fig. 8.5) towards him and studies it most carefully. 'Well, I can see that the process was unstable. I would suggest that the mean level of ammonia changed twice – at day 31 and day 55. As for the skewness, well I can see that there are several very low results. Is that what you mean?'

'Yes, there are some values well below average, but there are none which are well above average. If we drew a histogram you would find that these very low values gave it a long tail to the left. You recall that we had one long tail in the BOD histogram, but that was the result of process instability. With the ammonia results, we would get a skewed histogram even during a stable period. This is a histogram covering the first 30 days, during which the mean was steady.'

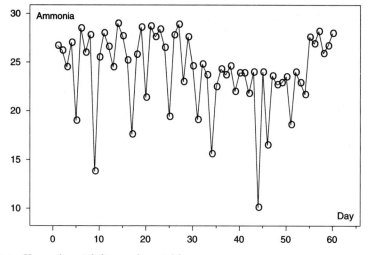

Fig. 8.5 Skewed variability and unstable process.

Tony Walters studies the histogram (Fig. 8.6). He is obviously thinking aloud again as he reads the print out below the picture. 'The mean is 25.40 and the standard deviation is 3.726. Why is the skewness coefficient negative?' He asks.

'That is because the left tail is the longer', I explain. 'In the first histogram (Fig. 8.1) the right tail was the longer and the skewness coefficient was positive. What do you think of the process capability index?'

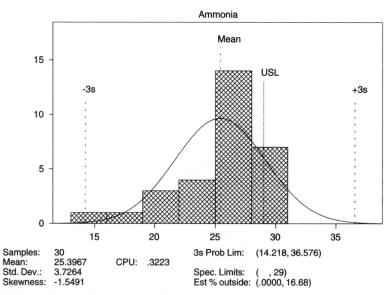

Samples:	30			3s Prob Lim:	(14.218, 36.576)
Mean:	25.3967	CPU:	.3223		
Std. Dev.:	3.7264			Spec. Limits:	(, 29)
Skewness:	-1.5491			Est % outside:	(.0000, 16.68)

Fig. 8.6 Skewed histogram and normal curve.

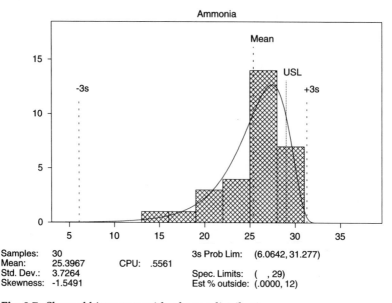

Fig. 8.7 Skewed histogram with a better distribution curve.

'Good heavens, the C_{pu} is 0.32', he exclaims. 'But the histogram does not protrude far beyond the consent limit of 29, does it?'

'Quite right, Tony. In the print out, it is predicted that 16.68% of the ammonia results will be above the consent limit. However, if you draw a line at 29 on the run chart (Fig. 8.5) you will see that none of the 30 results are above the line, and only one is on the line. Of course, the computer program bases its prediction on the normal curve, not on the histogram.'

'And the normal curve does not fit the histogram very well, so the prediction is misleading and the capability index is misleading', suggests Tony Walters. 'Did you ask the computer program to fit an alternative curve, which would better match the shape of the histogram?'

'Try this one', I suggest, handing my client the only remaining histogram in my folder (Fig. 8.7). 'I think we could reasonably claim that this distribution curve fits the histogram much better. Note that the predicted percentage has reduced to 12.0% and the capability index has increased to 0.56.'

'Well that is an improvement on the C_{pu} of 0.32, which was based on the normal curve. Though I am surprised that we can get an index as low as 0.56, when all the data is within the specification. How is it calculated? I suppose the formula must be different.'

'Yes the C_{pu} of 0.56 has come from a different formula. If we used the same formula that we used earlier we would arrive at the same index, because the mean, the standard deviation and the consent limit have not changed. After fitting the skewed distribution curve, Quality Analyst calculates the process capability index as follows:

$$C_{pu} = \frac{\text{USL} - \text{median}}{+3s \text{ value} - \text{median}}$$

$$= \frac{29.0 - 26.14}{31.28 - 26.14}$$

$$= 0.556$$

'Note that the revised formula for calculating the C_{pu} makes use of the median rather than the mean, and it uses the $+3s$ value given in the print-out. Perhaps I should explain these two modifications', I continue.

'Well, I have heard of the median', Tony Walters exclaims. 'Isn't it the figure that half of the ammonia results were less than?'

'Yes it is', I confirm. 'If we put the first 30 ammonia results in ascending order, we would find that the fifteenth was equal to 26.5 and the sixteenth was 26.6, so the median of the 30 results is between these two. Let us say the median is 26.55.'

'But you just used 26.14 in the calculation', interjects Tony Walters. 'Was that a rounding error?'

'No. There are two medians', I reply. 'The median of the data is 26.55, but the median of the distribution curve (Fig. 8.7) is 26.14. While the data and the curve have the same mean, they do not have the same median. Though, the difference between the two medians is quite small, isn't it? The important point is that it is wise to use the median rather than the mean when we have a skewed distribution. And skewed distributions are quite common, you know. Take salaries, for example. I feel sure that annual salaries in Middshire Water have a skewed distribution, with about 70% of employees earning below average. Of course, exactly 50% of employees earn less than the median salary.'

'Yes, I've noticed that the Royal Society of Chemistry always quote the median salary in their annual review of members' salaries', Tony offers in confirmation. 'So, it is better to use the median rather than the mean when we are calculating a capability index from skewed data. How about this $+3s$ value that you used?'

'Yes, let's compare the two pictures', I suggest, positioning the two diagrams (Figs 8.6 and 8.7) for ease of comparison. 'Unfortunately the two diagrams do not have identical scales on the x-axis. Nonetheless, we can clearly see that the two distributions have the same mean, but the $+3s$ values obviously differ and the $-3s$ values also differ. With the normal distribution diagram (Fig. 8.6) the $+3s$ line and the $-3s$ line are equidistant from the mean. In fact 's' is a symbol for standard deviation and the lines are placed three standard deviations above and below the mean. But I am sure you would agree that the $+3s$ line and the $-3s$ line (Fig. 8.6) do **not** constitute reasonable limits for the natural variation of the process.'

'No, they do not', my host agrees. 'Some of the data is very close to the

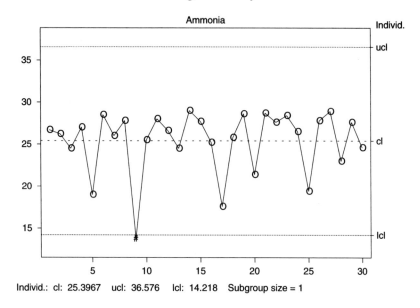

Fig. 8.8 An individuals chart based on the normal distribution.

$-3s$ line but none is close to the $+3s$ line. The two lines in the other diagram (Fig. 8.7) seem much more reasonable.'

'That's right, Tony. It just isn't reasonable to have lines which are equidistant from the mean when we have a skewed distribution. So the $+3s$ line and the $-3s$ line in the second diagram (Fig. 8.7) are placed so as to give the same size tails that you would see with lines drawn at three standard deviations from the mean on a normal distribution curve. You do not need to know how the computer program achieves this, but the two values in the print-out, 6.06 and 31.28, are very useful if you want to plot an individuals chart.'

From my file I extract two more diagrams (Figs 8.8 and 8.9) and lay them on the table. 'Which of these control charts do you think is most useful?', I ask.

'Well, the first one is rather silly', he observes, pointing at Fig. 8.8. 'Even though the process is stable, we find one point below the lower control line, but there are no points anywhere near the upper control line.'

I am not sure how much experience Tony has had with control charts. Clearly he is not overawed by the two charts I have put before him, so I feel it is safe to elaborate a little. 'The centre line (Fig. 8.8) is drawn at the mean, 25.4. With such a skewed distribution this results in far more points above the line than below. Now, in the other chart (Fig. 8.9), the centre line is drawn at the median, 26.55, so that we have 15 points below the line and 15 above. Note also that the control limits in the second chart (Fig. 8.9) are not equidistant from the centre line. They are drawn at the $+3s$ value and the $-3s$ value taken from the skewed distribution curve (Fig. 8.7). I would suggest

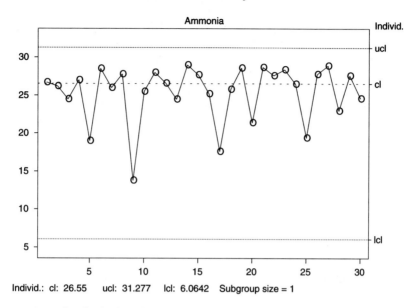

Fig. 8.9 An individuals chart based on the skewed distribution in Fig. 8.7.

that the second control chart (Fig. 8.9) will give more reliable indications of change than the first chart. It the ammonia level increased the second chart would detect the change more quickly. Furthermore, the second chart (Fig. 8.9) would give far fewer false alarms at the lower control limit.'

I am anxious not to be drawn into a full-scale discussion of the false indications that can be *given* by control charts. So I am quite relieved when there is a knock at the door and a young man with rather untidy hair enters the room. 'Aha, Edward', exclaims Tony Walters, 'do come in. This is Roland Caulcutt. He has just taught me far more about statistics than all those frightful books you lent me. It is just common sense, really.'

Edward Sutherland and I exchange greetings. He is certainly not so smartly dressed as Tony Walters. Indeed, one could be forgiven for assuming that the new arrival had ridden through the woodland on horseback in his journey from Central Laboratory. Perhaps Edward has little contact with customers, suppliers or senior managers.

We are about to take our seats around the table when another knock at the door heralds the arrival of coffee. I am not surprised to find that this is served in fine china cups and saucers. I have encountered, in other water companies, similar evidence of elegant living, carried over from a time when there was less commercial pressure. As we sip the excellent coffee Tony Walters explains that Edward has brought some data from various experiments that were carried out in order to assess the variability of the test methods. They hope that I can offer guidance on the interpretation of such data.

8.4 MEASUREMENT ERROR

Tony Walters opens the discussion by reminding me of something I said to him on the telephone. 'You expressed the view, which I have certainly heard elsewhere, that the increasing use of control charts is focusing more and more attention on measurement error.'

'That is right', I reply. 'One of your long-term objectives is the reduction of variability. Clearly this variability, or lack of consistency, increases your costs. But the variation has many causes, so which ones will you work on? You could incur considerable expense trying to eliminate one of the causes, only to find that you achieved very little reduction in variation at the output of the process. To be more specific, can I ask how much of the day-to-day variation in BOD is due to measurement error?'

Tony Walters clearly does not feel competent to answer my question. He turns to Edward Sutherland. It is equally clear that Edward does not have a ready answer. 'Well', he says, speaking very slowly, 'it is obvious that the test method is not perfect, but I could not say how much additional variation it introduces. I would have thought that the treatment plant was much more variable than the test method.'

'Can I show you my process model?', I ask, reaching for my briefcase and extracting an acetate slide (Fig. 1.3). 'We can regard sewage treatment as a process, with the product being the effluent which is discharged to the river. The variability in the BOD of the effluent is due to variation in the inputs which include the raw sewage, the settlement tanks, the operators, the procedures, etc. Measurement error introduces additional variation so that the daily determinations of BOD are more variable than the "true values" that we would obtain if we had a perfect test method. Of the total variation in the determinations a percentage will be due to the test method, but it may be a very small percentage. It would be foolish to make a substantial capital investment in a better method, if you had no idea how much variability was caused by the analytical method.'

'Well it could not be a complete waste of money, could it?', asks Edward Sutherland. 'Surely it would be better to buy new analytical equipment than to spend yet more money on training the operators or building yet another settlement tank?'

'You may be right Edward', I admit with some reluctance, 'but can you provide any evidence that would help the process manager to decide where best to invest?'

'No he cannot', Tony Walters asserts with a surprising bluntness. 'Everyone in Middshire Water maintains that it would be profitable to invest in his or her area, but no one produces any evidence. The simple truth is, Roland, we do not have a process manager who could weigh up the evidence if it were presented. Your process model has brought that fact home to me. Heaven knows how the annual budget for the Central Laboratory is arrived at, but I am sure that variability is not taken into account.'

Table 8.2 The results of five experiments

1*	28.3	27.7	28.0	28.0	27.0	27.8	28.5	28.2	28.2	27.7
	28.1	28.5	28.1	28.0	27.8	28.3	28.0	28.5	28.2	27.8
2†	A	B	C	D	E	F	G	H	I	J
	28.2	27.7	28.6	28.1	28.2	29.4	28.3	28.9	27.0	27.4
	28.4	27.7	28.8	28.0	28.5	29.4	28.8	28.2	27.1	27.8
3‡	27.0	26.0	26.2	27.5	26.8	28.5	28.8	26.5	25.2	27.0
	26.0	28.0	27.2	29.5	27.7	25.0	27.0	25.8	28.5	28.0
4§	29.0	28.6	29.5	29.5	28.7	28.1	30.0	29.2	29.0	28.6
	28.3	29.0	30.5	29.2	29.7	28.6	29.5	28.5	29.6	29.5
5**	N	26.5	28.5	25.7	28.3	27.2	26.3	27.0	26.5	
	Q	26.4	28.0	25.2	27.5	27.5	25.2	26.4	25.6	

*A sample of discharge was split into 20 subsamples. The subsamples were sent to the laboratory in the guise of normal samples, over a period of two days.
†A sample of discharge was split into 20 subsamples. Two subsamples were sent to each of ten laboratories (A–J).
‡A sample of discharge was taken each day for 20 days. All samples were sent to the same laboratory.
§Twenty samples of discharge were taken in quick succession. All samples were sent to the same laboratory.
**A sample of discharge was taken each day for eight days. Each sample was split into two subsamples, one being sent for analysis by the normal method (N) and the other being analysed immediately by a new quick method (Q).

'Well, gentlemen, I am afraid you could make similar statements about most, if not all, of the companies I visit.'

'Let us concentrate on the main item on the agenda', Tony Walters suggests. 'I believe you do have **some** evidence, Edward. Perhaps it will cast some light on the precision of our test methods.'

'Yes, I have gathered together the data from five experiments. These were carried out by different people at different times and, no doubt, for different purposes. Perhaps it would be dangerous to compare the results of one experiment with those of another, but it would be useful if you could explain, in simple terms, what conclusions might be drawn from experiments of this type.' As Edward Sutherland completes his well-rehearsed request, he hands me an A4 sheet on which the results of the experiments are summarized (Table 8.2).

I read the sheet with considerable interest. Here is something I can really get my teeth into. After a second reading of the sheet I am convinced that our discussion of this material could continue for the rest of the day. 'It is such a pity you did not send me this data so that I could analyse it in advance and produce some helpful diagrams', I suggest. 'These experiments throw up so many interesting points, but our progress will be retarded by my having to perform calculations and draw pictures.'

'Well, let us make a start and see how far we can go', suggests Tony Walters, who has also been studying the sheet intently. 'What I have learned from the first experiment is that you need to be deceitful if you wish to assess the error in a test method. Is it really necessary to disguise the samples sent to the laboratory?'

'I have witnessed many heated discussions between laboratory staff and production people in several chemical companies, concerning the need for openness in such matters. In an ideal world deceit would be unnecessary. However, we can consider a test method to be a process', I suggest, pointing to the process model (Fig. 7.1) which is still on the table. 'Clearly there will be at least two people involved whenever you take a sample and produce a determination of its biochemical oxygen demand (BOD). It is reasonable to suggest that the error in a determination is likely to be less if these people are taking special care. Do we want to assess the precision of the method when special care is being taken, or the precision of the method when people are behaving normally?'

'Can people not take special care with every sample?', asks Tony Walters.

'No they cannot', I reply most emphatically. 'One wily old production manager put it to me like this. "Suppose I send to the lab a bottle with a label saying – My viscosity is 80.0 centistokes. Please measure me. – Should I be surprised if the result sheet reads – Viscosity = 80.0 cSt?" What do you think, Edward?'

'Well, our laboratory people are really dedicated to their work and they are trained to follow good practices. I would like to say that they achieve peak performance with every sample, but I guess that cannot be the case. One thing I am sure of, they deeply resent anything which casts doubt on their integrity.'

'So the laboratory people in Experiment 1 did not realize that 20 identical samples were passing through', interjects Tony Walters, 'but what do the results tell us about the measurement error?'

'Let us calculate the mean and the standard deviation of the 20 results', I suggest, extracting a pocket calculator from my briefcase and typing in the numbers. 'There we are. The mean is 28.04 and the standard deviation is 0.3514. We can now use . . .'

'What formula did you use?', asks Edward Sutherland, before I can explain how we might make use of the standard deviation. 'Books on SPC seem to use $\bar{R}/d_n$, whereas other statistics books use a quadratic formula.'

'You are right, Edward', I confirm. 'Many books on SPC do recommend that you put data into subgroups, calculate the range for each subgroup, then calculate the mean range and divide this by Hartley's constant to obtain the standard deviation (Procedure B in Appendix A). I fully support the use of this formula, with certain reservations; see Chapter 4. However, with this data there is no obvious subgrouping. We do not even know the order in which the samples were analysed, so I simply typed the 20 results into my calculator and the automatic standard deviation routine gave me 0.3154. The calculator uses the quadratic formula (Procedure C in Appendix A) which you have seen in many statistics books.'

'But would the two formulae not give different standard deviations with the same data?', asks Edward with some concern in his voice.

'Yes, they would, almost certainly', I reply. 'Let us put the 20 results into 5 groups of 4. The ranges of the groups are 0.6, 1.5, 0.8, 0.5 and 0.7, giving a mean range of 0.82. Hartley's constant, for a group size of 4, is 2.059 (see Table A in Appendix B) which gives a standard deviation equal to 0.398. This is, of course, not equal to the 0.3154 from the calculator. With very few sets of data would the two formulae give the same result.'

'But which is right?', Edward Sutherland demands to know.

'Unfortunately, neither is right', I reply. 'If you intend to make use of statistical techniques you had better become used to being wrong. From the data we have calculated a standard deviation. This is an estimate of what we would have found if we had had much more data – unlimited data, in fact. Obviously an estimate is very likely to differ from the "true value" that we are trying to estimate. So it is very likely that two estimates will differ from each other.'

I pause to see if my clients are offended by the statistical perspective that I have adopted. Clearly Tony Walters is not disturbed, but Edward Sutherland appears to be rather tense.

'While we are discussing whether 0.398 or 0.3155 is the best estimate, we are failing to carry out a visual inspection of the data', I continue. 'This visual inspection might reveal that **both** estimates are likely to be badly in error.'

'You suggested earlier', Tony Walters interjects, 'that one should never calculate a capability index without drawing a histogram. At this point I would like to see a histogram of the data from Experiment 1.'

'Excellent, Tony. Excellent. Let us plot a histogram or, better still a dot plot, as we are doing it by hand. What are the highest and lowest values?', I ask.

'28.5 is the highest and 27.0 is the lowest', Edward Sutherland suggests.

I draw a line on a sheet of graph paper and mark off a scale from 27.0 to 28.5 in steps of 0.1.

'Would you like to read out the data?', I ask. Soon we have a rather crude, but very useful dot plot (Fig. 8.10).

'I see what you mean', exclaims Tony Walters, as I turn the graph paper so that my clients can better see the dot plot. 'One of the BOD results is obviously wrong. Should we discard it, then recalculate the mean and standard deviation from the remaining 19 results?'

Fig. 8.10 A dot plot of the data from Experiment 1.

'We cannot just discard any result that fails to support our assumptions or our prejudices', Edward asserts with obvious emotion. He and Tony turn to me, expecting a resolution of their disagreement.

'If we assume that the 19 clustered results represent the normal operation of the test method, then it is easy to believe that the outlier must have resulted from some abnormality. So I would like to recalculate the standard deviation without it. However, the outlier may be a very important result, in that it offers us a learning opportunity. We should try to discover why it differs so much from the normal results.'

'Perhaps we have reached an eating opportunity', Tony Walters suggests. 'There is a buffet set out in the next room. It might be a good idea to snatch what we want before the people in MR1 take their break. We can eat in here.'

8.5 REPEATABILITY AND REPRODUCIBILITY

Within 30 minutes we have dined and cleared away the remains. There has been little opportunity for idle chatter. 'You recall, gentlemen, that we had agreed to set aside the one result that falls outside the distribution within which the other 19 results appear to lie.'

While speaking I have re-entered the 27.0 into the calculator and used the INV key to remove it from the data set. 'The standard deviation reduces to 0.2601 if we remove the outlier', I announce. 'Let us call this 0.2601 the repeatability standard deviation. The 19 results were made on 19 identical samples with the test method being used under repeatability conditions. The word repeatability is defined in British Standard 5532, and should not be used carelessly. Repeatability implies that the determinations were made by the same person, using the same instrument, during a short period of time.'

'But it was not such a short period. The analyses were spread over two days', Tony Walters reminds us. 'I have been thinking about that time period and about the second rule of statistics. Should we not plot a run chart of the 19 results?'

Tony speaks these words with obvious satisfaction. Perhaps he realizes that his colleague is unlikely to be aware of rule two. Edward certainly looks puzzled. I attempt to explain: 'Earlier I expressed the view, that one should never make use of a histogram without also examining a run chart. To give this view a higher status I called it "rule two of statistics". Yes, it would be wise to plot a run chart if we knew the order in which the determinations were made. Unfortunately we are not sure of the order. Obviously, the standard deviation of the results would be inflated if there were a drift or a day-to-day change. But we cannot resolve all these uncertainties, without more information. Remember our objective is simply to illustrate how the results of such experiments might be used. Some time before lunch I was about to explain how we could use the standard deviation from Experiment 1 to estimate the repeatability of the test method. Shall I continue?'

'Please do, Roland', answers Tony Walters. 'Obviously our questions have disrupted your flow, but I think they do help us to derive the maximum benefit from your advice.'

'To calculate the repeatability estimate we simply multiply the repeatability standard deviation by 2.83. That is an easy formula to remember:

$$\text{Repeatability} = 2.83 \times (\text{repeatability SD})$$
$$= 2.83 \times 0.2601$$
$$= 0.74$$

Let me explain what exactly that means', I continue. 'The repeatability of 0.74 implies that two BOD determinations made on identical samples are unlikely to differ by more than 0.74, if the determinations are made by the same operator in the same laboratory during a short period of time. If we look again at the dot plot (Fig. 8.10) I think you will find very few pairs of results that differ by more than 0.74.'

Tony and Edward both snatch at the graph paper with unseemly aggression. Each is holding one corner as they pore over it. 'The largest value, 28.5, differs from the two lowest by 0.8', Edward suggests.

'The outlier differs by more than 0.74 from most of the other results. I suppose that proves that it does not belong with the others', adds Tony Walters.

'Yes and yes', I reply. 'So the concept of repeatability is relatively simple but not so useful as the associated concept, reproducibility. This applies when we wish to compare results from identical samples analysed in two different laboratories. For example, it would be useful to know the reproducibility of the test method if there were a dispute between yourselves and the National Rivers Authority concerning the level of BOD in a discharge. If the difference between your result and their result were less than the reproducibility then the difference could be attributed to testing error.'

'From time to time our laboratory participates in inter-laboratory trials. Usually the report of the trial quotes an estimate of the reproducibility of the test method. Could we calculate the reproducibility from the results of Experiment 2?', asks Edward Sutherland.

'Yes indeed', I reply. 'Experiment 2 is clearly an inter-laboratory trial. From the results we can calculate both the repeatability and the reproducibility. Let us do the repeatability first.'

'How would you calculate the repeatability standard deviation?', Edward Sutherland asks. 'Surely, we cannot just put the 20 results into a calculator? They have not come from the same laboratory.'

'You are so right', I confirm. 'We must consider each laboratory separately. We can calculate either the range or the standard deviation. The range will be quicker. The ten ranges are 0.2, 0.0, 0.2, 0.1, 0.3, 0.0, 0.5, 0.7, 0.1 and 0.4. Thus the mean range is 0.25. If we divide this by 1.128, that is Hartley's constant for a group size of 2 (see Table B.1 in Appendix B), this gives 0.2216 which is the repeatability standard deviation. Multiplying this by 2.83 gives the repeatability estimate of 0.63.'

'That is appreciably smaller than the estimate you calculated from the results of Experiment 1', Tony Walters exclaims. 'I suppose there is no point in my asking which is correct?'

'From Experiment 1 we obtained 0.74 and from Experiment 2 we obtained 0.63', I summarize. 'I would not say the two estimates were remarkably different. Perhaps the second estimate is the better of the two. It is based on a small number of results from each of 10 laboratories, whereas the first estimate is based on many results from only one laboratory. The one laboratory might not be typical, of course.'

'You implied that we could have used standard deviations rather than ranges. How would that work?' asks Edward Sutherland.

'We could calculate a standard deviation for each laboratory, then combine the 10 standard deviations using a well-known formula (Procedure C in Appendix A). Unfortunately we do not have time to do that now. However, the repeatability standard deviation by this alternative method would be very similar, I am sure. Shall we turn to reproducibility?', I ask, and after nods of approval from my clients, I continue. 'Well, the calculation is rather long winded. We first calculate a mean for each laboratory, then we obtain the standard deviation of the 10 means. From this we can calculate what is known as the between-laboratories standard deviation, which is then combined with the repeatability standard deviation to obtain the reproducibility standard deviation. Multiplying this by 2.83 gives the reproducibility estimate. The details of the calculation are set out in this sheet (see procedure C in Appendix A). Unfortunately, we do not have time for all that so I will make an intelligent guess that the reproducibility is somewhere between 1.5 and 2.0.' (Use of procedure C gives 1.92.)

'I suppose the reproducibility of a test method is always larger than the repeatability?', Edward asks.

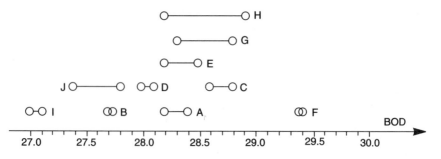

Fig. 8.11 A stratified dot plot of the data from Experiment 2.

'Oh yes, it is quite common for the reproducibility to be two or three times as large as the repeatability. So the difference between two determinations made in different laboratories could well be two or three times the difference you would find in the same laboratory.'

Tony Walters has said little during this discussion, but he now returns with a most important contribution. 'I think we have just violated rule 3 of statistics', he asserts. 'Never calculate a reproducibility estimate without drawing a suitable diagram.'

Edward Sutherland is clearly taken aback. I am delighted, as my smile must indicate. 'Excellent, Tony. What type of diagram would be appropriate?', I ask.

'I would suggest a dot plot, but with some means of distinguishing between the laboratories', Tony replies.

'What you are recommending is known as a stratified dot plot. We will draw one, without delay. What are the highest and lowest results from Experiment 2?'

Soon we have identified the highest and lowest results then I draw a rough dot plot as Tony Walters reads out the results. Edward Sutherland remains silent. Perhaps he is wondering how many more rules of statistics will emerge.

'That is a very powerful diagram', Tony says, after he and Edward have pored over it for some time. 'You can see the closeness of results from the same laboratory and you can see how much some laboratories differ from others. Actually, I am surprised that you think the reproducibility is only 2.0. The difference between a result from laboratory I and a result from laboratory F must be about 2.5.'

Before I can reply, Edward Sutherland quickly corrects his colleague's misunderstanding. 'You would not expect all the differences to be less than the reproducibility figure. Only 95% of them', he asserts, quite correctly. 'I think Roland's guess of 1.5 to 2.0 is OK. After seeing this dot plot I would estimate the reproducibility to be about 1.8 or 1.9.'

Tony Walters looks at his watch. Edward and I look at our watches. 'Good heavens', Tony exclaims 'It is nearly 16:00. Can you deal with Experiments 3, 4 and 5 today Roland?'

'I must go, I am afraid', Edward informs us. 'I was looking forward to what you might say about Experiment 5, Roland. Perhaps you will keep me informed, Tony.'

Edward Sutherland bids me farewell and departs hurriedly. Tony explains that his colleague has to be back to Central Laboratory by 17:00, and that the motorway road works are proving troublesome.'

'I expect that you would learn more from our discussing Experiments 3 and 4', I suggest. 'Perhaps I could write a few notes about Experiment 5 and post them to Edward.'

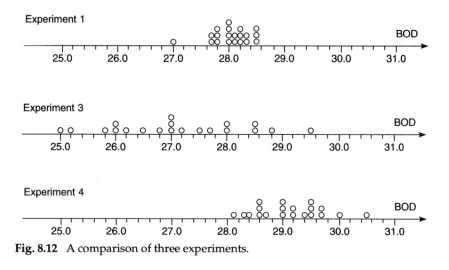

Fig. 8.12 A comparison of three experiments.

8.6 VARIABILITY DUE TO MANY CAUSES

'Let us set aside Experiment 2, the inter-laboratory trial, and compare the results from Experiments 1, 3 and 4', I suggest. 'What comments would you like to make about the variation in the three sets of data?' (see Table 8.2).

'Well I have learned today that it is better not to comment on any data until you have seen it in a pictorial form. So I would like to reserve judgement until I have seen a stratified dot plot.'

Tony Walters has an appetite for data plots which is very endearing. If all my consultancy clients and all the people who attend my courses, had this same passion for pictorial presentation there would be better communications within their companies. Unfortunately, there are many companies in which promotion is gained by impressing one's superiors rather than communicating clearly. In such a company data diagrams could be damaging.

With Tony Walters reading out the data it takes only a few minutes to plot the results of the three experiments. I explain to Tony that I am using the same scale for all three plots to facilitate comparisons. When he has studied the dot plot carefully (Fig. 8.12) and re-read the descriptions of the experiments (Table 8.2), he is ready to answer my question.

'In the first experiment the variability is due to the test method alone. In Experiment 4, the variation is due to the test method **and** real variation in the discharge. In Experiment 3 . . .', Tony pauses and returns to the data sheet (Table 8.2). 'Well, it is the same as Experiment 4, but the samples were taken over a longer period. Twenty days, compared with twenty minutes, say.'

'That is a very useful summary', I acknowledge. 'Experiment 3 exhibits long-term variability whereas Experiment 4 exhibits only short-term variability. It is true of many processes that two samples taken in quick succession are likely to be quite similar, but two samples taken several days apart are likely to differ much more.'

Clearly Tony Walters is not at all surprised by what I have said, so I continue: 'From the results of the three experiments we can obtain several standard deviations which will help us quantify the variation due to each of the sources or causes. Let us start by calculating the standard deviation of the 20 results from Experiment 4.'

Tony Walters reads the results while I key them into my pocket calculator. The mean BOD for Experiment 4 is 29.13 and the standard deviation is 0.6053.

'Now then, Tony, let me ask you a searching question. Why is the standard deviation for Experiment 4 (0.6053) much greater than the standard deviation for Experiment 1 (0.2601), or the repeatability standard deviation from Experiment 2 (0.2216)?'

Tony is in no hurry to reply. He studies the two dot plots (Figs 8.11 and 8.12) then he re-reads the sheet (Table 8.2). 'Well, the standard deviations are simply measuring the variability that we see in the dot plots. So the question is "Why do the widths of the dot plots differ so greatly?" Before answering that I would like to see run charts of the data. But we cannot plot run charts because we do not know the order in which the samples were taken or the order in which they were tested.'

'Suppose we did know the order and we had plotted the run charts and we found that the variation appeared to be random. No step changes, no gradual changes, no spikes, no cyclical variation, just random variation from sample to sample.'

'Then I would have to conclude', Tony says somewhat reluctantly, 'that the results from Experiment 4 were more variable than those from Experiment 1 because of real, but random, variation in BOD from sample to sample. Both sets of results contain variability due to the test method, of course, and we cannot be sure that the same laboratory was used in both experiments.'

'Let us assume that it was the same laboratory and the same operator and that the testing was carried out over a period of two days in both cases', I suggest, in order to progress the discussion. 'Let us also give names to these standard deviations and then we can relate them.'

I tear a sheet of paper from the flip chart and draw a table to show the relationships between the various standard deviations. As I build up Table 8.3 I explain the meaning of the multitude of standard deviations.

'All the variability in Experiment 1 ($SD_1 = 0.2601$) is due to the test method, but we do not have repeatability conditions or reproducibility conditions. We have something between the two extremes: a long sequence of tests carried out by the same person in the same laboratory over a two-day period. So we call it SD_{Test} and can write:

Table 8.3 Sources of variation in four experiments

	SD_1	SD_2	SD_3	SD_4
SD_{test}	✔	–	?	✔
SD_{repeat}	–	✔	?	–
SD_{reprod}	–	✔	?	–
SD_{short}	–	–	✔	✔
SD_{long}	–	–	✔	–

$$SD_{Test} = SD_1 = 0.2601$$

'If we now compare Experiments 1 and 4 we should be able to estimate SD_{Short} which quantifies the short-term variability in the effluent. It would be very convenient if we could use the simple equation:

$$SD_4 = SD_{Test} + SD_{Short}$$

but this would not be correct. A well-known rule of statistics tells us that standard deviations should not be added. We must square the standard deviations before we add, then we must take the square root.

$$SD_4 = \sqrt{(SD_{Test}^2 + SD_{Short}^2)}$$

Of course, we know SD_4 and SD_{Test} so we can rearrange the equation to bring SD_{Short} to the left of the equation.

$$SD_{Short} = \sqrt{(SD_4^2 - SD_{Test}^2)}$$

I hope you are not too disturbed by these equations, Tony?'

Clearly, Tony is not at all overawed by the sudden rush of algebra, for he seizes my calculator and works through the calculation:

$$
\begin{aligned}
SD_{Short} &= \sqrt{(SD_4^2 - SD_{Test}^2)} \\
&= \sqrt{(0.6053^2 - 0.2601^2)} \\
&= \sqrt{(0.3664 - 0.0677)} \\
&= \sqrt{(0.2987)} \\
&= 0.5466
\end{aligned}
$$

'For people who do not like algebra, I like to represent the equation by a right-angled triangle (Fig. 8.13). If we draw two lines at right angles, with lengths equal to 0.5466 and 0.2601 we should find that the hypotenuse has a length of 0.6053.'

'How would the triangle change if we improved the test method?', I ask. This is a very important question that I hope will lead Tony Walters to an understanding many managers clearly do not have.

'Obviously, the SD_{Test} side would reduce in length. Since the SD_{Short} line would not change, the SD_4 line would also be shorter', he replies.

'This only confirms what is obvious. That an improvement in the test method would reduce the variability in the results, the measured values that is, but would not directly affect the true variation in BOD in the

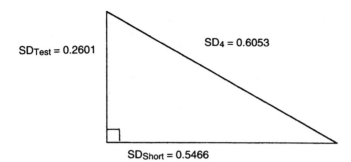

Fig. 8.13 Relating sources of variation.

discharge. (In practice we might see an indirect benefit from increased ability to control the process.) Let me ask you a more specific question. Suppose we were considering two possible improvements:

1. purchasing new analytical equipment which would halve the variability of the test method; or
2. purchasing a new control system which would reduce the true variation in the discharge by 10%.

Which of the two improvements would give us the greatest reduction in BOD results?'

'Well, 50% is much greater than 10%. Yesterday I would have said that the improvement in the test method would be more beneficial, but I am a much wiser person now so I will redraw the triangle and perform the appropriate calculations.'

Tony Walters redraws the original triangle (Fig. 8.13) to illustrate the two possible improvements (Fig. 8.14). He uses the calculator to obtain the length of the hypotenuse in each case. 'Good heavens', he exclaims as he completes the calculations. 'A 50% reduction in the test method variability is less beneficial than a 10% reduction in the true variation in the discharge. Now then, what is the general principle that I should be learning here? I suppose in general it is more beneficial to reduce the longer side of the triangle.'

'That is right', I concur. 'Compare the two sides of the triangle which are at right angles. If they are roughly equal in length then it will be beneficial

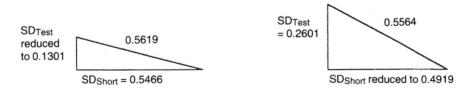

Fig. 8.14 Two possible improvements.

to reduce either. However, if one is much longer than the other, then there will be much greater benefit from reducing the longer of the two. To express that in more practical terms, we should work on those sources of variation which make a large contribution to the total variability and ignore those which make only a small contribution. Obviously any decisions about variation reduction would also be influenced by costs, opportunities, etc.'

'Have we time to consider Experiment 3?', asks Tony Walters looking anxiously at his watch. 'Yes, indeed', I reply. 'It would be a good idea to take the discussion one step further, before I leave. The problem with Experiment 3 is that we do not have an appropriate standard deviation for the test method. Note that the samples were tested in the same laboratory but on different days. During a 20-day period there may have been changes in staff, in reagents, etc.'

'Yes, I see what you mean', Tony replies after reading the sheet (Table 8.2) yet again and referring to the Table on the flip chart (Table 8.3). 'I suppose the appropriate testing standard deviation for this experiment would be greater than the repeatability standard deviation (0.2216) and greater than the SD_{Test} (0.2601) from Experiment 1, but less than the reproducibility standard deviation.'

'You are quite right. So it could be misleading to compare Experiment 3 with Experiments 1 or 4 because of the different testing regime. To help us proceed further let us assume that the 20 samples in Experiment 3 were tested over a period of two days. This obviously is not true, but the assumption will allow us to cross out the three question marks in Table 8.3 replacing only the top one with a tick. The columns for SD_3 and SD_4 are then very comparable' (Table 8.4).

'Quickly, Roland, let us calculate the standard deviation for Experiment 4', Tony suggests, picking up the sheet (Table 8.2) and reading out the results.

'The mean BOD is 27.11 and the standard deviation is 1.2169', I announce. Tony is already drawing a triangle. He draws a line and labels it '$SD_4 = 0.6053$'. 'Come along', he urges. 'What is the length of SD_{Long}?'

I open my mouth to answer, but realize that my hurried calculation has led me to a silly result. I close my mouth and repeat the calculation. 'That's better', I announce. 'SD_{Long} is equal to 1.0556. Come along, Tony. We haven't all night.'

Table 8.4 Sources of variation, simplified by an assumption

	SD_1	SD_2	SD_3	SD_4
SD_{test}	✔	–	✔	✔
SD_{repeat}	–	✔	–	–
SD_{reprod}	–	✔	–	–
SD_{short}	–	–	✔	✔
SD_{long}	–	–	✔	–

Fig. 8.15 Estimating long-term variability.

It is quite unusual for me to indulge in good natured banter with a client at our first meeting. Perhaps Tony Walters' obvious enthusiasm for dot plots, histograms and run charts has helped to create a rapport.

'This new triangle (Fig. 8.15) shows that the total variation in the results of Experiment 3 is dominated by the long-term variation in the treatment plant', Tony asserts. 'If we also look at the earlier triangle (Fig. 8.13) we can see that the contribution of the test method is quite small.'

'That's quite right', I confirm. 'What is more, you will see this even more clearly if we combine the two triangles. The line (Fig. 8.16) labelled SD_4 is a link between the two.'

'I must let you go Roland. Obviously this is a very useful technique that you have illustrated here. It can help us to make better decisions for process improvement if we can obtain reliable and appropriate data. I shall have to open discussions, the likes of which we have never had before.'

As we walk to our cars Tony Walters confides that he has learned more about statistics today than in the past 50 years. He thanks me for coming. I look forward to my next visit, but Tony Walters has much work to do in the interim.

8.7 SUMMARY

Middshire Water treat raw sewage to produce solid sludge, and liquid effluent. The solid sludge can be sold as fertilizer but the liquid effluent is

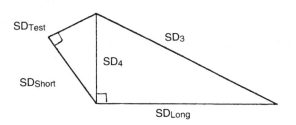
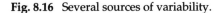

Fig. 8.16 Several sources of variability.

discharged to rivers. The National Rivers Authority monitor the effluent and set upper limits for the ammonia content, the suspended solids and the biochemical oxygen demand (BOD). It would be possible for Middshire Water to reduce the BOD to very low levels, well below the specified limit, but to achieve this they would require greater usage of electricity and greater plant capacity.

Better control of the treatment process will result in the specification being met at minimum cost. To achieve this control they must reduce the day-to-day variation. However, there are many causes of this variation. Against which cause, or source of variation, should they take up arms?

We have seen in this chapter that there is little to be gained by focusing on those causes that contribute very little to the overall variability of the product. It is much better to invest time and effort in working on a cause that gives rise to a major portion of the total variation. We used right-angled triangles to illustrate this point.

We also explored in this chapter the concepts of repeatability and reproducibility. These words should not be used loosely. They are defined in an International Standard. Inter-laboratory trials can be used to assess the repeatability and the reproducibility of any test method.

Much of what has been said in this chapter would apply to industries far removed from sewage treatment. The precision and accuracy of measurement systems is surely important in any industry – in the laboratory, on the shop floor, in market research, etc. We should not forget that almost all measurement systems involve human activity and written procedures. Both may be sources of extra variation.

It is no use hoping that variability will just go away. Our never-ending striving for quality improvement should include strategies for the reduction of variability. In Chapter 9 we will examine Taguchi methods that can help you to design products that are less susceptible to the damaging effects of external variation.

Planned experiments for quality improvement

The consultant visits Champfield Engineering to discuss the use of planned experiments with the Quality Manager. He recommends the use of factorial experiments which are very efficient and often reveal improvement opportunities that one-variable-at-a-time experiments would not uncover. Simple graphical and tabular methods are used to translate experimental results into practical conclusions.

9.1 INTRODUCTION

As I drive down the M1 it occurs to me that one or more of the components in my car may have been made by Champfield Engineering. I know that they do supply components to many British, American and Japanese vehicle manufacturers. Today I am visiting Champfield's factory at Woodburn. It would be ironical if a failure of one of their components caused me to be late for my appointment.

It is quite some time since I last visited an engineering company. I am really looking forward to seeing neat rows of freshly machined metal parts. I have been invited to Champfield's by Ross Boucher, who attended one of my three-day SPC courses about six months ago. Ross is the Quality Manager at the Woodburn factory. He wishes to discuss with me the use of planned experiments for quality improvement. I am not sure if anyone else will take part in the discussions or what type of processes we will focus upon. Nonetheless, I am quite excited to have this opportunity to spread enlightenment.

It is no exaggeration to say that researchers fall into two distinct groups . . . those who understand the benefits of planned experiments and those who do not. Unfortunately the first group is much smaller than the second, with the result that much research is carried out very inefficiently. I believe there should be more experimentation taking place in industry, but much of that which does occur, fails to lead to clear conclusions, unfortunately. So we need more **good** experiments, not more bad ones.

It is with thoughts such as these that I add interest to a boring motorway journey, but I must be careful not to miss my turn-off. Here it is. I leave the motorway and soon I am driving into the visitors' car park of Champfield Engineering's Woodburn factory. I am early, as usual, so I read my newspaper for a few minutes before approaching reception. There I have a further short wait, during which I skim through the house magazine: smiling faces, announcements of new contracts, recent successes in manufacturing and sporting activities. All is well at Champfield Engineering.

'Roland. Nice to see you again', Ross Boucher greets me as he breezes into the reception area. 'Have a good journey? Fine.'

I have previously spent three days with Ross. So I am aware that he often speaks rather quickly, asks many questions and answers quite a high proportion of them, himself. I smile and shake his hand. Before I can speak, however, he is into top gear again.

'Delighted you could come, Roland. Especially at such short notice. Come along to my office. I need some advice on planned experiments. You are the obvious person to turn to. Speaking of turning, it's left here. That's it, second on the right.'

Ross Boucher has a very large office overlooking open countryside. I am impressed, but I resist the urge to comment on either the office or the view, for fear that I might trigger another monologue. My objective for the day is to keep attention focused on the use of planned experiments in the manufacture of motor vehicle components.

9.2 ONE FACTOR AT A TIME

'Where shall we start?', I ask, taking advantage of a rare momentary hesitation by my host. 'Have you carried out any experiments?'

'Not me', Ross Boucher replies. 'But here are the results of an experiment, carried out by James Rexley in Development, trying to improve a welding process. He changed five factors. Sixteen welds in total. Is that a good design? I suppose not.'

Ross hands me an A4 sheet on which I can clearly see the plan of the experiment and the results (Table 9.1). I need time to study the table carefully, so I raise one hand as if to stem the flow of words. Ross remains silent as I read the information, line by line, then column by column.

The five centre columns contain the values of the five variables that were deliberately changed during the experiment. These are known as the independent variables or control variables or factors. I scan these five columns searching for a pattern which will indicate the nature of the plan, or the experimental design, as it is often called. As I spot the pattern Ross Boucher can contain himself no longer. 'What type of design is this? What conclusions can you draw? How can we increase the strength of the weld?', he asks.

Table 9.1 The first experiment

Weld	Voltage	Root gap	Bevel angle	Gas flow	Speed	Strength
1	8	0.4	80	55	30	262
2	8	0.4	80	55	30	239
3	8	0.4	80	55	30	242
4	8	0.4	80	55	30	208
5	8	0.4	80	55	30	232
6	8	0.4	80	55	30	255
7	10	0.4	80	55	30	269
8	10	0.4	80	55	30	278
9	8	0.5	80	55	30	236
10	8	0.5	80	55	30	282
11	8	0.4	85	55	30	190
12	8	0.4	85	55	30	221
13	8	0.4	80	50	30	240
14	8	0.4	80	50	30	233
15	8	0.4	80	55	35	272
16	8	0.4	80	55	35	291

'This plan is known as a one-factor-at-a-time experiment', I reply, in answer to his first question. 'You see that the first six welds are under standard conditions and then there are two welds with one of the independent variables having been deliberately changed, then two welds with another variable changed, etc. You notice that in each of the last 10 welds only one variable deviates from the standard conditions. To answer your other questions I would need to analyse the results in the final column and plot some simple graphs. But first I would like you to tell me more about the welding process and how the variables are measured.'

'Can't do that, Roland. Secret process, under development. Everything I can disclose is on the sheet. You just assume that we know what we are doing. Tell me how to analyse the data.'

'It is dangerous to divorce the data analysis from the process knowledge', I suggest. 'But, if we are simply using this experiment as an example, to illustrate the general principles of design and analysis, then I am happy to do so. The first step in the data analysis then, is to draw a dot plot or a run chart.'

I persuade Ross Boucher to read out the results in the strength column. As he does so I plot a rough dot plot on a sheet of graph paper (Fig. 9.1).

'Good picture. Good picture', Ross exclaims. 'What do you think? Should I increase voltage and increase speed? Very subjective. Have you a computer program that will do statistical tests? Of course you have.'

My client has answered his question correctly. I do have many computer programs that would facilitate the data analysis. However, I believe that Ross will learn much more if we use simple pictures and a pocket calculator. But, before we perform any calculations, I feel that we should carefully examine the stratified dot plot (Fig. 9.1).

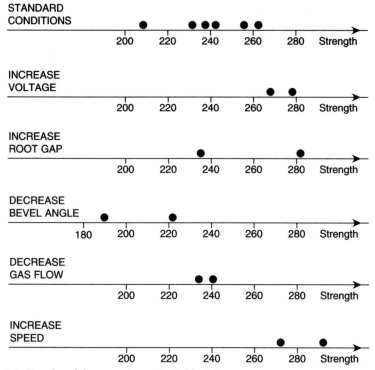

Fig. 9.1 Results of the experiment in Table 9.1.

'I can offer you a statistical test which does not require a computer or any calculation', I say, pointing at the dot plot. 'Compare the five groups of two results with the group of six results. Whenever both results lie outside the group of six we can reasonably conclude that the change in the independent variable has had an effect on the strength of the weld.'

'That's simple enough', Ross Boucher snaps. 'Is it a good test? Can't be. People would not do all these *t*-tests and *F*-tests if your simple test was as good. What is it called? Caulcutt's test, I suppose.'

Once again he has answered his own question, but this time, incorrectly. 'No', I reply. 'It is called Tukey's quick test. We do not have time to go into all the details now, but I have described it more fully in my book, *Data Analysis in the Chemical Industry*. True, it is not as powerful as some other tests but you have to acknowledge its simplicity. Actually, we are misusing Tukey's test with sample sizes of 2 and 6, but it still gives a useful indication.'

'It indicates that we should increase the voltage and increase the speed', Ross Boucher asserts. 'Is that right? We want to increase the weld strength, of course. Would other statistical tests give the same conclusions?'

'If you have reservations about Tukey's quick test, I would suggest that we calculate confidence limits for the effect of each of the five changes that were introduced. Are you familiar with confidence intervals?'

Table 9.2 Summary of strength results from Table 9.1

Operating conditions	Welds	Mean	SD
Standard	1–6	239.7	18.98
Increased voltage	7–8	273.5	6.36
Increased root gap	9–10	259.0	32.53
Increased bevel angle	11–12	205.5	21.92
Decreased gas flow	13–14	236.5	4.95
Increased speed	15–16	281.5	13.44

'I have heard of them. Ninety-five per cent confidence. Is that it? No, I don't really understand. You had better explain.'

'Well, first we need to calculate the mean and standard deviation for each group of results', I suggest. 'Would you mind reading out the strength figures again?', Ross reads, I calculate and soon we have the summary in Table 9.2.

I have noticed Ross Boucher becoming increasingly agitated as the calculation continues. He seizes the sheet on which I have written the means and standard deviations. 'You can not do that', he insists. 'You cannot calculate the standard deviation of two results. Only two numbers. You should use the range. I'm sure I've read somewhere that, when you have less than 6 results you should calculate the range, not the standard deviation. Don't you agree? No.'

I suspect that, if I remained silent, Ross would eventually ask all the important questions and provide most of the answers. However, on this occasion he is wrong, so I must speak.

'Clearly, I can calculate the standard deviation of two numbers. I have just done it. Furthermore it is perfectly valid. The standard deviation is better than the range when you have three or more numbers. The SD and the range are equally good when you have only two numbers. In fact the standard deviation of two results is equal to their range divided by the square root of 2. Obviously a standard deviation calculated from only two results, is not very reliable. But the range of two results is not reliable either. You can see how much the standard deviations differ (Table 9.2). It is not my fault that you have only two results for each change. That was how the experiment was planned. A better design would . . .'

'Is the SD of six results, three times as good as the SD of two results?', Ross asks before I can introduce more efficient experimental plans. 'No, it's nine times as good. Or is it?', he continues.

'You could say it is five times as good, depending on what you mean by good. Statisticians speak of degrees of freedom. You don't need to know exactly what degrees of freedom are, but with the standard deviation given by the automatic routine on your calculator, its degrees of freedom are one less than the number of numbers you typed in. So the SD of six results has five degrees of freedom, while the SD of two results has only one degree of freedom.'

'So, the 18.98 from the first six results is five times as good as the other standard deviations', Ross suggests. 'The average of the other SDs must be about 19, I suppose, but they do vary a lot. Can we bung them all together to obtain something better? No, I suppose not.'

'Yes, you can', I contradict, perhaps rather too bluntly. 'We can calculate what is called the combined standard deviation. It is rather a messy calculation because we must square the standard deviations before we add them, then we must take the square root. With this data there is a further complication because the groups are of different size, six and two.'

I take up my calculator again and soon we have the combined standard deviation. (The method of calculation is given in procedure C (Appendix A). It was used previously in Chapter 8.) This is equal to 18.94 and it has ten degrees of freedom.

'OK, Ross, we can now calculate confidence limits for the effect of each independent variable. The formula makes use of the combined standard deviation (CSD) and the difference between the means.'

Confidence limits for the true effect of an independent variable

These are given by:

$$(\bar{x}_1 - \bar{x}_2) \pm t \times CSD \times \sqrt{(\frac{1}{n_1} + \frac{1}{n_2})}$$

where
$\bar{x}_1$ is the mean response at the high level
$\bar{x}_2$ is the mean response at the low level
CSD is the combined standard deviation
n_1 is the number of results in $\bar{x}_1$
n_2 is the number of results in $\bar{x}_2$
t is from Table B.3 in Appendix B

Ross Boucher does not appear to be overawed by the formula. 'Let us do the calculations for increased speed', he suggests. 'The means we want are 281.5 and 239.7.' (See Table 9.2.)

'That's right', I confirm. 'What will be the values of n_1 and n_2?'

'Six and two or two and six', Ross replies. 'The combined standard deviation is 18.94, but what is the value of t?'

'That comes from a statistical table. (See Table B.3 in Appendix B.) For a 95% confidence interval, with 10 degrees of freedom, t will be equal to 2.23. The confidence limits are

$$(281.5 - 239.7) \pm 2.23 \times 18.94 \times \sqrt{(\frac{1}{2} + \frac{1}{6})} = 41.8 \pm 34.5$$

$$= 7.3 \text{ to } 76.3$$

We can be 95% confident that the effect of increasing the speed, from 30 to

35, is to increase the weld strength by something between 7.3 and 76.3.

I pause at this point, fully expecting that Ross Boucher will be staggered by the width of this confidence interval. The usefulness of confidence intervals and confidence limits is that they force you to face up to the uncertainty in an estimate. For example, we could declare that 'The effect of increasing the speed was to increase the weld strength by 41.8.' This statement, however, tells us nothing about the uncertainty that surrounds this figure. However, a confidence interval of 41.8 ± 34.5 puts things into perspective. The 34.5 takes account of the inherent variability of the welding process (CSD = 18.94) and the small sample sizes (2 and 6).

'That's because the experiment is so small', exclaims Ross Boucher. 'The interval is so wide because we have so little data, I suppose. But the cost of 16 of these special welds is very high. How many welds would we need for an interval of ±20, say? Hundreds, I suppose.'

'There is a formula we can use to estimate how much data we need to obtain a certain width of confidence interval', I reply. 'To make use of this formula we need some idea of the variability of the process. Of course, we already have that, in the combined standard deviation. So we can use the combined standard deviation to discover how many welds we need to estimate an effect with a certain precision. The formula is

$$n_1 = n_2 = 2 \left(t \times \frac{SD}{c}\right)^2$$

where n_1 and n_2 are the sample sizes

SD is a standard deviation

t is from Table B.3 in Appendix B

± c is the required width of confidence interval.

You want to know how many welds you must do for a confidence interval of ±20, so we put c=20, SD=18.94 and t=2.23 which gives

$$n_1 = n_2 = 2 \left(\frac{2.23 \times 18.94}{20}\right)^2$$
$$= 8.9$$

Thus we would need 9 welds at the low level of the factor and 9 welds at the high level of the factor. Eighteen welds in total.

'That is 18 welds to investigate one factor', Ross interjects. 'For five factors we would need 54 welds, wouldn't we? Yes, 9 at the standard conditions and 9 for each of the five changes. Is there no better way? Yes, there must be, or you wouldn't be here.'

'Yes there is a better way', I reply. 'You do not need 54 welds to investigate five factors, you only need 16, if you use a better experimental plan. But before we look at that, let us complete the data analysis for this one-factor-at-a-time experiment. Confidence limits for the effect of increasing the voltage are:

$$(273.5 - 239.7) \pm 2.23 \times 18.94 \times \sqrt{(\tfrac{1}{2} + \tfrac{1}{6})}$$
$$= 33.8 \pm 34.5$$
$$= -0.7 \text{ to } 68.3$$

So we can be 95% confident that the effect of increasing the voltage from 8 to 10, is to increase the weld strength by something between −0.7 and 68.3.'

'Good heavens', Ross Boucher exclaims. 'The weld strength might increase by as much as 68.3 or it might decrease. Surely not? Yes.'

'We have failed to prove that increasing the voltage had any effect on the weld strength', I assert. 'Note that we have not proved that the change in voltage had no effect. We have simply failed to prove, beyond reasonable doubt, that it did have an effect. If you forced me to give an estimate of the result of changing the voltage from 8 to 10, I would have to say that it appeared to cause an increase in weld strength of 33.8. However, I would wish to qualify this estimate by reminding you of the large standard deviation, 18.94, and the small sample sizes, 2 and 6. As the resulting confidence interval includes zero, we have failed to eliminate the possibility that there was no effect at all.'

'I like that', Ross responds. 'A confidence interval that includes zero implies that the change in voltage may have had no effect.'

He pauses, but it is clear that he will have more to say when he has come to terms with this new concept. His face lights up as he continues: 'That's what I was going to say. The 34.5 cropped up again. Will all the confidence intervals be ±34.5? Yes, of course they will. So any calculated effect which is less than 34.5 could be simply due to chance. Is that right, Roland? Don't tell me I am wrong again.'

'Quite right, Ross, quite right', I reply. 'The experimenter changed five factors, or independent variables. We can calculate confidence limits for each of the five effects, and each confidence interval will be ±34.5. Let me set them out in a table' (Table 9.3).

'So we calculated an estimate of the effect of each factor, but only one of the effects is statistically significant. We have proved, beyond reasonable doubt that the change in speed had an effect on the weld strength, but we have failed to prove that the other four factors had any effect. However, it is quite possible that two or even three of the other four factors *did* have an effect, but the evidence is inconclusive. If you want to put a name to it you

Table 9.3 Which factors affect the weld strength?

Factor	Calculated effect	Confidence interval	Conclusion
Voltage	33.8	33.8±34.5	Not significant
Root gap	19.3	19.3±34.5	Not significant
Bevel angle	−34.2	−34.2±34.5	Not significant
Gas flow	3.2	3.2±34.5	Not significant
Speed	41.8	41.8±34.5	Significant

could call the 34.5 the "least significant difference" or the "least significant estimate", because an estimate must exceed 34.5 if it is to be regarded as statistically significant.'

'Yes, yes, it's all clear now. But with sample sizes of 8 and 8 the least significant effect would have been 20', Ross Boucher declares. 'I think so. That is what we proved earlier, is it not? . . . when we used the formula? So Jim Rexley's experiment is inconclusive because it uses only 8 welds to assess each factor – six at the base line and two after the change. Is that right? And you are going to show me how to use all 16 welds to estimate the effect of each factor.'

'That is right, Ross', I reply. 'I am going to show you a different experimental plan which allows you to make better use of the 16 results. Perhaps we could have some coffee before we embark on this new journey.'

9.3 FACTORIAL EXPERIMENTS

As I sip my coffee and nibble a biscuit I observe that Ross Boucher has the ability to talk continuously, even while eating and drinking. Being rather hungry I take a second biscuit, then a third. It is while eating the latter, that I realize my client's monologue has ended and he has lapsed into silence. Perhaps he needs the stimulus of a threatened interruption to sustain his energy. That's unfortunate. I was enjoying listening to his suggestions for improving the education system.

The coffee pot has been drained. The biscuit plate is bare. It seems quite natural to return to our discussion of planned experiments. 'Let me offer you an alternative experiment, which also requires 16 welds, but which will give you better effect estimates. It is a more powerful experiment. There is a whole family of experiments known as two-level factorial experiments. We will start with the smallest and build up until we have one large enough for your needs.' With these words I extract from my briefcase several sheets which display various factorial experiments in a rather abstract format (Table 9.4).

'What on earth is that?', Ross Boucher demands to know. 'You could destroy your reputation as a communicator, sticking that under my nose. What are A and B? What do + and − mean? Are you sure it is an experiment?'

Table 9.4 A 2^2 factorial experiment

Run	A	B	Response
1	−	−	
2	+	−	
3	−	+	
4	+	+	

Table 9.5 A 2^2 factorial experiment

Weld	Voltage	Root gap	Strength
1	8	0.4	
2	10	0.4	
3	8	0.5	
4	10	0.5	

'Bear with me for one moment, Ross', I plead. 'Let me rewrite the plan on the flip chart. I will replace A and B with variable names and replace + and – with numerical values (Table 9.5).'

'That's better', Ross concedes. 'Why did you not present that in the first place? You could have turned me against these factorial experiments with those meaningless symbols.'

My client is correct. I should have started with the concrete and then moved to the abstract. I should be grateful that Ross Boucher had the courage to react honestly to an unpleasant experience. I am grateful. However I must now encourage him to accept the more abstract representation of the experiment, so that we can progress more quickly.

'There are certain advantages in using the plus and minus signs when discussing factorial experiments', I explain. 'These advantages will become clear later if you will allow me to use this rather abstract notation.' Ross Boucher nods agreement and I place on the table a plan for a 2^3 factorial experiment (Table 9.6).

'With a 2^3 factorial experiment we have three factors each at two levels', I continue. 'Two cubed is equal to eight, of course, which is the number of runs. I am sure you can see the patterns of plus and minus signs, so you could probably write down a plan for a two to the fourth experiment.'

'I guess it would have 16 runs with a D column containing eight minuses followed by eight plusses. Am I right? Yes. And a 2^5 experiment would have 32 runs. Is that right? But you said we could investigate five factors in 16 runs. You haven't miscalculated have you?' Ross asks rather belligerently.

'No, no. I have not miscalculated. We will use half of a 2^5 experiment. You draw up a 2^4 experiment on the flip chart, then I will add a fifth column to give us what we need', I propose.

Table 9.6 A 2^3 factorial experiment

Run	A	B	C	Response
1	–	–	–	
2	+	–	–	
3	–	+	–	
4	+	+	–	
5	–	–	+	
6	+	–	+	
7	–	+	+	
8	+	+	+	

Table 9.7 Half of a 2^5 factorial experiment

Run	A	B	C	D	E	Response
1	−	−	−	−	+	
2	+	−	−	−	−	
3	−	+	−	−	−	
4	+	+	−	−	+	
5	−	−	+	−	−	
6	+	−	+	−	+	
7	−	+	+	−	+	
8	+	+	+	−	−	
9	−	−	−	+	−	
10	+	−	−	+	+	
11	−	+	−	+	+	
12	+	+	−	+	−	
13	−	−	+	+	+	
14	+	−	+	+	−	
15	−	+	+	+	−	
16	+	+	+	+	+	

Ross Boucher writes – and + alternately in the A column (Table 9.7). Then he adds the B, C and D columns. We now have on the flip chart a 2^4 factorial plan which is both correct and rather beautiful. I am reluctant to deface this work of art with my rather inconsistent scrawl. 'Perhaps you would like to add the E column', I suggest. 'Just multiply the signs in the A, B, C and D columns. In the top row we have minus times minus, times minus, times minus, which gives a plus.'

Before I have finished speaking Ross Boucher is filling in the E column and we soon have the plan for a half of a 2^5 factorial experiment. 'So we have eight plusses and eight minuses again', he observes. 'I suppose you could put any of our five factors into any column, then do the 16 runs, and then put the strength measurements in the final column? Yes.'

I have grown accustomed to my client filling almost all available time with speech. Indeed, I have become so accustomed to his voice that I feel quite disturbed whenever he pauses for more than a few moments. Ross is now staring silently at the flip chart. What is he thinking, I wonder. He pulls from a drawer, a pile of papers and thumbs through them, rapidly.

'I knew it', he shouts. 'Jim Rexley planned one of these experiments. How is that for a coincidence? He left before the experiment was complete, but I have the results here. Just check it. I am sure it is one of these half to the fifth things.'

I carefully examine the tabulation on the sheet that Ross has handed to me (Table 9.8). Clearly this is what we call a half replicate of a 2^5 factorial experiment. The 16 runs are listed in exactly the same order as those in my matrix in Table 9.7. It is common practice to put the runs into random order before carrying out the experiment. Perhaps Jim Rexley or someone else randomized the runs on a separate sheet. If Ross had handed me the

Table 9.8 Half of a 2^5 factorial experiment

Weld	Voltage	Root gap	Bevel angle	Gas flow	Speed	Strength
1	8	0.4	80	50	35	297
2	10	0.4	80	50	30	293
3	8	0.5	80	50	30	255
4	10	0.5	80	50	35	246
5	8	0.4	85	50	30	216
6	10	0.4	85	50	35	185
7	8	0.5	85	50	35	311
8	10	0.5	85	50	30	287
9	8	0.4	80	55	30	236
10	10	0.4	80	55	35	233
11	8	0.5	80	55	35	315
12	10	0.5	80	55	30	280
13	8	0.4	85	55	35	235
14	10	0.4	85	55	30	242
15	8	0.5	85	55	30	260
16	10	0.5	85	55	35	276

randomized table it would have taken me much longer to check it out.

'You are right, Ross', I confirm. 'This is indeed a half of a 2^5 factorial experiment. Furthermore it is set out in the standard order. Have you analysed the results?'

Ross Boucher is thumbing through the papers again. He reads aloud a few words from each, and when he eventually reaches the bottom of the pile he concludes: 'No. There does not appear to be an analysis of the results. I did not think there would be, as the results were not available until after Jim left. No one else would know how to do the analysis.'

'Well I am delighted to tell you Ross that there is a very simple method

Table 9.9 Calculation of the effects

Run	A	B	C	D	E	Strength
1	−	−	−	−	+	297
2	+	−	−	−	−	293
3	−	+	−	−	−	255
4	+	+	−	−	+	246
5	−	−	+	−	−	216
6	+	−	+	−	+	185
7	−	+	+	−	+	311
8	+	+	+	−	−	287
9	−	−	−	+	−	236
10	+	−	−	+	+	233
11	−	+	−	+	+	315
12	+	+	−	+	−	280
13	−	−	+	+	+	235
14	+	−	+	+	−	242
15	−	+	+	+	−	260
16	+	+	+	+	+	276

of analysis, using the plus and minus signs that you kindly wrote on the flip chart. Perhaps you would add the weld strengths. Write them in a new column, down the right-hand side, while I find my calculator.'

Thank you Ross. Now then, to calculate an estimate of the effect of increasing the voltage we use the signs in the A column and the numbers in the strength column, as follows:

$$-297 + 293 - 255 + 246 - 216 + 185 - 311 + 287 - 236 + 233 - 315 + 280 - 235 + 242 - 260 + 276 = -83$$

Then we divide the result by 8 to obtain the estimate:

$$-83 \div 8 = -10.375.$$

So, we estimate that the effect of increasing the voltage from 8 to 10 was to decrease the weld strength by 10.375.'

'So, to estimate the effect of changing the root gap would we use the signs in the B column?' Ross Boucher asks. Before I can reply, he continues: 'Yes, of course. We want

$$(-297 - 293 + 255 + 246 - 216 - 185 + 311 + 287 - 236 - 233 + 315 + 280 - 235 - 242 + 260 + 276)/8$$

which is equal to 36.625. Am I right, Roland?'

'You are indeed, Ross', I reply, rather taken aback by the speed with which my client has carried out the calculation. Soon we have calculated estimates for the effects of the other three factors. I list them on the flip chart (Table 9.10).

I am about to invite Ross Boucher to compare these estimates with those from the one-at-a-time experiment, but he has clearly already made the comparison between Table 9.10 and Table 9.3. 'These conclusions are totally different to those from the previous experiment', he bellows. 'They are completely different, aren't they? Voltage, for example, is −10.4 compared with 33.8. Root gap is 36.6 compared with 19.3. How do you explain that? Confidence intervals, I suppose.'

'Let us take this slowly, step by step', I suggest. 'First, if you carry out two experiments you must not expect them to give exactly the same estimates. Second, we can calculate confidence limits for the true effects from the results of either experiment. For the one-factor-at-a-time experi-

Table 9.10 Analysis of the results in Table 9.9

Factor	Estimated effect
Voltage (A)	−10.4
Root gap (B)	36.6
Bevel angle (C)	−17.9
Gas flow (D)	−1.6
Speed (E)	3.6

we had ±34.5. I promised you approximately ±20 for the factorial experiment. So the factorial experiment is telling us that only root gap (B) is statistically significant, whereas the one-at-a-time experiment suggested that only speed (E) was significant. Clearly the two experiments have led to conflicting conclusions – so far, that is. But we have not yet completed our analysis of the data from the second experiment. When we do so, we may find much closer agreement.'

Ross Boucher is clearly suspicious. No doubt he would like to continue the data analysis, to see if I am able to reveal this closer agreement. However, I have glanced at my watch and he has done likewise, so we are both aware that lunch would be jeopardized by further lengthy discussion. 'The next steps in the analysis will blow your mind', I promise my client in a slow deep voice. 'I think you should raise your blood sugar level in order to maximize your enjoyment of the experience.'

We go to the works canteen, which serves a very acceptable meal. Perhaps this is the only dining room on site. There is certainly a wide mix of suited managers and overalled workers scattered throughout the room. I remind myself that everyone is a manager in a TQM culture.

Ross Boucher does much of the talking. He seems to be more relaxed now than he was earlier. His sentences are longer and he asks fewer questions. I certainly enjoy listening as he tells me about the exciting new developments at Champfield Engineering. They are reducing their dependence on motor vehicle components by moving into pipework for electricity generators, using the latest welding technology.

At the end of the meal we take cups of coffee through to a lounge area and I take the opportunity to prepare Ross Boucher for the topic we must discuss next, by asking him several questions. 'Why do you put sugar in your coffee? Why do you stir the coffee after adding the sugar? Why not put in less sugar and stir longer or, alternatively, put in more sugar and stir less?'

9.4 INTERACTION BETWEEN VARIABLES

Ross Boucher answers the coffee questions several times as we walk back to his office. He is in no doubt that the purpose of adding sugar is to increase sweetness. He is also quite certain that the stirring also increases the sweetness of the coffee. It is the third question that evokes a stream of answers as Ross searches for words that will adequately describe his coffee table behaviour.

'Let us plot a graph', I suggest, when we are safely returned to the privacy of my client's office. On the flip chart I plot two axes, labelled sweetness and sugar, then I plot points to illustrate the results of a hypothetical experiment. Finally I join the points with two straight lines (Fig. 9.2), then pose several questions. 'How much will the sweetness increase if

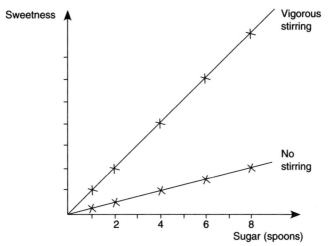

Fig. 9.2 An interaction between two variables.

I add an extra spoonful of sugar? How much will the sweetness increase if I vigorously stir the coffee? Why are the two lines not parallel?'

Perhaps Ross Boucher suspects that these are trick questions. He certainly constrains his natural quick-fire style as he stares fixedly at the graph. 'It depends', he says, at last. 'The effect of adding extra sugar depends on whether or not you stir. The effect of stirring depends on how much sugar has been added. One thing depends on the other.'

'A brilliant answer, Ross. Quite brilliant. You have identified the important feature of the relationship. The effect of one factor depends on the level of the other. We say that the two factors interact, or we say that there is an interaction between the two factors. This idea is so important I will write it on the flip chart.'

> When the effect of one factor, on the response, depends on the level of a second factor, we say that there is an **interaction** between the two factors.

'I must point out', I continue, 'that some of the words I have used are potentially misleading. Some people call the factors independent variables, but there is no guarantee that they will be independent. If there is an interaction between two factors then their effects are not independent. Furthermore, the variation of the two factors may not be independent. They may be correlated, with one changing whenever the other changes. One feature of factorial experiments is that the factors are not correlated; they are uncorrelated, or orthogonal, if you want a more difficult word. I don't think we have time to discuss these ideas today. They are dealt with in one of my other books *Statistics in Research and Development*.'

'**Correlation** between two factors is not the same as **interaction** between two factors. Is that what you are saying?', asks Ross Boucher. 'To find out

Table 9.11 The design matrix for half of a 2^5 experiment

Run	A	B	C	D	E	AB	AC	AD	AE	BC	BD	BE	CD	CE	DE	*Response*
1	−	−	−	−	+	+	+	+	−	+	+	−	+	−	−	297
2	+	−	−	−	−	−	−	−	−	+	+	+	+	+	+	293
2	−	+	−	−	−	−	+	+	+	−	−	−	+	+	+	255
4	+	+	−	−	+	+	−	−	+	−	−	+	+	−	−	246
5	−	−	+	−	+	+	−	+	+	−	+	+	−	−	+	216
6	+	−	+	−	+	−	+	−	+	−	+	−	−	+	−	185
7	−	+	+	−	+	−	−	+	−	+	−	+	−	+	−	311
8	+	+	+	−	−	+	+	−	−	+	−	−	−	−	+	287
9	−	−	−	+	−	+	+	−	+	+	−	+	−	+	−	236
10	+	−	−	+	+	−	−	+	+	+	−	−	−	−	+	233
11	−	+	−	+	+	−	+	−	−	−	+	+	−	−	+	315
12	+	+	−	+	−	+	−	+	−	−	+	−	−	+	−	280
13	−	−	+	+	+	+	−	−	−	−	−	−	+	+	+	235
14	+	−	+	+	−	−	+	+	−	−	−	+	+	−	−	242
15	−	+	+	+	−	−	−	−	+	+	+	−	+	−	−	260
16	+	+	+	+	+	+	+	+	+	+	+	+	+	+	+	276

the difference I need to read your book. Perhaps I will, but we must return to the welding experiment. If there are interactions in a coffee cup, I am sure they exist in a welding process. How can we find out whether or not the factors interact?'

'Well the first point to note is that you never will find interactions if you change one variable at a time. The first experiment (Table 9.1) is not only inefficient it is also incapable of revealing interactions. With the second experiment (Table 9.8) it is very easy. We make use of the plus and minus signs again. First we must extend our matrix to include ten interaction columns. These are obtained by selecting pairs of the A, B, C, D, E columns and multiplying them. This is one I prepared earlier (Table 9.11). If we write the weld strengths in the response column we can proceed.'

Ross Boucher examines the new matrix for some time. 'So, the AB column is the product of the A column and the B column', he murmurs. 'Minus times minus is plus, plus times minus is minus, . . . From the five original columns you have generated ten additional columns. Each one contains eight minuses and eight plusses, but all the columns are different. No two are the same. This is remarkable. Is this one of Taguchi's orthogonal arrays?'

I am surprised to learn that Ross Boucher is aware of Genichi Taguchi. He is a Japanese quality guru who has had considerable success in persuading engineers to use planned experiments in the development of products and processes. His followers use a whole package of statistical techniques known as Taguchi methods. Some of these techniques are very useful, but some are less useful, and I am hoping that Ross Boucher is not going to waste our valuable time by insisting that we discuss the less useful ones.

'You could describe this design matrix as an orthogonal array', I continue.

Table 9.12 Estimates of the interaction effects

Interaction	Estimate
Voltage × Root gap *AB*	−2.6
Voltage × Bevel angle *AC*	2.4
Voltage × Gas Flow *AD*	6.6
Voltage × Speed *AE*	−44.1
Root gap × Bevel angle *BC*	27.4
Root gap × Gas Flow *BD*	9.6
Root gap × Speed *BE*	12.9
Bevel angle × Gas Flow *CD*	5.1
Bevel angle × Speed *CE*	−3.1
Gas Flow × Speed *DE*	6.6

'If you replaced each minus by 2 and each plus by 1, you would have what Taguchi calls an L16 orthogonal array. We could discuss Taguchi methods later if time permits. Let us first estimate the interaction effects.'

Using the plus and minus signs in the AB column (Table 9.11) and the numbers in the response column we calculate an estimate of the first interaction effect:

$$(297 - 293 - 255 + 246 + 216 - 185 - 311 + 287 + 236 - 233 - 315 + 280 + 235 - 242 - 260 + 276)/8 = -2.625$$

Continuing in this way we estimate all ten of the interactions and I list them on the flip chart (Table 9.12).

Before my list is complete Ross Boucher has decided that two of the ten interactions are statistically significant. He recalls my earlier assertion that we would obtain a confidence interval of ±20 if we had 9 results at each level of a factor. It is true that the factorial experiment has only 8 results at each level, but Ross has recalculated the least significant effect to be

$$\pm t \times CSD \times \sqrt{\left(\frac{1}{n_1} + \frac{1}{n_2}\right)}$$
$$= \pm 2.23 \times 18.94 \times \sqrt{\left(\frac{1}{8} + \frac{1}{8}\right)}$$
$$= \pm 21.1$$

'I have two questions. Which will you answer first?', Ross asks. 'Why are we using the standard deviation value of 18.94 from the other experiment? Why didn't we calculate a standard deviation from the results of the factorial experiment? What values should we use for voltage, speed, root gap and bevel angle now that we have found the two interactions?'

'Can we leave the standard deviations till later, Ross? I would like to focus first on how we can give meaning to these interactions. Now that we know the two interactions are significant we will go back to the data. That will help us keep our feet on the ground. Because the interaction between voltage and speed gave us the largest estimate, 44.1, we will start with that

Table 9.13 Re-tabulation to illustrate interaction *AE*

Speed (E)	Voltage (A)	
	8	10
30	255, 216	293, 287
	236, 260	280, 242
35	297, 311	246, 185
	315, 235	233, 276

one. I will re-tabulate the data in the form of a two-way table. Perhaps you would read out the results, starting with the four welds that have a minus sign in both the A column and the E column in Table 9.11.'

'255, 216, 236 and 260', Ross Boucher replies, responding as quickly as he would to one of his own questions. 'For the four welds with a plus in both columns we have 246, 185, 233 and 276.'

With Ross Boucher in such sparkling form we soon have all 16 results correctly positioned in the two-way table (Table 9.13). My client seizes the sheet of paper on which I have produced the tabulation. He examines it at length. 'Will he spot the pattern?', I wonder. Perhaps one or two questions from me will help to focus his attention on the important feature of the table. 'What voltage would you use to obtain the highest weld strength?', I ask rather slowly. After a pause, I pose the complementary question, 'What speed would you use?'

'Yes, I see what you mean', Ross replies. 'What a superb table this is. All the high weld strengths are in two opposite corners. So we need either high voltage and low speed or low voltage and high speed. I guess we would prefer to use the higher speed to increase the throughput.'

'We can make the two-way table even more meaningful if we calculate some means and standard deviations and plot one or two graphs', I suggest. 'Come on, Ross. Read out the results again, starting with the four in the top-left corner.' Soon we have the means and standard deviations in Table 9.14.

'The numbers in brackets are standard deviations. Ignore those for the moment and focus on the means', I suggest. 'Of the four means in the centre of the table, the two largest are in opposite corners, which fits in with your earlier observation. Look at the two column means, 265.7 and 255.3. The difference between these column means is 10.4, which is equal to the estimate of the voltage effect we calculated earlier (Table 9.10). The difference between the row means is (262.3 − 258.7 =) 3.6. This is equal to the speed effect estimate we found using the matrix.'

'So you can calculate the estimates from the matrix of plus and minus signs or from the two-way table', Ross exclaims. 'The two-way table is more meaningful, but rather tedious. A pity it will not give you the interaction. Or will it?'

'It will indeed, Ross', I proudly announce. 'We have used the column means to estimate the voltage effect and the row means to estimate the

Table 9.14 Means, from which to calculate effect estimates

Speed (E)	Voltage (A)		
	8	10	Mean
30	241.8	275.5	258.7
	(20.04)	(22.96)	
35	289.5	235.0	262.3
	(37.14)	(37.89)	
Mean	265.7	255.3	260.5

speed effect. Now we will use the **diagonal** means to estimate the interaction effect.

Mean response on the $--$, $++$ diagonal $= (241.8 + 235.0)/2 = 238.4$

Mean response on the $-+$, $+-$ diagonal $= (289.5 + 275.5)/2 = 282.5$

Estimate of interaction effect $= 238.4 - 282.5 = 44.1$

I think this agrees with the estimate we obtained from the matrix.'

'It would be useful to have a computer program to calculate all the estimates, then produce two-way tables to illustrate the interactions', Ross suggests. 'Are there such programs? There must be. Do you have one?'

'You could do it on a spread sheet', I reply, 'but there are more specialized programs which will analyse the results to give you effect estimates, help you to decide which are significant, then produce two-way tables and graphs. I think the graphs are even more impressive than the tables. Shall we plot one or two?'

On the assumption that Ross Boucher will be in favour of plotting the graphs, I take a sheet of graph paper from my brief case and draw two sets of axes. On both graphs I label the vertical axis with the name of the response variable, weld strength. The horizontal axis is labelled with the name of an independent variable, voltage on one graph and speed on the other. Then I plot four points on each graph using the four means from the centre of Table 9.14.

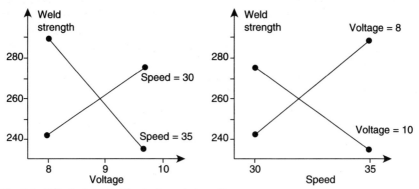

Fig. 9.3 Effect plots, to illustrate an interaction.

'The two effect plots are alternative ways of illustrating the interaction', I continue. 'You would not normally plot both. Either would suffice. Note that in both plots the two lines are not parallel. If there were no interaction between speed and voltage we would get two parallel lines in each plot. The more the slopes differ, the stronger the interaction. In this relationship we see that the slopes have opposite sign. One slope is negative the other positive. Thus an increase in voltage from 8 to 10 might increase the weld strength or it might decrease the weld strength, depending on whether the speed were 30 or 35.'

Ross Boucher is clearly impressed. He studies the two graphs in silence, for quite some time. Eventually he says, 'The potential for process improvement is enormous, if we use planned experiments to discover interactions. I can see now why there is such conflict between our engineers. One might say that increasing voltage causes an increase in weld strength, while another says that increasing voltage causes a decrease in weld strength. Of course, they can **both** be right, though each believes that the other must be wrong. Fascinating. How about the other interaction? Between root gap and bevel angle, was it?'

Soon we have split the 16 results into four groups of four and calculated the mean and standard deviation for each group. These are entered in the centre of a two-way table (Table 9.15) and are used to draw two effect plots. (Fig. 9.4)

'Different again', exclaims Ross Boucher, as I join the points on the effect plots. 'You say that you would not normally draw both of these plots, but I find them both useful. One shows the effect of changing root gap, with a constant bevel angle and the other shows the effect of changing the angle. I need to study these carefully.'

My client examines the four effect plots (Figs 9.3 and 9.4) for some time, then he declares: 'Well, it looks as if we need to have a gap of 0.5, a voltage of 8 and a speed of 35, to give us a high weld strength. If we stay within the range of this experiment, that is. But I would like to explore larger gaps, lower voltages and higher speed. What do you think? I suppose the main conclusion is that we need to do another experiment. What do you say?'

'I must agree, Ross. The main purpose of a two-level factorial experiment is to tell you what experiment to do next. By doing a succession of experiments we draw closer and closer to the optimum conditions. The angle and

Table 9.15 Illustrating interaction BC

	Bevel angle (C)		
Root gap (B)	*80*	*85*	*Mean*
0.4	264.8	219.5	242.2
	(34.99)	(25.49)	
0.5	274.0	283.5	278.8
	(30.89)	(21.42)	
Mean	269.4	251.5	260.5

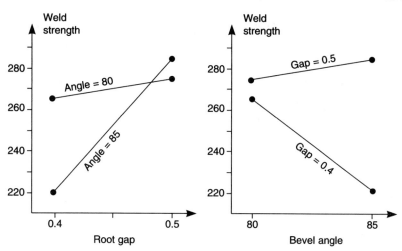

Fig. 9.4 An effect plot to illustrate interaction BC.

the gap and the speed and the voltage that give maximum weld strength, that is. Note that we are not mentioning gas flow. This factor does not appear to have any effect. Why is that, Ross?'

'I am sworn to secrecy', he replies. 'I have promised not to discuss with you the technology of welding. There is a lot of money tied up in this project.'

'I appreciate that. You can rest assured that I will not mention your technology elsewhere, without your permission. Allow me to make the general point that a factor which **does** have an effect will give a significant estimate only if it is varied by a sufficient amount. We certainly have not proved that changes in gas flow have no effect. But we have obtained an indication that a change in gas flow from 50 to 55, has little or no effect.'

Ross Boucher leans back in his seat. He clearly has a sense of achievement which, I assume, is based on his recent learning about interactions. 'Very good', he says, 'but there are still one or two questions outstanding. How do we obtain a standard deviation from a factorial experiment? I do not like borrowing a standard deviation from another experiment, as we did here. Why are the standard deviations in the two-way tables so large, compared with the 18.9 obtained from the first experiment? And another thing that is worrying me. Why should anyone do a full factorial experiment if a half experiment gives you all the interactions? Can you answer all these questions today?'

I look at my watch. 'Yes, I think I can cope with them quite easily. I am in no hurry to leave. Let me show you an incredibly powerful picture that will reduce your need for standard deviations.'

'First, we will have some coffee', Ross suggests. 'Shall I arrange that, while you plot the diagram? Yes, I will. Good.'

Ross Boucher leaves the room with satisfaction written all over his face.

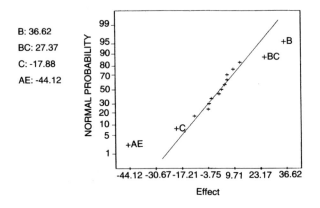

Fig. 9.5   A normal plot of the effect estimates.

I search my briefcase for another sheet of graph paper. I will need rather special graph paper for the diagram I am about to draw.

9.5 COST EFFECTIVE EXPERIMENTS

While Ross Boucher is out of the room I fail to find the normal probability graph paper that I usually have in my briefcase so I rush to my car, return with my laptop computer, call up a program, type in the results of the experiment (Table 9.8) and produce on the screen a plot of the effect estimates.

When Ross returns with the coffee he is surprised to find that I am interacting with a computer. I am also surprised, and delighted, to discover that the coffee is accompanied, not by the usual biscuits, but by hot buttered scones. What could be nicer, when faced with a long drive home and the prospect of a late dinner.

'Remember the 15 effect estimates (Tables 9.10 and 9.12) we calculated?', I ask. 'Well here they are on the screen, plotted as a rather special graph, known as a normal plot or a normal probability plot. You can see that eleven of the 15 points lie roughly on the straight line. Have you seen this sort of plot before?'

'Well, I have heard of normal plots and seen the funny graph paper you people use', Ross replies, staring at the screen. 'I suppose the points that are not near the line are the significant effects. Is that right? It must be.'

'Yes. If none of the factors had any effect on the weld strength we would expect all 15 points to be scattered around a straight line', I inform my client. 'However if one or two of the factors do have an effect, their points will be displaced from the line. The bigger the effect, the bigger the displacement.'

'So the interaction between voltage (A) and speed (E) has the biggest

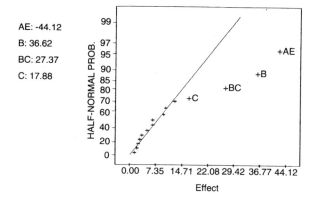

Fig. 9.6 A half normal plot of the effect estimates.

effect, then root gap (B), then the interaction between root gap (B) and the bevel angle (C)', suggests Ross. 'How about the fourth point labelled C, that's bevel angle? Is it on the line or off the line? What is your opinion?'

'Well, you are right to imply that it is a matter of opinion, Ross', I reply. 'This method of analysis is rather subjective. But it is very simple and it avoids any discussion of standard deviations. Some people claim that this approach is a little less subjective if we use a slightly different graph, known as a half normal plot or a Daniels plot.'

With this computer program it is very easy to replace the normal plot with a half normal plot, displaying the same 15 effect estimates (Fig. 9.6). With the half normal plot all the estimates are treated as positive and the vertical axis has a different scale. However, the interpretation is the same, in that we wish to identify those points which do not fit on the straight line.

'Yes, I think it is clearer. Don't you? This half normal plot is less ambiguous', suggests Ross Boucher. 'I am happy to accept that four of the 15 points are not on the straight line. Significantly deviant. Is that what you say? So, let us recap the sequence. You plan the experiment, then you carry out the experiment to obtain the results. From the results you calculate the effect estimates, then you put them in order of magnitude and plot them on half normal paper. The significant effects stand out like sore thumbs. You produce two-way tables and effect plots to help you interpret the significant effects and draw practical conclusions. You can even get a computer program that will do most of the work for you. Am I right?'

'You are indeed, Ross', I reply. 'What you have described is an excellent procedure for using factorial and fractional factorial experiments. I should . . .'

'Which brings us back to my earlier question – what are the disadvantages of doing only **half** of a factorial experiment rather than the whole thing?', Ross asks.

Table 9.16 What can we estimate from a 2^n factorial experiment?

No. of factors	No. of runs	We can estimate
2	4	A, B
		AB
3	8	A, B, C
		AB, AC, BC
		ABC
4	16	A, B, C, D
		AB, AC, AD, BC, BD, CD
		ABC, ABD, ACD, BCD
		ABCD
5	32	A, B, C, D, E
		AB, AC, AD, AE, BC, BD, BE, CD, CE, DE
		ABC, ABD, ABE, ACD, ACE, ADE, BCD, BCE, BDE, CDE
		ABCD, ABCE, ABDE, ACDE, BCDE
		ABCDE

'Well there is a price to pay for doing only half the work. However, in some cases it is a very small price. Let us start with small factorial experiments and build up to larger ones. I will write down all the things we can estimate. With a 2^2 factorial experiment we have 4 runs and we can calculate 3 estimates. Let us call them A, B and AB. We can estimate the main effect of each factor and the interaction between the factors. With a 2^3 factorial experiment we have 8 runs and we can calculate 7 estimates. Using the same notation these will be A, B, C, AB, AC, BC and ABC.'

'What is ABC?', Ross Boucher demands to know. 'I knew I should not have asked about half replicates. Are you going to baffle me with algebraic symbols?'

'Well I hope not', I reply, in what I hope are soothing tones. Ross has been subjected to many new ideas today. He must be exhausted. But I cannot answer this important question without resorting to abstract symbolism. 'Let me say that ABC probably does not exist and would be difficult to describe if it did. It is known as a three-factor interaction. It tells us how the interaction between A and B depends on C. If we now move on to a 2^4 experiment we will meet ABCD, which is a four-factor interaction. Most experimenters are happy to assume that these higher interactions do not exist. They want an experiment that will allow them to estimate the main effects. A, B, C, etc., and the two factor interactions, AB, AC, BC, etc. Let me set out in a table (Table 9.16) what we can estimate from each experiment.

'Let me see if I have this right, Roland? If I do a 2^5 factorial experiment, the 32 results will give me 31 estimates, but I only want 15 of these, so I could do half of a 2^5 factorial experiment and find everything I want at half the cost. Right or wrong?'

'Absolutely right', I confirm. 'Just one word of caution. You cannot just do any old half of the full experiment. The 16 runs that you actually do, must be carefully selected from the 32 runs that you might have done. This is a design matrix for a full 2^5 factorial experiment (Table 9.17). Any 16 rows from that matrix would constitute half of a 2^5 experiment, but you must choose the **best** 16 rows.'

Ross Boucher studies the sheet I have handed to him. The 32 rows and 31 columns are a design matrix for a full 2^5 factorial experiment. Which 16 runs should you do if you wish to estimate the five main effects and the 10 two-factor interactions? Clearly, runs 1 to 16 would not constitute a good half replicate, because that would leave us with 16 minus signs in the E column. Ross appears to be thinking along the same lines.

'I can see that it would be unwise to do the first 16 runs', he says slowly. 'That still leaves many possibilities. How do you choose? Is there a simple way? There must be.'

'There is a simple way', I reply. 'Eliminate the 16 rows which have a minus sign in the ABCDE column and you will be left with a good half replicate. Shall we do that? You have a pencil and a ruler. Draw a horizontal line through every row that has a minus sign in the last column.'

Ross Boucher draws the lines much more quickly than I could have done. Soon he has eliminated the unwanted runs. He studies the 16 rows that remain. 'How would I know whether this were good or bad?', he asks. 'Can you not talk me through it? Can you convince me that I am backing a winner?'

'I will do my best, Ross. Even though we now have only 16 rows we still have 31 columns. One of the columns, ABCDE, contains only plus signs. So we cannot estimate the five factor interaction. Now the other 30 columns fall into 15 pairs. If you select any column I should be able to find one other column that is identical. Better still, I will choose a column, say AB. Can you find another column that is exactly the same?'

Ross scrutinizes the table with intense interest. 'Plus, minus, minus, plus', he mutters, over and over again. 'Aha! That's it, BCD. What does it mean? The AB column and the BCD column are identical. So what?'

'We say that AB and BCD are aliased. They are an alias pair. The effect of interaction AB and the effect of interaction BCD cannot be separated. From the results of the experiment we calculate an estimate. It could be due to AB or BCD or both. However, if we assume that the higher interactions do not exist, then it must be due to AB.'

'I see. So what is B aliased with?', my client asks. 'Must we search for an identical column, or have you a quick way of finding it?'

'B will be aliased with ACDE, C with ABDE, BC with ADE, AE with BCD, . . .

'I see the pattern', Ross interjects. 'Obviously the . . . what do you call them? . . . main effects, will be stuck to the four-letter interactions. Is that right? And the two factor interactions will be stuck to the three letter interactions. This is a fascinating subject, but can you teach it painlessly to our development engineers?'

Table 9.17 Design matrices for 2^2, 2^3, 2^4 and 2^5 factorial experiments.

A	B	AB	C	AC	BC	ABC	D	AD	BD	ABD	CD	ACD	BCD	ABCD
-	-	+	-	+	+	-	-	+	+	-	+	-	-	+
+	-	-	-	-	+	+	-	-	+	+	+	+	-	-
-	+	-	-	+	-	+	-	+	-	+	+	-	+	-
+	+	+	-	-	-	-	-	-	-	-	+	+	+	+
-	-	+	+	-	-	+	-	+	+	-	-	+	+	-
+	-	-	+	+	-	-	-	-	+	+	-	-	+	+
-	+	-	+	-	+	-	-	+	-	+	-	+	-	+
+	+	+	+	+	+	+	-	-	-	-	-	-	-	-
-	-	+	-	+	+	-	+	-	-	+	-	+	+	-
+	-	-	-	-	+	+	+	+	-	-	-	-	+	+
-	+	-	-	+	-	+	+	-	+	-	-	+	-	+
+	+	+	-	-	-	-	+	+	+	+	-	-	-	-
-	-	+	+	-	-	+	+	-	-	+	+	-	-	+
+	-	-	+	+	-	-	+	+	-	-	+	+	-	-
-	+	-	+	-	+	-	+	-	+	-	+	-	+	-
+	+	+	+	+	+	+	+	+	+	+	+	+	+	+
-	-	+	-	+	+	-	-	+	+	-	+	-	-	+
+	-	-	-	-	+	+	-	-	+	+	+	+	-	-
-	+	-	-	+	-	+	-	+	-	+	+	-	+	-
+	+	+	-	-	-	-	-	-	-	-	+	+	+	+
-	-	+	+	-	-	+	-	+	+	-	-	+	+	-
+	-	-	+	+	-	-	-	-	+	+	-	-	+	+
-	+	-	+	-	+	-	-	+	-	+	-	+	-	+
+	+	+	+	+	+	+	-	-	-	-	-	-	-	-
-	-	+	-	+	+	-	+	-	-	+	-	+	+	-
+	-	-	-	-	+	+	+	+	-	-	-	-	+	+
-	+	-	-	+	-	+	+	-	+	-	-	+	-	+
+	+	+	-	-	-	-	+	+	+	+	-	-	-	-
-	-	+	+	-	-	+	+	-	-	+	+	-	-	+
+	-	-	+	+	-	-	+	+	-	-	+	+	-	-
-	+	-	+	-	+	-	+	-	+	-	+	-	+	-
+	+	+	+	+	+	+	+	+	+	+	+	+	+	+

'Yes, I believe so. I have taught the design of experiments to many engineers and scientists and managers. Perhaps, I should not say taught. I have helped them to learn, using very participative methods and lots of group activities. It is very important not to thrust upon people the abstract symbols until they ask questions which serve as a natural introduction.'

'I guess a half of a 2^4 experiment would be a failure. Is that so?' Ross asks. Clearly his energy level has declined considerably. He is now asking single questions, and waiting for me to answer. 'A half of a 2^4 experiment would have 8 runs. No matter which 8 you selected from the 16 runs of a full 2^4 design, you would find that some of the main effects and the two factor interactions were aliased with each other. Table 9.18 shows you the best you can manage.'

E	AE	BE	ABE	CE	ACE	BCE	ABCE	DE	ADE	BDE	ABDE	CDE	ACDE	BCDE	ABCDE
-	+	+	-	+	-	-	+	+	-	-	+	-	+	+	-
-	-	+	+	+	+	-	-	+	+	-	-	-	-	+	+
-	+	-	+	+	-	+	-	+	-	+	-	-	+	-	+
-	-	-	-	+	+	+	+	+	+	+	+	-	-	-	-
-	+	+	-	-	+	+	-	+	-	-	+	+	-	-	+
-	-	+	+	-	-	+	+	+	+	-	-	+	+	-	-
-	+	-	+	-	+	-	+	+	-	+	-	+	-	+	-
-	-	-	-	-	-	-	-	+	+	+	+	+	+	+	+
-	+	+	-	+	-	-	+	-	+	+	-	+	-	-	+
-	-	+	+	+	+	-	-	-	-	+	+	+	+	-	-
-	+	-	+	+	-	+	-	-	+	-	+	+	-	+	-
-	-	-	-	+	+	+	+	-	-	-	-	+	+	+	+
-	+	+	-	-	+	+	-	-	+	+	-	-	+	+	-
-	-	+	+	-	-	+	+	-	-	+	+	-	-	+	+
-	+	-	+	-	+	-	+	-	+	-	+	-	+	-	+
-	-	-	-	-	-	-	-	-	-	-	-	-	-	-	-
+	-	-	+	-	+	+	-	+	-	-	+	-	+	+	-
+	+	-	-	-	-	+	+	+	+	+	+	+	+	-	-
+	-	+	-	-	+	+	-	+	-	+	+	+	-	+	-
+	+	+	+	-	-	-	-	+	-	-	-	+	+	+	+
+	-	-	+	+	-	-	+	-	+	+	-	-	+	+	-
+	+	-	-	+	+	-	-	-	-	+	+	-	+	+	+
+	-	+	-	+	-	+	-	-	+	-	+	-	+	-	+
+	+	+	+	+	+	+	+	-	-	-	-	-	-	-	-
+	-	-	+	-	+	+	-	+	-	-	+	-	+	+	-
+	+	-	-	-	-	+	+	+	+	-	-	-	+	+	+
+	-	+	-	-	+	-	+	-	+	-	+	+	-	+	-
+	+	+	+	-	-	-	-	+	+	+	+	-	-	-	-
+	-	-	+	+	-	+	+	-	-	+	+	-	-	-	+
+	+	-	-	+	+	-	-	+	+	-	-	+	+	-	-
+	-	+	-	+	-	+	-	+	-	+	-	+	-	+	-
+	+	+	+	+	+	+	+	+	+	+	+	+	+	+	+

My client nods and looks at his watch. 'Good heavens. It is late', he says. I suspect that he intends to terminate our discussion, but I must force upon him one more table (Table 9.19), which seems to summarize much of what I have said. I regard it as a very useful starting point for anyone who wishes to plan an experiment with each factor having only two levels or values.

'The matrix we used earlier had 16 runs (Table 9.11) so it can be regarded as a half of a 2^5 experiment, which is how we looked upon it. But it could equally well be regarded as a full 2^4 experiment, or as a quarter of a 2^6, or as two replicates of a 2^3 experiment. All these possibilities are set out in Table 9.19. In my design of experiments course I ensure that everyone understands the advantages and disadvantages of every alternative. The experiments in boxes are the smallest experiments which will allow you to

Table 9.18 Half replicates of 2^n factorials

Experiment	No. of runs	Alias pairs
Half of 2^2	2	(A, B)
Half of 2^3	4	(A, BC) (B, AC) (C, AB)
Half of 2^4	8	(A, BCD) (B, ACD) (C, ABD) (D, ABC)
		(AB, CD) (AC, BD) (AD, BC)
Half of 2^5	16	(A, BCDE) (B, ACDE) (C, ABDE) (D, ABCE) (E, ABCD)
		(AB, CDE) (AC, BDE) (AD, BCE) (AE, BCD) (BC, ADE)
		(BD, ACE) (BE, ACD) (CD, ABE) (CE, ABD) (DE, ABC)

Table 9.19 Cost-effective factorial experiments

No. of runs	No. of variables 2	3	4	5	6	7	8	9
4	2^2	$\frac{1}{2}\times2^3$	—	—	—	—	—	—
8	2×2^2	2^3	$\frac{1}{2}\times2^4$	$\frac{1}{4}\times2^5$	$\frac{1}{8}\times2^6$	$\frac{1}{16}\times2^7$	—	—
16	4×2^2	2×2^3	2^4	$\frac{1}{2}\times2^5$	$\frac{1}{4}\times2^6$	$\frac{1}{8}\times2^7$	$\frac{1}{16}\times2^8$	$\frac{1}{32}\times2^9$
32	8×2^2	4×2^3	2×2^4	2^5	$\frac{1}{2}\times2^6$	$\frac{1}{4}\times2^7$	$\frac{1}{8}\times2^8$	$\frac{1}{16}\times2^9$
64	16×2^2	8×2^3	4×2^4	2×2^5	2^6	$\frac{1}{2}\times2^7$	$\frac{1}{4}\times2^8$	$\frac{1}{8}\times2^9$

Table 9.20 Calculation of standard deviations

Effect	Effect estimate	Sum of squares
AE	−44.1	7788.1
B	36.6	5365.6
BC	27.4	2997.6
C	−17.9	1278.1
BE	12.9	663.1
A	10.4	430.6
BD	9.6	370.6
AD	6.6	175.6
DE	6.6	175.6
CD	5.1	105.1
E	3.6	52.6
CE	−3.1	39.1
AB	−2.6	27.6
AC	2.4	22.6
D	−1.6	10.6
Total	—	19 501.9

estimate all the main effects and the two factor interactions. I am sorry to force this upon you so late in the day when you want to get away.'

'But you have not answered my other question', Ross Boucher protests. 'How about the standard deviations. Why are the standard deviations in the two-way tables so large? How can we calculate a standard deviation from our factorial experiment?'

9.6 INHERENT VARIATION

My client is obviously tired. However, his need for rest, or change, is clearly secondary to his need to hear answers to these questions. I will attempt to provide adequate answers as quickly as possible without exhibiting an unseemly haste.

'Your colleague, Jim Rexley, carried out the experiment with 5 factors in 16 runs (Table 9.8). Clearly there is considerable variation in his results. This variation in weld strength is partly due to the changes in the factors, but some of the variation is simply the inherent variation of the process. If, for example, he had produced 16 welds using identical conditions, there would still be variation in the weld strengths. His previous experiment (Table 9.1) would suggest that the standard deviation of repeat welds should be about 19. You want to know how we can find an estimate of this inherent variation from the results of the factorial experiment. The easiest way is to gather the effect estimates into yet another table (Table 9.20), separating the significant effects from the others.'

'To calculate the sum of squares, in this experiment, you simply square the effect estimate, then multiply by 4. (You would need a different multiplier if you had 8 results or 32 results.) If we divide the total sum of squares by 15, then take the square root, we obtain the overall standard deviation, 36.06. (This is the same standard deviation you would find if you put the 16 results from Table 9.8 into your calculator.) Now, adding the sums of squares for the 11 insignificant effects gives 1072.7. Dividing this by 11 and taking the square root gives a much smaller standard deviation, 13.73. This is usually described as the residual standard deviation. Note that it is much smaller than the 36.06. It is even smaller than the 18.94 from the first experiment. You may remember I called that the combined standard deviation, but it could equally well have been described as a residual standard deviation.'

Ross Boucher is silent. He is looking at the table containing the sums of squares. 'A lot of the variation in weld strength is due to these four effects. The four we selected from the half normal plot. Is there a simple way to quantify this?', he asks.

'Yes. We can add up the sums of squares for the four effects and express this as a percentage of the total sum of squares. This would be known as the percentage fit.

$$\text{Percentage fit} = \frac{17\,429.3}{19\,501.9} \times 100 = 89.4\%$$

We have explained 89.4% of the variation in weld strength. Alternatively, you could say that the deliberate changes in voltage, root gap, bevel angle and speed have caused 89.4% of the variation. Much of the variation being due to the interactions, of course.'

I pause at this point, fully expecting that Ross will reiterate the one outstanding question. He remains silent, apparently deep in thought. Perhaps he has forgotten the question. After some time I decide to remind him.

'You asked why the standard deviations in the two-way tables (Tables 9.14 and 9.15) were so large. For example, in the voltage–speed table the four standard deviations were 20.04, 22.96, 37.14 and 37.89. In the other two-way table the standard deviations were 34.99, 25.49, 30.89 and 21.42. All of these are greater than the residual standard deviations, which were 18.9 from the first experiment and 13.73 from the second. Well, the simple explanation is that the standard deviations in the two-way tables are not simply due to the inherent variation of the process. They contain extra variation due to certain factors. The standard deviations in the voltage–speed table are not influenced by the change in speed, or the change in voltage, or their interaction, but they may well be inflated by the changes in root gap and bevel angle.'

'Yes, yes, I can see that', says Ross Boucher. 'Thank you. Thank you for your explanation. Thank you for your many explanations throughout the day. I think I now have an appreciation of the benefits available from the use of planned experiments. It is a great pity I did not discover planned experiments some years ago. I would like you to train several of our engineers. You can run a course here, on our premises, can't you? Yes. Unfortunately we cannot arrange dates yet, because I need to persuade one or two managers that their people should be using planned experiments. Perhaps you could persuade them better than I could. Could you run a one-day course for managers? Yes, of course, you have run one-day courses in other companies.'

Ross Boucher and I take leave of each other. We have both had a tiring day and I still have a long drive ahead of me. I feel quite satisfied with the progress we have made and I feel sure Champfield Engineering will benefit from my visit.

9.7 SUMMARY

Many researchers are quite unaware of the benefits to be gained by using factorial experiments. The great strength of these experiments is that they are very efficient, they allow you to detect interactions and they enable you to check the statistical significance of your findings.

The efficiency of factorial experiments, compared with one-factor-at-a-time experiments, follows from the fact that each effect estimate is calculated from all of the results. Thus we make maximum use of the data. The data analysis is achieved by the use of a matrix of plus and minus signs.

Interaction effects can be estimated if we add product columns to the matrix. An interaction occurs when the effect of one variable depends on the level of a second variable. Discovering interactions can open up opportunities for quality improvement and/or cost reduction. The normal plot and the half normal plot are simple but powerful graphical tools for identifying the main effects and interactions which are significantly greater than the inherent variability of the process.

The design of experiments, and the analysis of experimental results, are large subjects. In this chapter I have only brushed the surface, limiting the discussion to 'two-level factorial experiments', in which each independent variable has only two levels or values. These are very useful experiments. They are particularly useful when used as a sequence of small experiments to help you draw closer to optimum operating conditions. For a fuller description of two-level factorials and details of other types of experiments including Taguchi methods you could consult one of my earlier books *Statistics in Research and Development* or *Engineering, Quality and Experimental Design* by Grove and Davies, or *Statistics for Experimenters* by Box, Hunter and Hunter.

Chapter 10

Achieving quality improvement

The consultant attempts to summarize the advice he has offered to clients in Chapters 2 to 9. This summary is presented as a list of dos and don'ts, with references to the appropriate sections in earlier chapters.

10.1 INTRODUCTION

Chapters 2–9 of this book are written as conversations between a quality consultant and his clients. I hope that my writing in this style has resulted in a more readable and user friendly book. However, I suspect that this conversational style may also carry the disadvantage that it makes back reference more difficult. For example, you may recall having read a passage on process variability that seemed very helpful at the time, but you failed to mark it with your highlighting pen. How will you ever find it again?

You could use the index, of course, but even the most carefully prepared index is dependent on both reader and author sharing a common vocabulary.

In the hope that this summary chapter will assist the reader much better than an index, I am writing it as a list of dos and don'ts, and with each I will attempt to highlight an important point that was made in one or more of the earlier chapters. References to the appropriate sections, should also help any reader who wishes to return to the original discussion.

Perhaps a summary chapter written in this style will prove particularly useful to a reader who already has considerable knowledge of statistical process control, quality improvement, measurement error, etc. Such an experienced reader could start at Chapter 10 and allow the more interesting dos and don'ts to lead him or her to the most useful sections.

10.2 QUALITY IMPROVEMENT

Do not ignore the teachings of the quality gurus

In many chapters I have referred to the writings of William Edwards Deming, Joseph Juran, Philip Crosby, John Oakland, Frank Price, and other quality experts. There is much wisdom in these texts, which are based on many decades of experience in the pursuit of quality improvement. Of course, you do not have to accept the whole package of advice that any guru offers. On the other hand, it would be foolish to reject the whole package because you disagreed with one or two recommendations.

Do not blindly follow the teachings of any one quality guru

No quality guru, or quality consultant, knows more about your company and its many processes, than you do. Deming and other experts express themselves in generalities. You and your colleagues must translate these generalities into specifics, to forge a TQM philosophy that will help your company to progress. Unfortunately, some companies become very attached to the teachings of one guru, rejecting all others, and blindly follow their chosen leader. Perhaps this has proved successful in some companies, but it is obviously very dangerous. Furthermore, an approach which is helpful in one industry may be quite inappropriate in another. Total quality management has many elements. I believe you must include all of those elements, but with a blend that is suitable for your particular company, at this particular stage of its development. (See section 1.2.)

Do not confine your reading on this subject to a list of dos and don'ts

Lists are very useful. They can help to convey a large amount of information in a structured manner. They are particularly effective in conference presentations, where the number of words per slide is strictly limited. However, I would suggest that many of the lists which appear in conference proceedings, and in training manuals may prove to be very ambiguous, if you refer back to them at a later date. Unaccompanied by the spoken word, a list may have little or no meaning. I hope that you will find useful the list of dos and don'ts in this chapter. But I also hope that you will find the energy to read the sections in earlier chapters which this list refers to.

Do not assume that statistical process control (SPC) is simply a set of techniques

Many people think of the conventional mean chart when they encounter the phrase 'statistical process control'. This is most unfortunate for SPC embraces a long list of techniques; see sections 7.3 and 7.4. But SPC is not simply a set of techniques. It is also a way of thinking about variability. Of course it is much easier to list the techniques than to describe the philosophy for understanding variability. But the latter is the more important of the two. Deming asserted repeatedly that every manager needs to understand variability. Do you fully appreciate the distinction between common and special causes? (See section 4.2.)

Do not assume that the sole purpose of statistical process control charts is to help you gain better control of a process

It is unfortunate that statistical process control (SPC) is so-called. The word 'statistical' leads many people to avoid the subject for fear of contact with abstract mathematical statistics. The word 'control' leads many people to assume that the sole purpose of SPC is control. However, an even more important purpose of SPC is improvement. The techniques of SPC are tools for learning about processes, but the passion for learning must be shared by everyone within the process, if process improvement is to be maximized. (See sections 4.2, 7.5 and 8.3.)

10.3 PROCESS CAPABILITY AND STABILITY

Do not regard a machine, or any other piece of hardware, as a process

Processes can be defined in many ways. Various quality experts have given us process models. All of these models remind us that a process has many components including plant, people, procedures, measurement, materials, etc. If your company has invested many millions of pounds in a piece of hardware, it is easy for you to lose sight of the obvious fact that this equipment will produce nothing without the contribution of operators, supervisors, and managers. I believe that many companies fail to derive the best possible return on their investment in hardware, because they fail to make the equally important investment in people. (See section 1.4.)

Do not forget that every process must have an aim

The aim of a process must be to supply the product and/or service that the customer requires. Thus to define a process satisfactorily we need to define the customer and the customer's requirements. It is important that everyone working within the process should fully understand these requirements. However, it may be very difficult to see a whole process from within, thus a process manager has a responsibility to help those working within the process to see the whole picture and to appreciate how this process can be regarded as part of a larger process. (See sections 1.4 and 7.2.)

Do not forget that many processes contain feedback loops, delays and interactions between variables

Many industrial processes have what Peter Senge (1990) calls 'dynamic complexity'. This is characterized by actions having very different effects in the short term and the long term, or very different effects in two locations. Because of this dynamic complexity people may never experience the full consequences of their actions and thus may persist with behaviour that is not beneficial to the company. Often it will be more beneficial to focus on the simplification and the improvement of a process than to carry out a witch hunt to find one person responsible for an unsatisfactory outcome. (See sections 1.4, 7.2 and 9.4.)

Do not assume that the same action will always produce the same result

All processes are subject to random variation, so we would not expect to see exactly the same result when an action on the process is repeated. However, with some processes we may find that the same action appears to have a very different result, perhaps the opposite result. This is entirely understandable if you appreciate the concept of interaction between variables. We say that there is an interaction when the effect of one variable depends on the level of a second variable. Thus, if you are unaware that the second has changed you may be surprised by the result achieved when you change the first variable. (See section 9.4.)

Do become familiar with some of the many process capability indices which are quoted by customers and suppliers

Many companies are trying to reduce the variability of their products by reducing the variability of their purchased materials or components. One way to achieve this reduction of input variation is to move towards single sourcing, but how are you to decide which to discard? It seems obvious that you should discard the suppliers who are least capable of meeting your requirements on quality, delivery and price. Process capability indices, such as C_p and C_{pk}, express the capability of a supplier in one number. Clearly, having only one number for each supplier facilitates decision making. (See section 2.4.)

Do not discuss process capability indices unless you know how the standard deviations were calculated

Process capability indices compare the width of the specification with the natural tolerance of the process. The latter is quantified as some multiple of the process standard deviation. Not everyone realizes that the standard deviation of a set of data can be calculated in several ways. Each of the many calculation procedures will give a different result, so it is important to know which method was used before you attempt to interpret a process capability index. If the index is based on the short-term standard deviation, then it indicates only the short-term capability. [See sections 4.3 and Procedures A and C of Appendix A.]

Do not discuss a capability index without examining a histogram of the data from which the index was calculated

To calculate a process capability index we use a standard deviation which has been calculated from process data. Unfortunately, this standard deviation tells us nothing about the shape of the distribution of the data. A histogram, or a dot plot, of the data might reveal that the distribution was skewed or bi-modal, or contaminated with outliers, for example. Remember that a process capability index can be quite misleading if the data pattern deviates significantly from the normal distribution shape.

Never base decisions on a histogram without examining a run chart, or a control chart, of the data

A histogram shows the shape of a distribution and gives some indication of the mean and the spread of the data, but it tells us nothing about the stability of the process. The histogram does not indicate whether all the variation is due to random causes or some of the variation is due to an assignable cause. When we draw a histogram we lose the ordering of the data. Thus the same histogram could represent any one of a huge number of run charts. If you use a histogram to assess the capability of a process you would be wise to check the stability of the process by examining a run chart or a control chart. (See section 2.5 and Procedure B of Appendix A.)

Do not assume that a process which was stable for a short period will remain stable for ever

When you examine the stability of a process, following Procedure B (Appendix A) perhaps, you may find evidence of instability during the period when the data were recorded. However, you are also likely to find that the process appeared to be stable during part of this time period. It seems reasonable to assert that no process is permanently stable, while on the other hand, no process is chronically unstable. Perhaps it is better to regard stability as a state of grace which results from sustained effort to eliminate assignable causes of variation, and which can only be safeguarded by constant vigilance. Clearly, control charts have a role to play in both the achievement and the maintenance of stability.

Do remember that some processes, even when in a stable state, will produce variability that does not resemble a normal distribution

Some processes exhibit random variation which appears to follow a normal distribution. During a period of instability, the effect of the assignable causes can distort the distribution so that it becomes bi-modal or skewed. However, there are processes which exhibit skewed variability even when they are stable. If you have such a process, and you assume that its variation has a normal distribution, you may make bad decisions about the capability of the process and how it can best be controlled. (See section 8.3.)

10.4 MEASUREMENT, VARIABILITY AND CONTROL CHARTS

Do not assume that everything of importance can be measured, or that everything which is measured is important

You cannot measure the smile on your customer's face. However, you can probably measure some aspects of quality that are important to your customer. Measuring, controlling and improving something which is of secondary importance may be preferable to complete inaction. Furthermore, the attempt to remove chaos from these secondary variables may produce surprising improvements in the more important but immeasurable variables.

Do not forget that all measurements contain error

Whenever you analyse a set of data you should bear in mind that part of the variability in the measurement is due to the measuring process itself. The percentage of the variation that can be attributed to measurement error may be very small, of course. Unfortunately, this is not always the case. Some test methods, or measurement processes, may be so lacking in precision that they introduce substantial additional variation. Thus it may be important to reduce the inherent variability of a measurement process and/or improve its stability before you can effectively reduce the true variation in the product. On the other hand, if the measurement error is negligible, it might be foolish to invest in further improvement of the test method. (See section 8.4.)

Do try to put the measurement of quality into the hands of those who can take action to improve quality

Unfortunately, the measurement of quality is often carried out by measurement specialists. These specialists may be located remote from the scene of production, may have no responsibility for the control of quality and no interest in quality improvement. Their remoteness and detachment can also contribute delay in the quality measurements being received by those who can best make use of the data. Furthermore, this division of labour can promote suspicion and lack of confidence in the measurements. It is desirable that the people responsible for the quality and quantity of production should take ownership of the measurement process wherever possible. Any decrease in precision may be more than compensated for by a reduction in testing time and an increase in motivation among those who really can improve quality.

Do attempt to find out how the variability in your product or service affects your customer's process

Perhaps the variability in your product is so small that it goes unnoticed in your customer's process. On the other hand, the people within your customer's process may be fighting a never-ending battle against the effects of your variability. It is often possible to gain a competitive advantage by jointly studying the macro-process that spans both companies. For this you will need a close partnership and a willingness to speak each other's language. Clearly the communication is inadequate if your process operator does not know what effect his/her action will have when your product enters the customer's process. (See section 1.4.)

Do not continue to accept the variability which is present in the materials you receive from your suppliers

The variability in your raw materials or components is one of the many causes of variation in the quality of your product. Do you have any estimate of how much output variation is due to this input variation? It may be a large percentage. Do you have an estimate of how much time and effort is expended by your staff in trying to counteract this input variation? It may be considerable. Your suppliers can reduce their variability. Perhaps this can be achieved at little or no cost. Certainly their efforts will be assisted by a closer relationship in which you attempt to explain your real needs. (See section 8.6.)

Do not under-estimate the benefits of single sourcing the inputs to your processes

Companies in the assembly industries must always have known that you cannot make good assemblies (such as motor vehicles) from bad components, But they were much slower to realize that you cannot make reliable assemblies from highly variable components. Having made this realization, however, they now demand more and more consistency from their suppliers. Furthermore, they have completely eliminated many suppliers as they moved towards single sourcing. Gone are the days when it was considered wise to use multiple suppliers for each component, so as to play one against the other in order to drive down prices. Now the emphasis is on close partnership with each supplier fully understanding customers' needs and aiming to be on target with minimum variation. Single sourcing has ensured that more time is available to strengthen each partnership and has eliminated the additional variability from supplier to supplier. (See section 8.6.)

Do realize that variability in a delivery, or a 'lot', of your product may well increase as the size of the lot increases

It is probably true of many manufacturing processes that two 'items' produced during a short time interval are likely to differ less than two items produced on different days, or different weeks, say. Thus a small quantity of product produced during a short period is likely to be less variable than a larger quantity produced during a longer period. If this is true of your process, how will you answer the customer who questions the consistency of your product? Will you quote a short-term standard deviation or a longer-term standard deviation? If you are asked for a process capability index, which standard deviation will you use in the calculation? (See section 4.5.)

Do not adopt an over-simple definition of 'stable' or 'in control' when you are assessing the stability of your process

Many people would say that a process is in control if a sufficiently large set of results gives points which all lie within the action lines on both mean and range charts. Some people would include warning lines and supplementary rules in this definition. Almost everyone would use $\sigma = \bar{R}/d_n$ to calculate the standard deviation when setting up the charts, I believe there are processes which will never be in control, if we use the above definition. These processes exhibit medium-term random variation over and above the short-term random variation which is assessed by $\sigma = \bar{R}/d_n$. (See section 4.3.)

Do choose the most appropriate type of control chart for assessing and monitoring your process

The conventional mean and range charts are ideally suited for assessing the stability of any process. With such an exercise we have all the data to hand before the plotting starts. Naturally grouped data should be left in their natural groups. One-at-a-time data can be artificially grouped using any reasonable group size. When control charts are used for monitoring the performance of a process, it is very important to choose charts which match the characteristics of the process. For a process which produces one-at-a-time data we use an individuals chart or a moving mean chart, supported by a moving range chart. For a process which yields naturally grouped data we use the conventional mean and range charts. The cusum chart can be adapted for use with any type of process. When choosing control charts you need to consider the power of the different alternatives, their ease of use, training implications, etc. (See Procedure B of Appendix A and sections 3.2, 4.2, 4.4 and 6.3.)

Do not assume that every user of control charts adopts the same rules for interpretation of the charts

Almost all users of control charts agree that one point outside the action lines constitutes an indication of change, or loss of control. Some users would agree that two consecutive points outside the warning lines gives a clear indication. Others would suggest that eight consecutive points plotted on the same side of the centre line constitutes an action signal. There is not, however, universal agreement on these, or the many other supplementary rules listed in books on statistical process control. (See section 4.4.)

Do not accept the commonly held view that there is only one correct formula for calculating a standard deviation when setting up control charts, or calculating process capability indices

The most widely used method for calculating a standard deviation when setting up control charts is to group the data, find the range for each group, then use $\sigma = \bar{R}/d_n$. Let us call this the short-term standard deviation. Clearly this method produces useful charts with many processes, but it is not always successful. Some processes display medium-term random variation which is additional to the short-term random variation and may be due to other causes. To avoid being sent on a wild goose chase you must include this medium-term variation in the standard deviation by using a different method of calculation; see section 4.3. Similar problems can arise when calculating a process capability index. Should you use the short-term standard deviation or employ some other method? A computer program, such as the 'Quality Analyst' package used throughout this book, may be able to use several formulae to calculate a standard deviation. When reading the output from a program you should ensure that you know which formula it has used.

Do not assume that a control chart will immediately detect every change in your process

Control charts are very useful, especially if they are used by the right people. They can help us to detect changes in a process. They can facilitate the learning that brings process improvement. However, they do not possess the magical powers that many people attribute to them. It is important to realize that some of the decisions indicated by a control chart will be wrong. Furthermore, the wrong decisions fall into two types. You may conclude that the process has changed, when, in fact, it has not. You may conclude that the process has not changed, when, in reality, it has. Average run length graphs can show us how often these wrong decisions are likely to occur. (See section 4.4.)

> *Do not accept that a process must be stable (i.e. in control) before you can monitor its performance with a control chart or carry out an experiment*

Lucky is the manager whose process is in control. Clearly, a stable process is more predictable, its variation can reasonably be expected to stay within the limits of a known distribution. Of course, the stability of the process may not be due to good fortune. It may be the result of much study and persistent elimination of assignable causes. Unfortunately, many processes are not in this happy state and it is fair to say that, when you first investigate the stability of your process, you are unlikely to be entirely happy with what you find. You could be plunged into deeper gloom, if you read a text which advises that you will be powerless to improve the process until after you have brought it into a state of statistical control. You may reach the depths of despair if the text, or consultant, suggests that it is a trivial matter to eliminate the assignable causes. From your perspective it may not be obvious what action you should take. Do not despair, I believe that you do not need to follow a prescribed procedure. The persistent use of control charts or any other of the 'seven tools' will help you to improve your process if you establish a learning culture.

10.5 EXPERIMENTS AND OTHER TOOLS FOR IMPROVEMENT

> *Do be aware of the distinction between a survey and an experiment*

In a survey the researcher simply observes, records and draws conclusions. An experiment is more pro-active. In an experiment the researcher deliberately changes the process and draws conclusions about what effect these changes have had. A good experiment contains an element of prediction, for the researcher forecasts what will happen before the changes are introduced. Naturally, we are even more impressed by the experimenter's ability to predict the future than we are by the 'surveyor's' ability to explain the past. (See Chapter 9.)

Do not assume that experiments can be carried out only by scientists

An experiment is more likely to be successful if the experimenter has an understanding of the scientific method and/or the Deming cycle; see section 7.5. However, you do not require a degree in physics, or a white laboratory coat, in order to make use of this scientific approach to process learning. Indeed, it can be argued that the scientific method is programmed into our minds at birth. Observe a baby in its pram carrying out experiments with intense concentration and great persistence. Clearly, the very young are not content to learn solely from surveys, whatever their parents' wishes.

Do be aware of the limitations inherent in the common practice of changing only one factor at a time

If you want to know what effect a variable has on the quality of your product you change the variable and observe the effect. If you wish to study the effects of many variables it seems natural to change them all, but only one at a time. It can be demonstrated, however, that changing one variable at a time is very inefficient. Furthermore, by changing one at a time you will learn nothing about interactions between the variables. Fortunately, there are experimental plans which enable us to change many variables simultaneously in a systematic way, so that we can use all of the results very efficiently to estimate the effects of the variables and their interactions. They are known as factorial experiments and fractional factorial experiments. (See sections 9.2 and 9.3.)

Do not commit all of your available resources to one grand experiment

Many inexperienced researchers are incredibly optimistic. They have faith that their next experimental run of the process will find the optimum conditions, giving maximum quality at minimum cost. These miracles rarely occur. A more mature researcher may go to the opposite extreme, putting his or her faith in one large planned experiment, which will reveal all there is to know about the process. Such grand experiments can misfire in many ways, with disappointing results and no hope of saving the project, for all the resources have been squandered. Adopt a hill climbing approach, with only 30% of your budget devoted to your first experiment. The second experiment can be planned after the results of the first experiment have been analysed. Thus you will gradually approach the optimum conditions, using at each stage the most appropriate type of experiment. (See section 9.5.)

Do not underestimate the usefulness of the simple run chart

Every one of the 'seven basic tools' can help you to improve quality and reduce costs. The power of these simple tools is out of all proportion to their complexity. Perhaps the simplest and most powerful of all is the run chart. I have never met a process operator who could not understand a run chart. I have never met a manager whose decisions could not be improved by plotting his or her data as a run chart. If you have not yet introduced statistical process control into your organization, start today by asking your 'shop floor' people to plot run charts. Soon they will be discussing variability and the effect this might have on your customers.

Do look for relationships between the variables you can control and the variables your customer regards as important

Does your process have a control lever labelled 'quality' and another labelled 'cost'? If so, you should have little difficulty increasing quality or decreasing cost. I suspect that such processes are very rare. I have never met one. With most processes we can only control quality indirectly, by manipulating other variables that are known to influence quality. Thus our knowledge of the relationships between many variables is the key to quality control and improvement. All of the 'seven basic tools' can help us to increase this knowledge, but the scatter diagram is particularly useful when we are attempting to relate measured variables. And do not overlook the most neglected of Ishikawa's seven tools, stratification. (See sections 7.3 and 7.4.)

Do take time to study your data carefully, making use of pictures to increase your understanding and to facilitate communication

The basic tools for quality improvement turn data into pictures. Clearly these pictures assist communication and help the manager to make better decisions. Why then, are they not more widely used in business and industry? There must be many reasons. I stumbled upon one reason quite by accident during a discussion in a hotel bar. 'My boss will not be impressed by simple pictures', I was told. 'He will be more impressed with a highly technical report that he does not understand. If I do not impress him, I will not be promoted.' Clearly the speaker worked for a company that did not have a learning culture. (See sections 7.3, 7.4, and 7.5.)

Do attempt to make use of the cusum technique if you have not already done so

The cusum technique was developed largely in Britain, but it is so powerful that even the Americans have accepted it. And yet it is so simple. It can be implemented very easily on a spreadsheet. When interpreting a cusum chart you must remember to focus on slopes or you may draw false conclusions. For complete safety it is better to let the cusum chart tell you when the changes occurred, than go back to a run chart to confirm the nature of the changes. (See section 6.2.)

10.6 PEOPLE AND LEARNING

Do not accept that employees are motivated solely by money, laziness and fear

Twenty years ago it was widely believed that Britain's economic problems could be blamed on the 'workers'. At that time it was easy to share the views of those managers who subscribed to MacGregor's Theory X, which predicted that the typical worker would consistently demand more money for less work and would avoid all responsibility. Recently it has been shown that this same workforce, when placed under Japanese management, can demonstrate world class performance. Now MacGregor's Theory Y is more widely accepted, but perhaps the pendulum has swung too far. Quality gurus criticize management quite ruthlessly and it is widely accepted that 'there are no bad workers, only bad managers'. I have always felt that this maxim is terribly unfair to the many hard-working and conscientious managers I have had the pleasure of working with over the years. Furthermore, I think that the study of processes suggests an extension to the maxim ... 'There are no bad managers, only bad processes.' If we define a worker as someone who is within the process and a manager as being outside the process, and also accept that we have processes within processes, within processes ... then it follows that everyone is a manager and everyone is a worker and there are only bad processes. (See sections 1.4 and 1.5.)

Do not assume that all people are identical in their needs, their motivation and their objectives

It is unwise to assume that everyone within your company will respond in the same way to the announcement of a TQM initiative, or to the publication of a company mission statement, or to impending change. I believe that all human behaviour is motivated by self-interest, but self-interest is uniquely defined for each person and is constantly changing. Thus any manager who believes that every employee will automatically change direction and follow the new company objectives, could be mistaken. If the manager is covertly asking 'What's in it for me?', why shouldn't everyone else be asking the same question? (See section 1.5.)

Do attempt to establish a company culture in which all employees will strive to satisfy the needs of your stakeholders

A young employee of a well-known company recently told me in confidence, 'I do not waste my time trying to satisfy customers. I aim to satisfy my boss. The customer is not going to offer me a promotion, is he?' Clearly, some vital linkages are missing from the culture of this company. If the young employee believed that by pleasing the customers and the suppliers and the shareholders, he would also be pleasing his boss, and ultimately pleasing himself, then his contribution would be more valuable to the company.

Do not underestimate the need for co-operation between people within your organization

It is being realized by more and more managers that profitability is constrained by a lack of understanding of key processes. Thus you and your competitors are in a learning race. You probably are not quite sure when the race started, but it is clear that some companies had a head start, no one knows when the race will end and every so often the competitor at the back of the field drops out. In this race you cannot afford to ignore any method of learning and sharing existing knowledge is clearly important. Unfortunately, your people may be reluctant to share their hard earned secrets. It is these secrets, born of experience, which enable each employee to believe that he or she is making a unique contribution, and is, therefore, indispensable. Clearly a learning culture must be a sharing culture, in which fear is reduced to a minimum. (See sections 1.5 and 7.5.)

Do not underestimate the power of leadership

It is widely believed that a manager gains more and more power as he or she climbs up the organizations. Undoubtedly, there is some truth in this belief, but the senior managers with whom I discuss TQM claim that they have little power to make things happen. Clearly, they control large budgets and they have the power to hire and fire and to influence the careers of those they choose to sponsor or block, but they claim to be almost powerless when culture change is under discussion. On the other hand, it is equally clear that the process operators, their supervisors and their junior managers, with whom I also have the pleasure of discussing TQM, are very attentive to the many messages that come down from above. These messages seem to have two outstanding characteristics in all large organizations. First, there are so many, that it is impossible to act on all of them. Second, it is difficult to decide which are most important. (I do not recall ever seeing a memo which stated that something was not important.) So the junior staff would dearly love to be able to answer the question, 'What is really important?' Perhaps they seek an answer to this question, not in the words of memos, but in the behaviour of managers. If a senior manager frequently leaves head office to visit the sites, and while there he frequently uses the word 'quality' in a meaningful way, then quality will be seen as truly important. How could we describe such management behaviour? Would the word 'leadership' be appropriate?

Do not forget that all data comes from the past, but all managers must look to the future

The present is just a fleeting moment of time that separates the past from the future. Why, then, do we express so many statements in the present tense? We might say, for example, 'This process is stable.' What we really mean is that the process was stable during the period when this data was recorded, and will remain stable for some time to come, we hope. Many gurus have expressed the view that more management decisions should be based on data. Clearly the data must come from the past, while the decisions must form the basis for action in the future. Thus managers are linking the past and the future, but they must also link cause and effect. Their decisions must specify actions on the causes that will produce the effects our customers want. I believe that managers deserve more credit for undertaking this difficult role and they certainly deserve data of the highest quality, presented in the simplest possible format. As Wheeler says in his video 'The Japanese Control Chart': 'The problems of the past are lessons for the future, only when they are documented and studied.' (See Chapter 1 and section 7.5.)

Do consider the possibility that the most sustainable competitive advantage is the ability to learn faster than your competitors

In many industries there is a frantic rush to develop new products, to improve the quality of existing products and to increase the efficiency of all processes. Success appears to depend on learning how to do things better and more quickly. The learning can only be done by people, of course. Small wonder, then, that many senior managers have expressed the view that their company's greatest asset is its staff. Small wonder that many companies are trying to develop a learning culture. (See sections 1.3 and 7.5, and Senge (1990).)

Do not assume that the quickest ways of learning are the most effective

In the almost frantic endeavours to improve your processes faster than your competitors, it is natural to seek the quickest methods of learning. Perhaps the speediest way your process operators and your technicians can gain a greater understanding of their process, is for them simply to **accept** what they are told. Learning by accepting can be very quick. But who are the experts who can tell them what they need to know? It is most unlikely that external consultants will have all the answers. You would be wise to assume that your employees will just have to do their own research using the scientific method, or the Deming cycle. It is not as quick as learning by accepting, but it is much more reliable. (See section 7.5.)

Do consider the possibility that the effective knowledge of a team may be greater than the total knowledge of all the members, or less than the knowledge of any one member.

In this book I have said little about teams, despite the fact that teamwork is an essential component of TQM. I have focused more upon the tools and techniques that team members must use to control and improve their processes. Of course, there is no certainty that people, once trained in these techniques, will actually use them. Similarly, there can be no guarantee that bringing together a group of people will create an effective team. If the chairman of the group concentrates solely upon converging to the common ground that links the members' existing views, then the effective knowledge of the team may be minimal. If, on the other hand, a facilitator can help the group to diverge to a greater pool of views and opinions which are discussed openly, rather than defended, then the effective knowledge of the team can greatly exceed that of any one member. Clearly the facilitator's role differs from that of the chairman or team leader. A company which aspires to a learning culture will need a number of group facilitators if team learning is to take its rightful place alongside the learning of individuals.

10.7 SUMMARY

I must confess that, as I wrote this final chapter, I became aware that I was not merely summarizing but also adding some new ideas that had not appeared earlier. This was not planned. It just happened. Obviously I was influenced by having learned a little more about quality improvement during the year that it took me to write the book. In fact I think I learned quite a lot in 1993.

Dr William Edward Deming, the quality guru whose teachings inspired much of my writing claimed that he learned more in 1992 than any one of his previous 91 years. Unfortunately Dr Deming died on 20th December 1993 while I was writing this chapter. Clearly his influence will continue. Perhaps his ideas will help you improve your processes.

Appendix A: Useful procedures

PROCEDURE A – TO ASSESS THE CAPABILITY OF A PROCESS

1. Collect data over a suitable time period for the quality measures that you and your customers regard as important. (It is impossible to prescribe how long this period should be. If the data covers a very short period you will be able to assess only the short-term capability. Ideally you should have at least 30 results.) The following instructions need to be repeated for each quality measure, or variable.
2. Draw a histogram, or a dot plot of the data. Mark the specification limit(s) and the target value on the histogram. (The target value is often midway between the specification limits, but there may be only one specification limit and there may be no target value.)
3. Plot a run chart, an individuals chart or a mean chart. Plot a range chart of the data. (See Procedure B.)
4. If the charts plotted in step 3 show that the process was stable, as defined in Procedure B, then the histogram from step 2 gives a good indication of the process capability during the period when the data was gathered.
5. If the charts plotted in step 3 show that the process was unstable, then the histogram from step 2 could be misleading. The histogram will show the process to be less capable than it would have been if it had been stable and centred. You should attempt to answer the following questions:
    (a) Can we identify the assignable causes that created the instability and can we prevent them from acting in the future? If the answer is 'Yes' then you can look forward to a more stable and more capable process in the future. If the answer is 'No' then you may have to live with this instability and the histogram from step 2 may give a fair indication of your process capability. However, you cannot be confident that the instability in your data is typical of future performance.
    (b) Does the run chart, individuals chart or mean chart indicate that the process was stable for part of the period covered by the data? If the answer is 'Yes', then you could base your capability analysis on the stable period. Whether this revised analysis gives a fair indication of future performance, will depend on your ability to reproduce this stability in the future.

(c) Are you prepared to show your data plots to your customers and use them as a basis for discussing your performance and their expectations?

6. Calculate the standard deviation of your data so that you can then calculate process capability indices. There are several formulae you can use; see Procedure B and C. Your choice of formula for the standard deviation will depend on what is the accepted practice in your industry and/or upon what you are trying to prove. If you use a 'short-term standard deviation' you will obtain an indication of short-term capability. Many computer programs use the 'overall standard deviation' when calculating process capability indices, even though they use the 'short-term standard deviation' when setting up control charts.

7. If you have an upper specification limit, calculate C_{pu}. If you have a lower specification limit, calculate C_{pl}. If you have both upper and lower limits, calculate C_p and C_{pk}. Note that these capability indices can be misleading if either:
   (a) your process was not stable;
   (b) your histogram is not approximately normal in shape; or
   (c) you used very little data.

In any discussion of process capability indices, whether they were produced by your suppliers, your customers or yourself, you should attach great importance to supporting pictures such as histograms and run charts.

PROCEDURE B – TO ASSESS THE STABILITY OF A PROCESS

1. Collect data over a suitable time period. (How much data do you need? Ideally, at least 80 results, but you may have to settle for less. If your data falls into natural groups, it is desirable to have at least 20 groups.)
2. One-at-a-time data should be put into suitable subgroups, e.g. 20 groups with 4 results in each. Naturally grouped data should be kept in its natural groups.
3. Calculate the mean and range of each group.
4. Calculate the overall mean, $(\overline{X})$, which is the mean of the group means.
5. Calculate the mean range $(\overline{R})$, which is the mean of the group ranges.
6. Divide the mean range by Hartley's constant to obtain the standard deviation (σ). (This is sometimes referred to as the short-term standard deviation.) Hartley's constant is given in Table B.1 (Appendix B).
7. Calculate centre, action and warning values for a provisional mean chart using:

Centre value $= \overline{X}$

Upper action value $= \overline{X} + \dfrac{3\sigma}{\sqrt{n}}$

$$\text{Upper warning value} = \overline{X} + \frac{2\sigma}{\sqrt{n}}$$

$$\text{Lower warning value} = \overline{X} - \frac{2\sigma}{\sqrt{n}}$$

$$\text{Lower action value} = \overline{X} - \frac{3\sigma}{\sqrt{n}}$$

Where n is the number of results in each group. Set up a provisional mean chart and plot on it the group means.

8. Calculate centre, action and warning values for a provisional range chart using:

    Centre value $= \overline{R}$
    Upper action value $= A\overline{R}$
    Upper warning value $= B\overline{R}$
    Lower warning value $= C\overline{R}$
    Lower action value $= D\overline{R}$

Where A, B, C and D are taken from Table B.2 in Appendix B. Set up a provisional range chart and plot on it the group ranges.

9. Calculate centre, action and warning values for a provisional individual's chart using:

    Centre value $= \overline{\overline{X}}$
    Upper action value $= \overline{\overline{X}} + 3\sigma$
    Upper warning value $= \overline{\overline{X}} + 2\sigma$
    Lower warning value $= \overline{\overline{X}} - 2\sigma$
    Lower action value $= \overline{\overline{X}} - 3\sigma$

Set up a provisional individuals chart and plot on it the individual results. One-at-a-time data should be plotted as in Fig. 3.2. Data which falls into natural subgroups should be plotted as in Fig. 4.4.

10. Study the three charts plotted in Steps, 7, 8 and 9. If there are any action indications in any one, or more, of the three charts, then you should identify the nature of the additional variation and consider its possible causes. Common sense is invaluable, but you might find the following questions useful.

    (a) Does the variation show any clear pattern such as a step change or a gradual trend (as in Fig. 3.2 or Fig. 5.11)?

    (b) Is any action indication due simply to an outlier in the data? If the answer is 'Yes', it might be wise to ignore the indication rather than to investigate an incident that is unlikely to recur.

    (c) Is the additional variation such that the action indications appear to occur at random (as in Fig. 4.3)? If the answer is 'Yes', you should consider recalculating the standard deviation as in Chapter 4.

    (d) Would it be possible in the immediate future and with your available resources, to find the causes of the additional variation and prevent them occurring in the future?

(e) Would it be better to focus on part of the data, when the process appeared to be in control? Would this focus give you a more useful standard deviation?

(f) Can you now set up control charts which will help you to monitor the future performance of the process?

PROCEDURE C – TO CALCULATE A STANDARD DEVIATION

The standard deviation of a set of data is a measure of the spread, or scatter, or variation of the data. Clearly the simplest measure of spread is the **range**, which is the difference between the largest and smallest values in the data set. However, the standard deviation of a set of data is a more reliable measure of spread than the range. So the standard deviation is often preferred, though it is not so easy to understand, or to calculate. For a fuller discussion of ranges and standard deviations see my earlier books *Statistics in Research and Development*, or *Data Analysis in the Chemical Industry*.

A further complication associated with the standard deviation is that it can be calculated in several ways, and the many different formulae will almost certainly give different results with any set of data. This raises the question, 'Which is the best formula to use?' The answer will depend on many factors.

Some of the formulae require the data to be in groups, which are often referred to as subgroups. Of course, some data fall naturally into groups because of the way in which they were gathered. These are known as natural subgroups. (See Chapters 4 and 5.) Many data do not have natural subgrouping and may best be described as 'one-at-a-time-data', but they can be put into subgroups of some arbitrary size: two, or three or four, etc. It is important that all the subgroups are of the same size.

To calculate the standard deviation of grouped data, three formulae are in common use:

1. $\sigma = \bar{R}/d_n$
2. $\sigma = \bar{\sigma} c_n$
3. $\sigma = \sqrt{\left[\dfrac{\sum \sigma^2}{m} \right]}$

When using formula (1) we calculate the range of each subgroup, then average the ranges, then divide the average range ($\bar{R}$) by Hartley's constant (d_n). Hartley's constant comes from Table B.1 in Appendix B.

When using formula (2), we first calculate the standard deviation of each group using formula (4); see below. Then we average the standard deviations and finally we multiply the average standard deviation ($\bar{\sigma}$) by c_n. The constant c_n depends on the subgroup size and is from Table B.1 of Appendix B.

When using formula (3), we first calculate the standard deviation of each subgroup using formula (4); see below. Then we square each standard deviation, add up the squares and divide by the number of groups (m). Finally we take the square root.

Formulae (1), (2), and (3) all give an estimate of what could be called the **short-term standard deviation**; see Chapter 4. If there were no variation within the groups, each would give a standard deviation of zero, no matter how much variation there was between groups. Which of the three formulae is likely to give the best estimate of the short-term standard deviation of the process? It can be shown that formula (3) is the best, with little to choose between the other two, especially with subgroup sizes such as 2, 3, 4, 5 or 6.

A fourth method of calculating standard deviation, which does not require grouping of the data, makes use of the following formulae:

4.
$$\sigma = \sqrt{\left\{ \frac{\sum (x - \bar{x})^2}{n - 1} \right\}}$$

5.
$$\sigma = \sqrt{\left\{ \frac{\sum x^2 - n\bar{x}^2}{n - 1} \right\}}$$

Formulae (4) and (5) will always give the same result, with any set of data, provided no rounding errors are introduced. It is formula (5) which is programmed into many electronic calculators and which is activated by pressing the σ_{n-1} key. There is no generally agreed name for this method, but many people refer to the formula as the 'quadratic formula', and it would be reasonable to refer to the result as the 'overall standard deviation'.

The overall standard deviation, from formula (4) or (5), will often be greater than the short-term standard deviation from formula (1), (2) or (3). This is because the quadratic formula embraces all the variation in the data, not just the short-term variation.

There are many situations in which it is desirable to partition the total variation into several parts, or components, with one component due to each of several causes. For example, part of the total variation in product quality is due to variation in raw materials, part is due to variation in the test method, etc. Thus it may be possible to break down the overall standard deviation into several smaller standard deviations. (See Chapter 8.)

An important example of subdividing variation is the analysis of the results of a precision experiment, or inter-laboratory trial, when we calculate the repeatability standard deviation, the between-laboratories standard deviation, and the reproducibility standard deviation. The data from an inter-laboratory trial falls into natural subgroups, of course. The results from each laboratory are entered into formula (1), (2) or (3) to obtain the repeatability standard deviation (σ_r). A mean is calculated for each laboratory, then the standard deviation of these means ($\sigma_{\bar{x}}$) is obtained by feeding the means into formula (4) or (5). The between-laboratories standard deviation

(σ_L) is calculated from equation (6), then the reproducibility standard deviation from equation (7).

6.
$$\sigma_L = \sqrt{\left[\sigma_x^2 - \frac{\sigma_r^2}{n} \right]}$$

7. $\sigma_R = \sqrt{[\sigma_L^2 + \sigma_r^2]}$

Appendix B: Useful statistical tables

Table B.1

Sample size n	Hartley's constant d_n or d_2	c_n
2	1.128	1.253
3	1.693	1.128
4	2.059	1.085
5	2.326	1.064
6	2.534	1.051
7	2.704	1.042
8	2.847	1.036
9	2.970	1.032
10	3.078	1.028
11	3.173	1.025
12	3.258	1.023

Hartley's constant is used to convert a range, or a mean range, to a standard deviation. Data is put into groups of equal size (n), the range is calculated for each group, and the mean range is divided by Harley's constant to obtain the standard deviation.

$$\sigma = \frac{\overline{R}}{d_n}$$

The constant c_n is used to calculate a standard deviation from the mean of the standard deviations of several groups or samples

$$\sigma = \overline{\sigma} \, c_n$$

Table B.2

Sample size	Constants for range chart			
n	A	B	C	D
2	4.12	2.81	0.04	0.00
3	2.98	2.17	0.18	0.04
4	2.57	1.93	0.29	0.10
5	2.34	1.81	0.37	0.16
6	2.21	1.72	0.42	0.21
7	2.11	1.66	0.46	0.26
8	2.04	1.62	0.50	0.29
9	1.99	1.58	0.52	0.32
10	1.93	1.56	0.54	0.35
11	1.91	1.53	0.56	0.38
12	1.87	1.51	0.58	0.40

The constants, A, B, C and D, are used to obtain appropriate values for placing action and warning lines on a range chart or a moving range chart.

Upper action line $= A\bar{R}$
Upper warning line $= B\bar{R}$
Lower warning line $= C\bar{R}$
Lower action line $= D\bar{R}$

where $\bar{R}$ is the mean range from several groups, each containing n values.

Table B.3 – Confidence intervals and the *t*-test

Degrees of freedom	Confidence level					
	90%	*95%*	*98%*	*99%*	*99.8%*	*99.9%*
1	6.31	12.71	31.82	63.66	318.31	636.62
2	2.92	4.30	6.97	9.93	22.33	31.60
3	2.35	3.18	4.54	5.84	10.21	12.92
4	2.13	2.78	3.75	4.60	7.17	8.61
5	2.02	2.57	3.37	4.03	5.89	6.87
6	1.94	2.45	3.14	3.71	5.21	5.96
7	1.90	2.37	3.00	3.50	4.79	5.41
8	1.86	2.31	2.90	3.36	4.50	5.04
9	1.83	2.26	2.82	3.25	4.30	4.78
10	1.81	2.23	2.76	3.17	4.14	4.59
11	1.80	2.20	2.72	3.11	4.03	4.44
12	1.78	2.18	2.68	3.06	3.93	4.32
13	1.77	2.16	2.65	3.01	3.85	4.22
14	1.76	2.15	2.62	2.98	3.79	4.14
15	1.75	2.13	2.60	2.95	3.73	4.07
16	1.75	2.12	2.58	2.92	3.69	4.02
17	1.74	2.11	2.57	2.90	3.65	3.97
18	1.73	2.10	2.55	2.88	3.61	3.92
19	1.73	2.09	2.54	2.86	3.58	3.88
20	1.73	2.09	2.53	2.85	3.55	3.85
25	1.71	2.06	2.49	2.79	3.45	3.73
30	1.70	2.04	2.46	2.75	3.39	3.65
40	1.68	2.02	2.42	2.70	3.31	3.55
60	1.67	2.00	2.39	2.66	3.23	3.46
∞	1.64	1.96	2.33	2.58	3.09	3.29

References and further reading

REFERENCES

Bannister, D. and Fransella, F. (1986) *Inquiring Man*, Croom Helm, London.
Caulcutt, R. (1991) *Statistics in Research and Development*, 2nd edn, Chapman & Hall, London.
Deming, W.E. (1986) *Out of the Crisis*, MIT, Cambridge, MA.
Deming, W.E. (1993) *The New Economics*, MIT, Cambridge, MA.
Harris, T. (1973) *I'm OK, You're OK*, Pan Books.
Hertzberg F. (1968) One more time: How do you motivate employees?, *Harvard Business Review*, Jan-Feb, pp. 53–62
Kelly, G. (1955) *Theory of Personal Constructs*, Norton.
McGregor, D. (1960) *The Human Side of Enterprise*, McGraw-Hill, New York.
Maslow, A.H. (1970) *Motivation and Personality*, Harper and Row, New York.
Neave, H.R. (1990) *The Deming Dimension*, SPC Press, Knoxville, Tennessee.
O'Connor, J. and Seymour, J. (1990) *Introducing Neuro-Linguistic Programming*, Mandala.
Oakland, J.S. (1993) *Total Quality Management*, 2nd Edn, Butterworth-Heinemann, Oxford.
Senge, P.M. (1990) *The Fifth Discipline*, Doubleday, New York.

FURTHER READING

Bissell, D. (1993) *Statistical Methods for SPC and TQM*, Chapman & Hall, London.
Box, G.E.P., Hunter, W.G. and Hunter, J.S. (1978) *Statistics for Experimenters*, Wiley, New York.
Caulcutt, R. (1989) *Data Analysis in the Chemical Industry*, Ellis Horwood, Chichester.
Caulcutt, R. and Boddy, R. (1983) *Statistics for Analytical Chemists*, Chapman & Hall, London.
Crosby, P.B. (1979) *Quality is Free*, McGraw-Hill, New York.
Duncan, A.J. (1986) *Quality Control and Industrial Statistics*, 5th Edn, Irwin, Homewood, Ill.
Grant, E.L. and Leavenworth, R.S. (1988) *Statistical Quality Control*, 6th Edn, McGraw-Hill, New York.
Hammer, M. and Champy, J. (1993) *Re-engineering the Corporation*, Nicholas Brealey, London.
Juran, J.M. (1988) *Juran on Planning for Quality*, The Free Press, New York.
Kohn, A. (1993) *Punished by Rewards*, Houghton Mifflin, New York.
Oakland, J.S. and Followell, R.E. (1990) *Statistical Process Control*, 2nd Edn, Heinemann Newnes, Oxford.
Oakland, J.S. and Porter, L.J. (1994) *Cases in Total Quality Management*, Butterworth Heinemann Oxford.

Perls, F.S. (1971) *Gestalt Therapy Verbatim*, Bantam, Toronto.

Quinn, F. (1990) *Crowning the Customer*, O'Brien Press, Dublin.

Shewhart, W.A. (1931) *Economic Control of Quality of Manufactured Product*, Van Nostrand. Republished in 1980 by ASQC, Milwaukee.

Shewhart, W.A. (1939) *Statistical Method from the Viewpoint of Quality Control*, Dover Publications, New York.

Wheeler, D.J. (1993) *Understanding Variation*, SPC Press, Knoxville, Tennessee.

Wetherill, B.G. and Brown, D.W. (1991), *Statistical Process Control, Theory and Practice*, Chapman & Hall, London.

Index

Learning Resources
Centre